To my grandchildren
Kylie, Jesse and Max

Human Ecology

Human Ecology

BASIC CONCEPTS FOR SUSTAINABLE DEVELOPMENT

Gerald G Marten

Earthscan Publications Ltd
London • Sterling, VA

First published in the UK and USA in 2001
by Earthscan Publications Ltd

ISBN: 1 85383 714 8 paperback
         1 85383 713 X hardback

Typesetting by PCS Mapping & DTP, Newcastle upon Tyne
Printed and bound in the UK by Bell & Bain Ltd, Glasgow
Cover design by Andrew Corbett; hands and globe image designed by Julie Marten
Photograph of the Earth taken from Apollo 17, NASA

For a full list of publications please contact:
Earthscan Publications Ltd
120 Pentonville Road, London, N1 9JN, UK
Tel: +44 (0)20 7278 0433
Fax: +44 (0)20 7278 1142
Email: earthinfo@earthscan.co.uk
http://www.earthscan.co.uk

22883 Quicksilver Drive, Sterling, VA 20166-2012, USA

Earthscan is an editorially independent subsidiary of Kogan Page Ltd and publishes in association with
WWF-UK and the International Institute for Environment and Development

A catalogue record for this book is available from the British Library

Library of Congress Cataloging-in-Publication Data
Marten, Gerald G., 1939-.
    Human ecology : basic concepts for sustainable development / Gerald G. Marten.
        p. cm.
    Includes bibliographical references and index.
    ISBN 1-85383-713-X (cloth) — ISBN 1-85383-714-8 (pbk.)
    1. Human ecology. 2. Sustainable development. 3. Nature—Effect of human beings on. 4.
Human–plant relationships. 5. Human–animal relationships. 6. Biotic communities. I. Title.

GF75 .M37 2001
304.2—dc21

2001023293

Contents

List of Figures and Boxes

FIGURES

BOXES

Foreword

Ecologically sustainable development has become a universal concern. It is a challenge that merits the attention and action of us all. Efforts to promote sustainable development are proceeding on a variety of fronts, but it is still far from a reality.

A crucial ingredient for sustainable development is a well-informed public. All actions that impact the environment come ultimately from individuals. It is public opinion that stimulates governments, corporations and other sectors of society to appropriate action. Even political leaders who are strongly committed to sustainable development cannot impose it upon people who do not understand or appreciate its importance. Conversely, even the most reluctant of political leaders cannot fail to pursue sustainability when their people demand it.

Most people are concerned about the environment but feel overwhelmed by the complexity and scale of the problems. Given the diversity of competing perspectives and interests, it is often difficult to know what information to trust. The numerous forces, both social and ecological, that stand in the way of sustainable development have so much momentum that changing the present course of environmental deterioration seems unlikely without major changes in people's attitudes and behavior. The imperative of sustainable development is forcing us to think in new ways, but the way to an ecologically sustainable future is not at all clear.

Ecologically sustainable development may only be possible once we have grasped the fundamental interdependence of human society and the natural environment. Human ecology, as the science of human–environment interaction, provides a whole-system perspective that bridges the gap between the natural and social sciences. It is a broad perspective that can help to clarify environmental issues and suggest how to deal with them. While human ecology has proved its worth as an interdisciplinary approach to solving environmental problems, it has not yet attained a clear identity with an established body of theory. The time has come for human ecology to become a major scientific discipline in its own right. The stake that we all have in an ecologically healthy future is far too great to settle for less.

Human Ecology: Basic Concepts for Sustainable Development is a valuable step towards making human ecology a scientific discipline which everyone can and should understand as a guide to their own actions. Dr Marten presents a coherent set of concepts about how ecosystems function and how human social systems interact with ecosystems. This will help readers to make sense of the complexity of human–environment interactions, enabling them to make connections not previously noticed in many areas of their lives. The examples that Dr Marten uses to illustrate the concepts are drawn from actual situations that cover a wide range of topics and take us to diverse parts of the world. They allow us to see how to make the jump from theory to practice.

For example, once aware of 'complex adaptive systems', readers will begin to notice ordered patterns in the changes occurring all around them. Once aware of 'landscape mosaics', readers will pay more attention to the implications of changes in their landscape for the future quality of their lives. The 'switch' character of ecosystem function clarifies how inappropriate use of environmental resources can lead to irreversible degradation. The concept of 'coadaptation' between social systems and ecosystems helps to explain why modern society has environmental problems, while pointing to fundamental changes necessary to deal with the problems.

Dr Marten provides us with the conceptual tools to understand and evaluate the complexities we face, so that we are better equipped to choose actions with positive outcomes in both the short and long term. The ultimate pay-offs can be realized when the ecological and systems concepts in this book are applied to sustainable development. The book explains how the existing economic system and other contemporary social institutions promote unsustainable human-environment interaction and describes social institutions that can contribute to ecologically sustainable interaction. It provides examples of successful actions by government, the private sector and civil society to develop healthier relationships with the environment.

The scope and clarity of this book make it accessible and informative to a wide readership. Its messages should be an essential component of the education for all students from secondary school to university. The book will be equally meaningful to anyone concerned with the environment who desires a fundamental understanding of the forces shaping the future of his children and grandchildren and all who care about the millions of people whose lives have been destroyed or undermined by environmental deterioration. In short, this is a book that provides a clear and comprehensible account of concepts that can be applied in our individual and collective lives to pursue the promising and secure future to which we all aspire.

Maurice Strong
Chairman, Earth Council
Former Secretary General, United Nations
Conference on Environment and Development

Preface

Twenty years ago I worked with a network of agronomists, social scientists and ecologists in South-East Asia. The agronomists were using Green Revolution technology to develop new production systems for small-scale agriculture in the region. Change was essential to feed a growing population. The new methods offered impressive possibilities for increasing food production and farmer incomes but in many instances the farmers were not using them. The agronomists were understandably disappointed and sought the help of social science colleagues to find out what they could do to convince farmers to take advantage of the opportunities.

The social scientists spent a lot of time talking to farmers and soon discovered that the farmers were generally more innovative than conservative. Many routinely experimented with new crops and cultivation techniques in a corner of their farm, adopting them on a larger scale when it was apparent they would do well. The farmers knew from experience that new crop varieties frequently did not perform so well on the marginal land that many of them had to use. Even if the land were suitable, improved varieties would require an ample water supply and expensive inputs such as fertilizers and pesticides in order to achieve high yields, inputs which were beyond the means of many poor farmers. The farmers were also afraid that new cultivation methods could lead to unanticipated long-term problems that they did not have the resources to deal with. Their apprehensions turned out to be justified, as soil problems appeared after several years in some areas with new agricultural systems. Most farmers felt they could not afford to make irreversible mistakes because they had no alternatives for earning a living besides their farms.

As the agronomists and social scientists learned more from the farmers, they came to appreciate how important it was for the new agricultural technology to fit into the everyday realities of the farmers' lives and how important it was for it to be ecologically sustainable. They also discovered that they had much to learn from the farmers' traditional agricultural methods, which had proved ecologically sustainable for centuries. All of this made the agronomists realize they would be more successful working with a broader perspective than in the past. The result was a collaborative research network of agronomists, social scientists, ecologists and farmers, each of which had something to contribute to the task of developing agriculture that farmers really could use.

This story illustrates just one of the thousands of challenges facing humanity as economies, technologies, cultures and the ways that people use natural resources change in today's rapidly evolving world. These challenges are encapsulated by the concept of 'sustainable development', frequently defined as meeting the needs of the present without compromising the ability of future generations to meet their own needs. Some consider sustainable development to be the major challenge of our time, but it is difficult for concerned individuals to know what they can actually do to help make it happen.

Human ecology, the science of interrelationships between people and the environment, can help to sharpen our perceptions of what is happening with the environment, and how people and the environment function together. This kind of understanding is one essential step toward effective action.

The term 'human ecology' has a long and varied history. It was first used in the 1920s, when a small group of urban sociologists used ecological concepts to explain what they were observing in cities. The sociologists found ecological metaphors to be of use because some of the early ecological concepts were in fact general systems concepts that were also valid for human society. This form of human ecology, which was prominent until the 1970s, was totally different from the human ecology in this book.

In the 1960s and 1970s, biological ecologists who were alarmed by the human population explosion and its implications for environmental destruction used the term 'human ecology' to emphasize that humans are subject to the same ecological limitations as other animals. At the same time, anthropologists directed attention to the shaping of culture by environment, and some anthropologists initiated human ecology field studies using prominent ecological concepts of the time, such as population regulation and energy flow. As awareness of environmental problems increased during the 1970s, scholars in a diversity of academic disciplines began to speak of 'human ecology'. These different forms of human ecology, conforming to the different disciplines in which they arose, generally had little in common with one another beyond dealing with people and the environment.

By the 1980s, biological ecologists and social scientists were working together in multidisciplinary research teams addressing practical problems involving the environment. For many of these scientists, including myself, human ecology was a perspective for problem solving that focused on interactions between human societies and the environment. By tracing chains of effects through ecosystems and human society, and by understanding more generally how people interact with ecosystems, human ecology could help to:

- anticipate the long-range environmental consequences of human actions;
- avoid disastrous surprises from the environment;
- generate ideas for dealing with environmental problems; and, in general,
- maintain a liveable and sustainable relationship with the environment.

The number of scientists studying human–environment interaction increased over the years, and the diversity of their backgrounds and perspectives expanded correspondingly.

This book grew out of an undergraduate course in the School of Policy Studies at Kwansei Gakuin University in Japan. The purpose of the course was to offer students a conceptual foundation for making human ecology and sustainable development an integral part of their personal and professional lives. The book reflects my own view of human ecology and attempts to provide a clear, understandable and coherent system of concepts for comprehending how ecosystems function and how human societies interact with ecosystems. The book draws on a variety of existing ideas, integrating long-standing ecological principles with concepts assembled more recently under the rubric of complex systems theory. The last part of the book focuses on social processes, social institutions and technologies that conflict with, or contribute to, ecologically sustainable development. While I hope this book will see extensive use in the classroom, it will be of equal value to anyone who is concerned about the environment and seeks the kind of understanding that can help to do things that make a positive difference.

Most of the concepts in this book are firmly established but a few are still the subject of unresolved scientific debates. One example is the concept of emergent properties (introduced in Chapter 4). Some scientists, including myself, consider each level of biological organization to have 'a life of its own' that emerges from the organization of the parts rather than simply from the characteristics of the parts themselves. Other scientists consider emergent properties to be theoretical constructs that lack rigorous scientific confirmation. I use emergent properties because they encourage the kind of whole-system thinking that I consider essential for ecologically sustainable development.

The concepts in this book are communicated by means of examples and stories, often accompanied by diagrams. I have sometimes used a 'broad brush' approach in the examples as the focus is on communicating the concepts rather than analysing particular situations in detail. The book includes a list of Further Reading which provides readers with the opportunity to explore central concepts and key examples in greater detail. It also offers an opportunity to explore details and perspectives of human ecology that are not covered in depth in this book.

A full appreciation of human ecology comes only with exploring the details of human–environment interaction in specific cases. The 'Things to Think About' exercises at the end of each chapter are intended to stimulate concrete translations of concepts to the reader's own circumstances. Reports in the annual *State of the World* and *Worldwatch Paper* series (Worldwatch Institute, Washington, DC) are valuable sources of information for some of these exercises. To realize the fullest benefits, readers should develop their own examples – their own 'stories' – in as much detail as possible. In that way, human ecology will come to life, and readers will begin to develop concrete visions of the possibilities for ecologically sustainable development in their own community.

Technical terms, as well as words used somewhat differently from their general meaning, are presented in bold type the first time they appear in the text. Their meanings are explained in the glossary.

Acknowledgements

While most of the ideas in this book derive from many years of ecological science, it is appropriate to recognize at least some of the specific sources of concepts and examples presented here. I should first note my intellectual debt to Kenneth E F Watt and C S Holling who pioneered the rigorous application of systems analysis to ecology. While the cyclical character of natural and social processes has been recognized for thousands of years, Holling's analysis of cycles in ecological systems stimulated the 'complex system cycles' in this book; the conflict between 'stability' and 'resilience' also originated with Holling. The book's central conceptual framework based on interaction between human social systems and ecosystems originated with Terry Rambo, who illustrated the concept with the example of cooking fuel and deforestation in India that is used in this book. I am particularly grateful for Terry Rambo's intellectual companionship over the years. The nail puzzle in Figure 4.4 was brought to my attention by Virginia Fine. The 'Gaia hypothesis' came from James Lovelock. Coadaptation and coevolution between the social system and ecosystem after the Industrial Revolution is based on Richard Norgaard's *Development Betrayed*. Some of the perceptions of nature in Chapter 9 are based on ideas developed by Gene Barrett. The discussion of the impact of 'portable capital' on renewable resource use is based on ideas originally put forth by Colin Clark. The phrase 'tragedy of the commons' was first used by Garret Hardin. The role of social complexity in the rise and fall of civilizations is based on Joseph Tainter's *Collapse of Complex Societies*. Conditions for sustainable common property management and the example of fisheries in Turkey are from Eleanor Ostrum's *Governing the Commons*, and the account of traditional forest management in Japan is based on publications by Margaret McKean. Melanie Beck, Paul Edelman, Joe Edmiston, Winston Salzer, Suzanne Good and Russ Dingman provided information on nature protection in the Santa Monica mountains. Scott Halstead provided information on the epidemiology of dengue hemorrhagic fever and Vu Sinh Nam provided information on his copepod programme for dengue control in Vietnam. Kerry St Pe provided information on the Barataria-Terrebonne National Estuary Program. Richard Carriere, Richard Borden, Anthony Clayton and Ann Marten commented on the overall manuscript at different stages of its development. Gary Haley and Julie Marten did computer graphics for the figures.

INTRODUCTION

WHAT IS HUMAN ECOLOGY?

Ecology is the science of relationships between living organisms and their environment. **Human ecology** is about relationships between people and their environment. In human ecology the environment is perceived as an **ecosystem** (see Figure 1.1). An ecosystem is everything in a specified area – the air, soil, water, living organisms and physical structures, including everything built by humans. The living parts of an ecosystem – microorganisms, plants and animals (including humans) – are its **biological community**.

Ecosystems can be any size. A small pond in a forest is an ecosystem, and the entire forest is an ecosystem. A single farm is an ecosystem, and a rural landscape is an ecosystem. Villages, towns and large cities are ecosystems. A region of thousands of square kilometres is an ecosystem, and the planet Earth is an ecosystem.

Although humans are part of the ecosystem, it is useful to think of human–environment interaction as interaction between the human **social system** and the rest of the ecosystem (see Figure 1.1). The social system is everything about people, their **population** and the psychology and **social organization** that shape their behaviour. The social system is a central concept in human ecology because human activities that impact on ecosystems are strongly influenced by the society in which people live. Values and knowledge – which together form our worldview as individuals and as a society – shape the way that we process and interpret information and translate it into action. Technology defines our repertoire of possible actions. Social organization, and the social institutions that specify socially acceptable behaviour, shape the possibilities into what we actually do. Like ecosystems, social systems can be on any scale – from a family to the entire human population of the planet.

The ecosystem provides services to the social system by moving materials, energy and information to the social system to meet people's needs. These **ecosystem services** include water, fuel, food, materials for clothing, construction materials and recreation. Movements of materials are obvious; energy and information are less so. Every material object contains energy, most conspicuous in foods and fuels, and every object contains information in the way it is structured or organized. Information can move from ecosystems to social systems independent of materials. A hunter's discovery of his prey, a farmer's observation of his field, a city dweller's assessment of traffic when crossing the street, and a refreshing walk in the woods are all transfers of information from ecosystem to social system.

Material, energy and information move from social system to ecosystem as a consequence of human activities that impact the ecosystem:

- People affect ecosystems when they use resources such as water, fish, timber and livestock grazing land.
- After using materials from ecosystems, people return the materials to ecosystems as waste.
- People intentionally modify or reorganize existing ecosystems, or create new ones, to better serve their needs.

human
ecology

Figure 1.1
Interaction of the human social system with the ecosystem

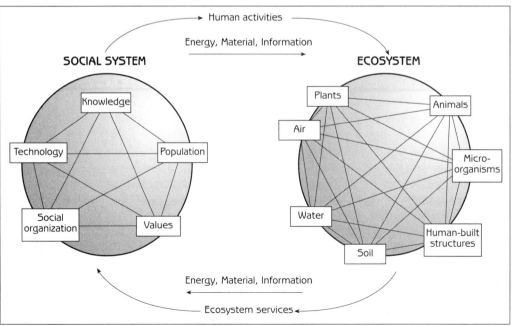

With machines or human labour, people use energy to modify or create ecosystems by moving materials within them or between them. They transfer information from social system to ecosystem whenever they modify, reorganize, or create an ecosystem. The crop that a farmer plants, the spacing of plants in the field, alteration of the field's biological community by weeding, and modification of soil chemistry with fertilizer applications are not only material transfers but also information transfers as the farmer restructures the organization of his farm ecosystem.

An example of social system–ecosystem interaction: destruction of marine animals by commercial fishing

human ecology

Human ecology analyses the consequences of human activities as a chain of effects through the ecosystem and human social system. The following story is about fishing. Fishing is directed toward one part of the marine ecosystem, namely fish, but fishing has unintended effects on other parts of the ecosystem. Those effects set in motion a series of additional effects that go back and forth between ecosystem and social system (see Figure 1.2).

Drift nets are nylon nets that are invisible in the water. Fish become tangled in drift nets when they try to swim through them. During the 1980s, fishermen used thousands of kilometres of drift nets to catch fish in oceans around the world. In the mid 1980s, it was discovered that drift nets were killing large numbers of dolphins, seals, turtles and other marine animals that drowned after becoming entangled in the nets – a transfer of information from ecosystem to social system, as depicted in Figure 1.2.

Figure 1.2
Chain of effects through ecosystem and social system (commercial fishing in the ocean)

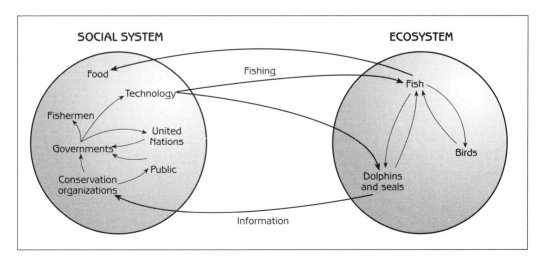

When conservation organizations realized what the nets were doing to marine animals, they campaigned against drift nets, mobilizing public opinion to pressure governments to make their fishermen stop using the nets. The governments of some nations did not respond, but other nations took the problem to the United Nations, which passed a resolution that all nations should stop using drift nets. At first, many fishermen did not want to stop using drift nets, but their governments forced them to change. Within a few years the fishermen switched from drift nets to long lines and other fishing methods. Long lines, which feature baited hooks hanging from a main line often kilometres in length, have been a common method of fishing for many years. The long lines that fishermen now use put a total of several hundred million hooks in the oceans around the world.

The drift net story shows how human activities can generate a chain of effects that passes back and forth between social system and ecosystem. Fishing affected the ecosystem (by killing dolphins and seals), which in turn led to a change in the social system (fishing technology). And the story continues today. About six years ago it was discovered that long lines are killing large numbers of sea birds, most notably albatross, when the lines are put into the water from fishing boats. Immediately after the hooks are reeled from the back of a boat into the water, birds fly down to eat the bait on hooks floating behind the boat near the surface of the water (see Figure 1.3). The birds are caught on the hooks, dragged down into the water and drown. Because some species of birds could be driven to local extinction if the killing is not stopped, governments and fishermen are investigating modifications to long lines that will protect the birds. Some fishermen are using a cover at the back of their boat to prevent birds from reaching the hooks, and others are adding weights to the hooks to sink them beyond the reach of birds before the birds

human ecology

Figure 1.3
Long line fishing

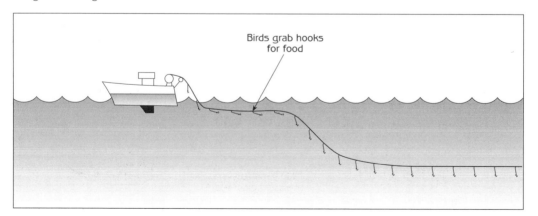

Birds grab hooks
for food

can get to them. It has also been discovered that birds do not go after bait that is dyed blue.

This story will continue for many years as new effects go back and forth between the ecosystem and social system. Another part of the story concerns seals and other fish-eating animals that may be declining to extinction in some areas because heavy fishing has reduced their food supply. The effects can reverberate in numerous directions through the marine ecosystem. It appears that the decline of seals in Alaskan coastal waters is responsible for the disappearance of impressive kelp forests in that region. Killer whales that previously preyed on seals have adapted to the decline in seals by switching to sea otters, thereby reducing the sea otter population. Sea urchins are the principal food of sea otters, and sea urchins eat kelp. The decline in sea otters has caused sea urchins to increase in abundance, and the urchins have decimated kelp forests that provide a unique habitat for hundreds of species of marine animals. (Another episode in the story of commercial fishing and marine animals is presented at the end of Chapter 11.)

human ecology

Cooking fuel and deforestation in India

The problem of deforestation in India provides another example of human activities that generate a chain of effects back and forth through the ecosystem and social system. The following story shows how a new technology (biogas generators) can help to solve an environmental problem.

For thousands of years people in India have cut branches from trees and bushes to provide fuel for cooking their food. This was not a problem as long as there were not too many people; but the

Figure 1.4 Deforestation and cooking fuel (chain of effects through ecosystem and social system)

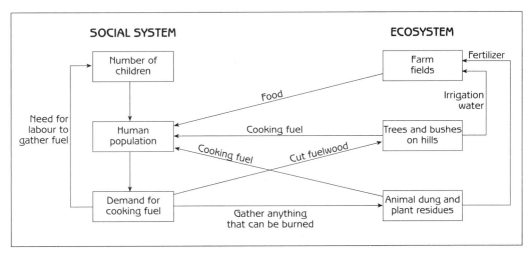

situation has changed with the radical increase in India's population during the past 50 years (see Figure 1.4). Many forests have disappeared in recent years because people have cut so many trees and bushes for cooking fuel. Now there are not enough trees and bushes to provide all the fuel that people need. People have responded to this 'energy crisis' by having their children search for anything that can be burned, such as twigs, crop residues (bits of plants left in farm fields after the harvest) and cow dung. Fuel collection makes children even more valuable to their families, so parents have more children. The resulting increase in population leads to more demand for fuel.

human ecology

Intensive collection of cooking fuel has a number of serious effects in the ecosystem. Using cow dung as fuel reduces the quantity of dung available for use as manure on farm fields, and food production declines. In addition, the flow of water from the hills to irrigate farm fields during the dry season is less when the hills are no longer forested. And the quality of the water is worse because deforested hills no longer have trees to protect the ground from heavy rain, so soil erosion is greater, and the irrigation water contains large quantities of mud that settles in irrigation canals and clogs the canals. This decline in the quantity and quality of irrigation water reduces food production even further. The result is poor nutrition and health for people.

Figure 1.5
Chain of effects through social system and ecosystem when biofuel generators are introduced to villages

This chain of effects involving human population growth, deforestation, fuel shortage and lower food production is a vicious

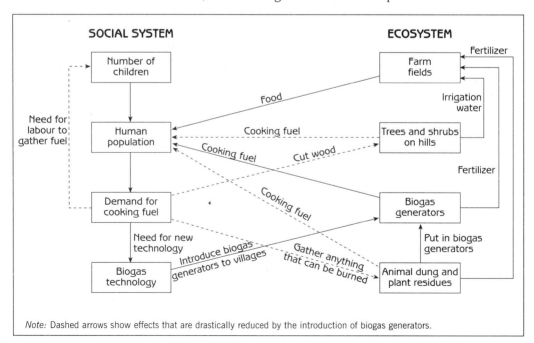

Note: Dashed arrows show effects that are drastically reduced by the introduction of biogas generators.

cycle that is difficult to escape. However, biogas generators are a new technology that can help to improve the situation. A biogas generator is a large tank in which people place human waste, animal dung and plant residues to rot. The rotting process creates a large quantity of methane gas, which can be used as fuel to cook food. When the rotting is finished, the plant and animal wastes in the tank can be removed and put on farm fields as fertilizer.

If the Indian government introduces biogas generators to farm villages, people will have methane gas for cooking, so they no longer need to collect wood (see Figure 1.5). The forests can grow back to provide an abundance of clean water for irrigation. After being used in biogas generators, plant and animal wastes can be used to fertilize the fields, food production will increase, people will be better nourished and healthier, and they will not need a large number of children to gather scarce cooking fuel.

sustainable development

However, the way that biogas generators are introduced to villages can determine whether this new technology will actually provide the expected ecological and social benefits. Most Indian villages have a few wealthy farmers who own most of the land. The rest of the people are poor farmers who own very little, if any, land. If people must pay a high price for biogas generators, only wealthy families can afford to buy them. Poor people, who do not have biogas generators, will earn money by gathering cow dung to sell to wealthy people for their biogas generators. Poor people may not care much about the ecological benefits from biogas generators because a better supply of irrigation water offers the greatest benefits to wealthy farmers who have more land.

As a consequence, the benefits from biogas generators could go mainly to the wealthy, widening the gap between the wealthy and the poor. Poor farmers, who see few benefits for themselves, might continue to destroy the forests, and the community as a whole might receive little benefit from the new technology. To improve the situation, it is important to make sure that everyone can obtain a biogas generator. Then everyone will enjoy the benefits, and the vicious cycle of fuel scarcity and deforestation will be broken.

SUSTAINABLE DEVELOPMENT

Unintended consequences such as the ones in the story about fishing and marine animals are not unusual. Many human activities impact the environment in ways that are subtle or inconspicuous or involve changes that are so slow that people do not notice what is happening until the problem is serious. Problems may appear suddenly, and sometimes at a considerable distance from the human actions that cause them.

Minamata disease is a typical example of an unintended consequence. Until the 1960s, mercury was widely used for industrial processes such as paper and plastics production. Plastic factories in Japan's Minamata region routinely dumped mercury waste into the adjacent coastal waters. Though mercury was known to be highly toxic, no one worried because the ocean was so large. However, bacteria around factory outlets were transforming the mercury into even more toxic methane mercury, which accumulated year after year in the coastal ecosystem. The mercury was biologically concentrated as it passed along each step of the **food chain** from **phytoplankton** (microscopic plants) to **zooplankton** (tiny animals), small fish and finally fish large enough for people to eat. No one realized that the mercury concentration in fish was more than a million times the concentration in the surrounding ocean water.

During the 1950s more than 1000 people in the Minamata region were afflicted with an illness that killed several hundred, left survivors with devastating neurological damage and produced severe deformities in babies. Once mercury-contaminated fish were identified as the cause of the problem, the local people mounted a campaign for the factories to do something about it. After several years the government finally ordered the factories to stop dumping mercury; but the large quantity of mercury already in the coastal ecosystem continued to circulate through the food web. It was nearly 50 years before fish in the Minamata region were safe to eat again. This dramatic incident eventually led to worldwide elimination of mercury from large-scale industrial processes, though mercury is unfortunately still in use for gold mining in parts of Africa, Latin America and Asia.

A recent tragedy in North Korea illustrates how serious an ecological mistake can be. Several million people have died of starvation during the past five years because of agricultural failure due to floods. The causes are complex, but deforestation seems to be a major part of the story. Deforestation started 100 years ago with the exploitation of Korea's forests by Japanese colonialism, and it continued with the partitioning of Korea after World War II. Because the North was the industrial region of Korea and the South the agricultural region, isolation of the North forced it to increase its food production by expanding agriculture into forest lands. Large-scale use of wood for household and industrial fuel, and logging of trees for timber export, reduced the forest in the North even further.

sustainable development

Forests perform a valuable function by capturing rainwater and releasing it to streams and rivers that provide water for cities and agriculture. Forest soils with a carpet of decomposing leaves absorb rainwater like a sponge, holding the water for gradual release to streams throughout the year. When **watersheds** lose their forest, the soil can lose its capacity to absorb rainwater as it did before. Rainwater flows quickly off the watershed, causing floods during the rainy season and a diminished supply of water during the dry season. Deforestation in North Korea proceeded for nearly a century before the disastrous consequences were apparent. Devastating floods and crop destruction have now become regular events. This mistake will not be corrected quickly because reforestation takes such a long time. Even worse, the same forces that caused deforestation have created a vicious cycle that intensifies deforestation even more. Deforestation has reduced agricultural production, creating a need to import fertilizers and food and forcing North Korea to cut even more trees to pay for the imported goods with revenues from timber export.

sustainable development

Sustainable development can be defined as meeting present needs without compromising the ability of future generations to meet their own needs. It is about leaving the opportunity for a decent life to our children and grandchildren. Ecologically sustainable development is about keeping ecosystems healthy. It is about interacting with ecosystems in ways that allow them to maintain sufficient functional integrity to continue providing humans and all other creatures in the ecosystem the food, water, shelter and other resources that they need. North Korea has not been ecologically sustainable because it failed to maintain the proper balance of forested watersheds essential for a healthy landscape. Nor is it ecologically sustainable development to exterminate marine animals, destroy forests to obtain cooking fuel or pollute marine ecosystems with mercury.

Sustainable development does not mean sustaining economic growth. Economic growth is impossible to sustain if it depends upon ever increasing quantities of resources from ecosystems with limited capacities to provide the resources. Nor is sustainable development a luxury to be pursued after economic development and other priorities such as social justice are achieved. Damaged ecosystems that lose their capacity to meet basic human needs close off opportunities for economic development and social justice. A healthy society gives equal attention to ecological sustainability, economic development and social justice because they are all mutually reinforcing.

Intensity of demands on ecosystems

There is a close connection between the sustainability of human–ecosystem interaction and the intensity of demands that people place on ecosystems. We all depend on ecosystems for material and energy resources. Some resources such as mineral deposits and fossil fuels are **non-renewable**; other resources such as food, water and forest products are **renewable**. People use these resources and return them to the ecosystem as waste, such as sewage, garbage, or industrial effluent (see Figure 1.6).

In general, greater demands on ecosystems in the form of more intense resource use are less sustainable. Intense use of non-renewable resources exhausts the supply more quickly. Intense use of renewable resources can damage the ability of ecosystems to provide the resources (explained in more detail in Chapters 6, 8 and 10.) Sustainable interaction with ecosystems is only possible if demands are kept within bounds. This has not been the case in recent decades as human population growth, as well as industrial and economic growth and burgeoning material consumption, have dramatically increased the scale of natural resource use. As environmental awareness has increased, there have been changes in the social system to reduce the intensity of demands on ecosystems. There has been a shift in recent years from technologies that are wasteful of resources toward technologies that use resources more efficiently and reduce pollution.

A small population can enjoy high levels of consumption without placing excessive demands on the environment. Too many

sustainable development

Figure 1.6
Human use of natural resources

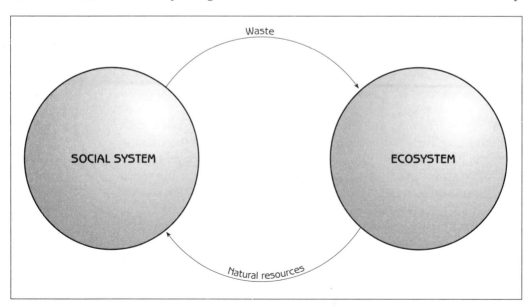

Waste

SOCIAL SYSTEM

ECOSYSTEM

Natural resources

> ### Intensity of demands on ecosystems = Population x Level of consumption x Technology
>
> *Intensity of demands on ecosystems:*
>
> - the total quantity of material and energy resources required for industrial and agricultural production; plus
> - pollution generated by industrial and agricultural production.
>
> *Population:* the number of people who use the industrial and agricultural products.
>
> *Level of consumption:* the per capita quantity of industrial and agricultural production. It is closely connected to a society's material affluence.
>
> *Technology:* the quantity of resource used and pollution generated per unit of industrial and agricultural production.

Box 1.1
Intensity of demands on ecosystems

organization of this book

people can employ the most efficient technologies imaginable and still be forced to make unsustainable demands on the environment while living in poverty. The level of consumption of wealthy nations is enormously greater than that of poor nations. The significance of the population in wealthy nations lies not only in the large numbers of people that they already have but also the fact that their heavy demands extend to ecosystems beyond their own boundaries. Developing world nations aspire to economic development with higher levels of industrial production and consumption, aspirations that are thwarted by rapid population growth now typical in that part of the world.

ORGANIZATION OF THIS BOOK

The first half of this book explains how ecosystems and social systems function and interact as self-organizing **complex adaptive systems**. It explains system concepts and ecological principles essential to the discussions of human–ecosystem interaction later in the book. Chapter 2 uses the growth and regulation of animal populations to illustrate positive and negative feedback – key concepts for understanding the dynamics of ecosystems and social systems. Chapter 3 relates the history of human population growth, explaining the causes and consequences of the unprecedented growth that we see today.

Chapters 4 and 5 explain how ecosystems organize themselves and how the same organizing principles apply to human social systems. Chapter 6 explains how ecosystems are continually changing due to natural processes and the impact of human activities. It shows how human activities can cause unintended changes in ecosystems – changes that are sometimes undesirable and irreversible.

The focus in the last half of the book shifts to interactions between social systems and ecosystems. Chapter 7 introduces a central concept for human–ecosystem interaction – the coevolution and coadaptation of social systems and ecosystems. As a rule, social systems that are coadapted to ecosystems are ecologically more sustainable. Chapter 8 describes the biological processes that move materials and energy through ecosystems – and between people and ecosystems. It explains how the quantity of materials and energy that ecosystems can provide for human use is affected by the way that people use them. Chapter 9 outlines perceptions and values that shape human actions toward ecosystems, and Chapter 10 surveys the numerous reasons why modern society interacts in an unsustainable manner with the ecosystems on which it depends for survival. Chapter 11 outlines principles for sustainable interaction with ecosystems and presents examples of social institutions that make sustainable interaction a reality. Chapter 11 finishes by emphasizing the need to build into modern society a dynamic adaptive capacity for sustainable development. Chapter 12 presents two case studies which illustrate ecologically sustainable development. The first is about ecological technology and the second is a regional environmental management programme.

things to think about

THINGS TO THINK ABOUT

1. Figure 1.4 summarizes the story of cooking fuel and deforestation in India. Look at each of the arrows in the figure and write down the effect that it represents, so that you can trace the chain of effects through the village social system and ecosystem. For example, the arrow from 'Human population' to 'Demand for cooking fuel' can be described as 'Increase in human population increases the demand for cooking fuel'. Then look at the arrows in Figure 1.5. Starting with 'Demand for cooking fuel', note how the direction of the effects in Figure 1.5 is different from Figure 1.4 because biogas technology is in the story. Start with the arrow from 'Demand for cooking fuel' to 'Biogas technology', which represents 'High demand for cooking fuel leads to biogas technology'. The arrow from 'Biogas technology' to 'Biogas generators' represents 'Biogas generators are introduced to villages'; and so on.

2. Put together an example of a chain of effects through ecosystem and social system, using information from newspaper or magazine articles and your own personal knowledge. Show the example with a diagram.
3. Think of examples of unintended consequences from the environment, using information from newspaper or magazine articles and your own personal knowledge. Why did it take so long for people to realize what was happening? Why did the problem become apparent so suddenly?
4. Look at the equation for 'intensity of demands on ecosystems' and think how population, consumption and technology are changing in your country. What are some important ways that changes in population, consumption and technology are changing your nation's demands on ecosystems? What is the contribution of each to the magnitude of the change in demands on ecosystems?
5. Do you think ecologically sustainable development is possible for your country? Is it possible for the world as a whole? Even if ecologically sustainable development is possible, do you think it will really happen? Does ecologically sustainable development appear to be more likely in some places than others?

things to think about

POPULATIONS AND FEEDBACK SYSTEMS

Why do environmental problems sometimes appear so suddenly? The explanation lies with positive and negative feedback – powerful forces that shape the behaviour of all biological systems from cells to social systems and ecosystems. Feedback is the effect that change in one part of an ecosystem or social system has on the very same part after passing through a chain of effects in other parts of the system. **Negative feedback** provides **stability**. All ecosystems and social systems have hundreds of negative feedback loops that keep every part of the system within the bounds necessary for the whole system to continue functioning properly. **Positive feedback** stimulates *change*. Positive feedback is responsible for the sudden appearance of environmental problems and many other rapid changes in the world around us.

An ecosystem's biological community consists of populations of every species of plant, animal and microorganism in the ecosystem. People interact directly or indirectly with populations whenever they interact with ecosystems. This chapter explains how positive feedback causes populations to increase rapidly when there is a surplus of resources. It also explains how negative feedback restrains the population of every species in a biological community within limits that the ecosystem can support.

EXPONENTIAL POPULATION GROWTH

A simple story about **exponential population growth** can show why environmental problems sometimes appear so suddenly. Water hyacinth is a floating plant that has spread from South America to waterways around the world. It can cover the water so completely that it obstructs the movement of boats.

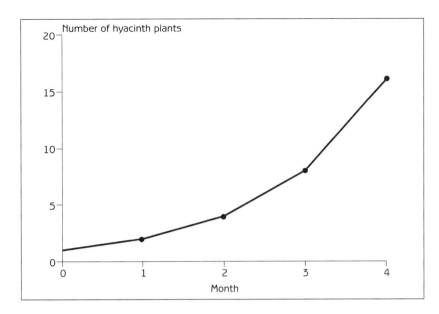

Figure 2.1
Growth in the water hyacinth population during the first four months after introducing a single hyacinth to a lake

exponential population growth

Imagine a lake that is 10 kilometres in diameter. It takes eight billion hyacinth plants to cover a lake of this size completely. To start with, our lake has no water hyacinth. Then we introduce one hyacinth plant onto the lake. After one month, this plant forms two plants. After another month the two plants have multiplied to four (see Figure 2.1), and the doubling continues month after month. Two years pass, and the hyacinths have multiplied to 17 million plants. Nobody pays attention to them because 17 million plants cover only 0.2 per cent of the lake.

Six months later, 30 months after we put the single plant on the lake, there are one billion hyacinth plants, which cover about 13 per cent of the lake (see Figure 2.2). Now people notice the hyacinths. Although there are not enough hyacinth plants to be a

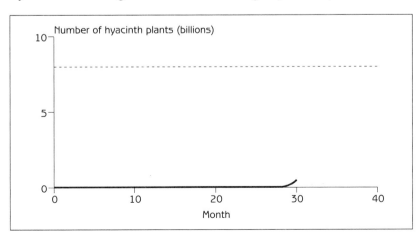

Figure 2.2
Water hyacinth population after 30 months

exponential
population
growth

Figure 2.3
Exponential
growth of the
water hyacinth
population

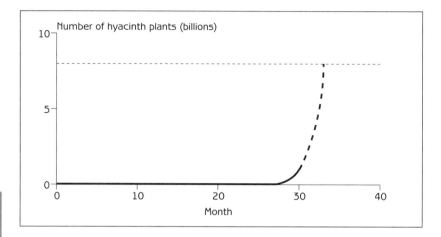

problem for the movement of boats, some people are worried. Other people say, 'Don't worry. It took a long time to get this many hyacinths. It will be a long time before there are enough to cause a problem.' Which people are right? Is the problem a long time in the future, or will there be a problem soon? In fact, with hyacinth doubling every month, the lake will be completely covered after only three more months (see Figure 2.3).

This is a true story. Water hyacinth has become an uncontrollable nuisance in many places, including the world's second largest lake – Lake Victoria in East Africa – where fish from the lake are a major source of animal protein for millions of people. Parts of Lake Victoria are now so badly clogged with water hyacinth that fishing boats cannot move through the water. Thousands of fishermen are out of work, and the supply of fish has declined drastically.

The water hyacinth story is about floating plants on a lake, but it is also about the human population on planet Earth. The rapid filling of the lake with water hyacinths after their population became noticeable is comparable to the exponential population growth that is now filling the planet with humans. The Earth's carrying capacity for humans may be about eight billion people; the planet's human population is already six billion. No one knows exactly how many people the Earth can support on a sustainable basis. Its carrying capacity for humans depends on technology, including future technology. It also depends on the impacts of human activities on ecosystems, activities that for the first time are happening intensively on a global scale. Nonetheless, the basic implication of the water hyacinth story for the human population is the same whether the Earth's carrying capacity is six billion, eight billion, ten billion or even somewhat more.

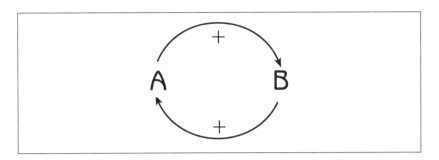

Figure 2.4
A positive
feedback loop

POSITIVE FEEDBACK

positive
feedback

The water hyacinth story is an example of **positive feedback**– a circular chain of effects that increases change. Many changes in ecosystems appear to be sudden because of positive feedback. When part of a system increases, another part of the system changes in a way that makes the first part increase even more. There is positive feedback whenever *A* has a positive effect on *B*, and *B* has a positive effect on *A* (see Figure 2.4). Positive feedback is a source of instability; it is a force for change.

Exponential growth is an example of positive feedback (see Figure 2.5). **Exponential population growth** occurs when there is a surplus of food, space and other resources that allows a plant or animal population to grow without limit. More population leads to more births, and more births lead to an increasing population. The water hyacinth story is not just about floating plants in a lake. It illustrates how the exponential growth of human populations in recent years, and the exponential growth in natural resource use and pollution due to industrialization, can suddenly reach the limits of ecosystems to provide the resources and absorb pollution.

Positive feedback increases change, but it does not always cause an increase. If a change is downward, positive feedback can make the downward change even greater. This can happen with

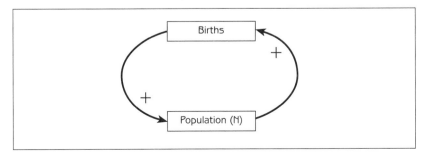

Figure 2.5
The positive
feedback loop
that generates
exponential
population
growth

populations. When the number of animals in the population of an **endangered species** becomes so small that it is difficult for the animals to find mates, births are fewer and the population decreases. The decrease in population makes it even more difficult to find mates, and the population decreases even more. Positive feedback causes a decline in population that leads to extinction.

Positive feedback does not happen only in plant and animal populations. It is common in human social systems. Mutual stimulation of friendly or antagonistic relations between individuals or groups is an example of positive feedback. Undesirable positive feedback is called a 'vicious cycle'. The Cold War arms race between the United States and the former Soviet Union provides an example of positive feedback. When the United States developed more and better weapons, the former Soviet Union was alarmed by the increase in American military strength and was stimulated to develop more and better weapons. The United States, alarmed by the increase in Soviet military strength, developed even more weapons. Positive feedback caused an ascending spiral of weapons in both countries. The process reversed when the Cold War ended, and the United States and former Soviet Union agreed to fractionally reduce their weapons. Though international arms reduction has been a very complex process, a major part of the story has been reciprocal stimulation of the United States and former Soviet Union to progressively reduce the quantity of weapons that they have directed against each other. Just as the ascending spiral was due to positive feedback, the descending spiral has also been due to positive feedback.

An example of positive feedback that causes one thing to replace another

Positive feedback can cause one thing to increase and another thing to decrease. When there is competition between two parts of a system, positive feedback causes one part to replace the other. The victory of VHS videocassettes over Betamax is a good example. Twenty-five years ago, when videocassette recorders (VCRs) were first placed on the market, there were two completely different electronic systems for the VCRs. The systems were VHS and Betamax, and they were not compatible with each other. Only VHS tapes could be used on VHS recorders, and only Betamax tapes could be used on Betamax recorders.

The public did not know which system to choose because the cost and quality of each was about the same. As a consequence, some people purchased VHS recorders, and others purchased

positive feedback

Betamax recorders. At first, about half the people had VHS, and the other half had Betamax, so about half of the movie video tapes at video stores were VHS tapes, and about half were Betamax tapes. This situation continued for several years. Then the number of VHS recorders and VHS tapes started to grow exponentially, and the number of Betamax recorders and Betamax tapes declined equally rapidly. Betamax disappeared, and everyone now uses VHS.

Why did VHS win the competition? Figure 2.6 shows what happened. The big change started when slightly more than half the people had VHS recorders. Movie companies then made more movie video tapes with the VHS system because more people had VHS recorders and therefore bought VHS tapes. More people then selected VHS when purchasing a new video recorder, because more movies were available on VHS tape. As a consequence, there were even more VHS recorders and fewer Betamax recorders, so the movie companies put even more movies on VHS tapes and fewer on Betamax tapes. In other words, an increase in VHS had a chain of effects through the system that caused VHS to increase even more, and a decrease in Betamax had a chain of effects through the system that caused Betamax to decrease even more. These were the positive feedback loops that carried VHS to victory and caused Betamax to disappear.

positive feedback

Figure 2.6
Positive feedback loops that caused VHS to replace Betamax

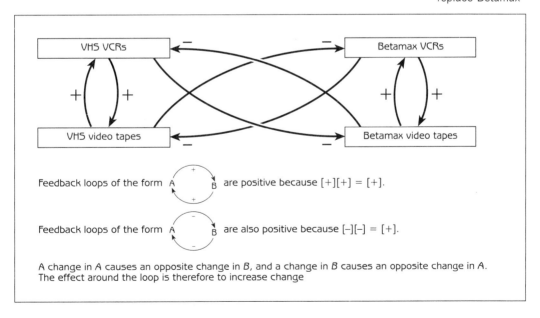

Feedback loops of the form A ↻ B are positive because [+][+] = [+].

Feedback loops of the form A ↻ B are also positive because [–][–] = [+].

A change in A causes an opposite change in B, and a change in B causes an opposite change in A. The effect around the loop is therefore to increase change

NEGATIVE FEEDBACK

Negative feedback is a circular chain of effects that opposes change. It keeps things the same. When part of a system changes too much from what it should be, other parts of the system change in a way that reverses the change in the first part. The function of negative feedback is to keep the parts of a system within limits that are necessary for survival. Negative feedback is a source of **stability**; it is a force against change.

negative feedback

Homeostasis is an example of negative feedback in biological systems. Homeostasis is control of an organism's internal physical and chemical condition within limits required for the organism's survival. Figure 2.7 shows how negative feedback is used to control human body temperature.

If body temperature increases above 37° Celsius, negative feedback reduces the body temperature by:

* reducing metabolic heat generation; and
* increasing heat loss from the body (more blood supply to the skin and more sweating).

If body temperature decreases below 37° Celsius, negative feedback increases the body temperature by:

* increasing heat generation (shivering); and
* decreasing heat loss (less blood supply to the skin and less sweating).

Keeping the body temperature close to 37° Celsius is essential for a person's survival.

Negative feedback is common in social systems. For example, people use negative feedback to drive a car. If the car starts to go off the road, you steer it in the opposite direction to bring it back

Figure 2.7
Control of body temperature by negative feedback

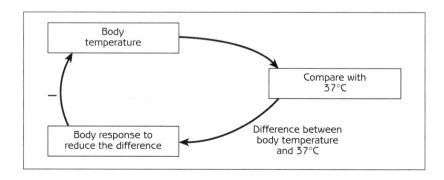

onto the road. In other words, when the trajectory starts to change, your negative feedback as a driver reverses the change by bringing the car back. Engineers use negative feedback for machines. If an aeroplane starts to descend toward the ground when it should not, the 'automatic pilot' in the aeroplane makes it go upward so it stays at the correct altitude.

POPULATION REGULATION

population regulation

Imagine a forest that has no deer. Then one male and one female deer come to the forest. After one year they have two fawns. A year later the young deer are old enough to reproduce, and each pair produces two more fawns. The deer population continues to double each year, and after ten years there are 1000 deer. Deer need plenty of food to grow and produce offspring. However, there is not as much food as before, because the larger numbers of deer are eating so much of it. The deer are less healthy, more susceptible to disease and sometimes die at a young age because they do not have enough food. Moreover, a malnourished deer may produce only one fawn instead of two.

This story tells us that deer are limited by their food supply:

- When population increases, the food supply decreases.
- When population decreases, the food supply increases.

- When the food supply increases, births increase and deaths decrease.
- When the food supply decreases, births decrease and deaths increase.

- Therefore, when population increases, the food supply decreases, the birth rate (births√population) decreases and the death rate (deaths√population) increases.
- When population decreases, the food supply increases, birth rate increases and death rate decreases.

Population regulation and carrying capacity

The story of the deer is the story of all plants and all animals, including people. Why do plants and animals have the abundance that they have? Why aren't there more? Or less? The explanation is

Figure 2.8
Population
regulation by
food supply
Note: The negative
feedback loop through
food supply and births
is [–][+][+] = [–].
The negative feedback
loop through food
supply and deaths is
[–][–][–] = [–]

population
regulation

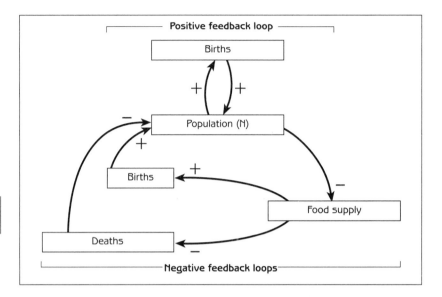

population regulation. Population regulation uses negative feedback to keep plant and animal populations within the limits of the **carrying capacity** of their environment. Carrying capacity is the population that the food supply in the environment will support on a long-term (sustainable) basis. Because the resources that sustain populations are limited, no population can exceed the carrying capacity of its environment for long.

Figure 2.8 shows how positive and negative feedback affect a population. With the positive feedback loop, an increase in the population leads to more births, which increases the population even more. With the negative feedback loop, an increase in the

Figure 2.9
The relation of
population
change to
carrying capacity
N = population
number
ΔN = the change in
population number
ΔN = [total number
of births in the
population] – [total
number of deaths in
the population]
When births >
deaths, then ΔN>0,
and the population
number increases
When deaths>births,
then ΔN<0, and the
population decreases

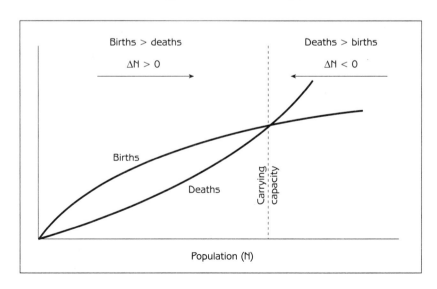

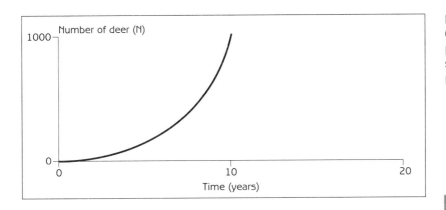

Figure 2.10
Growth of a deer
population after
starting with one
pair of deer

population
regulation

population reduces the food supply. Less food means more deaths and fewer births.

Figure 2.9 shows how negative feedback regulates a population near carrying capacity. If the number of plants or animals in a population is less than carrying capacity, births are greater than deaths and the population increases until it reaches carrying capacity. If the population is larger than carrying capacity, deaths are greater than births, and the population decreases until it reaches carrying capacity. Once a population is close to carrying capacity, births are more or less equal to deaths, and the population does not change much.

Returning to the story of the deer, Figure 2.10 shows what happened to the deer population during the first ten years. $\Delta N/\Delta t$ (the change in the deer population each year) is small during the first few years, when the deer population is small. $\Delta N/\Delta t$ is larger in the ninth year when the deer population is much larger. The population growth curve is exponential because of positive feedback, but exponential growth cannot continue forever. What will happen during the next 20 years?

An S-shaped 'sigmoid' curve for population growth (shown in Figure 2.11) is what usually happens when deer or any other plants or animals start a population in a new place. The exponential growth in the first part of the sigmoid curve is followed by population regulation as the number of plants or animals approaches carrying capacity and negative feedback takes over. In many instances a population increases gradually and then fluctuates in the vicinity of carrying capacity (the solid curve in Figure 2.11). It does not stay precisely at carrying capacity because:

- negative feedback is not highly precise; and
- other factors besides food supply can have an impact on births and deaths.

Figure 2.11
The sigmoid
curve for
population
growth and
regulation

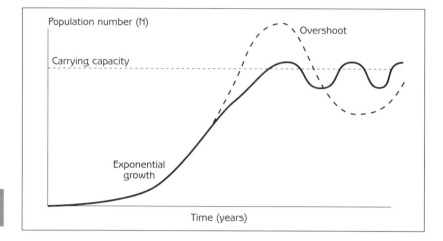

Sometimes a population grows so rapidly that it **overshoots** carrying capacity before negative feedback can stop the increase (the dashed curve in Figure 2.11). If a population overshoots, it usually depletes its food so severely that negative feedback in the form of more deaths and fewer births quickly reduces it below carrying capacity.

THE PRACTICAL SIGNIFICANCE OF POSITIVE AND NEGATIVE FEEDBACK

Every ecosystem and human social system has numerous positive and negative feedback loops. Both kinds of feedback are essential for survival. Negative feedback provides stability; it keeps important parts of the system within the limits required for proper functioning. Positive feedback provides the capacity to change drastically when necessary. The development and growth of all biological systems – from cells and individual organisms to ecosystems and social systems – is based on the interplay of positive and negative feedback. Ecosystems and social systems can stay more or less the same for long periods, but sometimes they change dramatically and rapidly. They function best when they have an appropriate balance between the forces that promote change and the forces that provide stability.

People constantly interact with these forces of change and stability. People depend upon negative feedback to 'take care of things' and keep everything functioning smoothly most of the time. When people try to improve their situation ('development' or 'solving problems'), they use positive feedback to help make the changes they want. However, in addition to working for people, positive and negative feedback can also work against them. Sometimes people try to improve things or solve a problem, and no matter what they do, there is no improvement because they are working against negative feedback that prevents the changes that they want. Other times, people prefer things to stay the way they are, but positive feedback amplifies seemingly harmless actions into changes that they do not want. If we pay attention to the positive and negative feedbacks in our social systems and ecosystems, we can use the feedbacks to our advantage instead of struggling against them. In the case of ecosystems, this means fitting our activities with ecosystems to do things 'nature's way', so nature does most of the work and keeps things going. The concrete meaning of 'doing things nature's way' will become more apparent in subsequent chapters.

things to think about

THINGS TO THINK ABOUT

1. Think of examples of positive feedback at different levels of social organization in your social system: family and friends, neighbourhood, city, national, and international. Draw diagrams to show circular chains of effects (ie, feedback loops). Do some of the feedback loops generate sudden changes?
2. Think of examples of the replacement of one thing by another in your social system or ecosystem during recent years. Draw a diagram to show the chain of effects and feedback loops that generated the replacement.
3. Think of examples of negative feedback at different levels of social organization in your social system. Draw diagrams to show the circular chains of effects.
4. Figure 2.10 shows what happened to the deer population during the first ten years in the 'story of the deer'. Compare $\Delta N/\Delta t$ in the first year (when the deer population is small) with $\Delta N/\Delta t$ in the tenth year (when the deer population is much larger). During which time is $\Delta N/\Delta t$ larger? What kind of population change does this graph show during the first ten years? Does positive feedback or negative feedback dominate the form of the graph when the population is small? Will the same kind of population change continue forever? Draw the graph in Figure 2.10 to show what you think will happen during the next 20 years. Is negative feedback important when the deer population is small or when it is large?
5. Think of examples in your nation or community that illustrate:
   • using positive feedback to make desired changes;
   • positive feedback that generates undesirable changes despite efforts to stop the change;
   • negative feedback that keeps things the way people want them to be;
   • negative feedback that obstructs efforts to change things that people consider undesirable.

3

HUMAN POPULATION

According to archaeological evidence, the first humans (*Homo habilis*) appeared in Africa about three million years ago. They used simple stone tools. Humans (*Homo erectus*) expanded their populations through Europe and Asia at least a million years ago. The modern human species (*Homo sapiens*) appeared in Africa about 1.3 million years ago and remained only in Africa for many years. *Homo sapiens* extended its population to Europe, Asia and Australia about 40,000–50,000 years ago. The first humans known to live in the Western Hemisphere migrated there from Asia about 13,000 years ago.

Homo sapiens have existed for at least 60,000 generations. The entire human population of the planet was probably less than ten million people during nearly all of that time. About 10,000 years ago humans began to increase their numbers in a few parts of the world, an increase that continued gradually until 300 years ago. By 1700 AD, there were about 600 million people around the world. The population has multiplied to six billion people during the 12 generations since 1700.

Why did the human population increase so rapidly during the past few centuries, after growing so little for such a long time? Have modern science and technology freed humans from population regulation and the limitations of carrying capacity that apply to other animals? This chapter provides an overview of human population history, starting with the small population of hunter-gatherers that constituted humanity for almost all of its history. It describes the expansion of human population as the **Agricultural Revolution** spread around the globe, and the explosive increase in population that followed the **Industrial Revolution**. The chapter finishes with implications for the future.

HUMAN POPULATION HISTORY

From hunting and gathering to agriculture

The physical and mental abilities of modern humans – and their ecological position in the ecosystem – were formed by several million years of evolution as hunters and gatherers. Humans lived in natural ecosystems that contained many different kinds of plants and animals, only some of them suitable as human food (Figure 3.1a). With their hunting and gathering technology, humans were able to capture only a small part of the ecosystem's total biological production as food for their own consumption. The carrying capacity for humans was similar to that of other animals, and human populations were no larger than the populations of other animals. Humans probably consumed about 0.1 per cent of the biological production in the ecosystems in which they lived.

human population history

This changed after the Agricultural Revolution, which enabled people to create their own small ecosystems for food production. Agriculture in its simplest form first appeared about 12,000 years ago in the Middle East. People encouraged wild plants that they used as food to grow near their dwellings, making food gathering easier. They eventually domesticated some of the plants by selecting individual species with desirable characteristics such as edible parts that were larger or easier to process for consumption. They also domesticated some of the wild animals that they used as food. In this way, people were able to increase the percentage of the ecosystem's biological production that was available for human consumption (see Figure 3.1B), and the carrying capacity for humans increased.

Figure 3.1
Distribution of biological production among plants and animals in the ecosystem food web

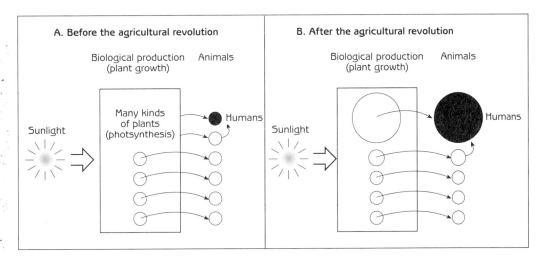

A. Before the agricultural revolution

Biological production (plant growth)   Animals

Many kinds of plants (photsynthesis)   Humans

Sunlight

B. After the agricultural revolution

Biological production (plant growth)   Animals

Humans

Sunlight

The Agricultural Revolution started in the Middle East because that region had the most plants and animals suitable for domestication. Only a few hundred plants and a few dozen animals among all the species in the world were suitable for domestication, and nearly all of them were domesticated at least 5000 years ago. No major new crop or livestock animal has been domesticated anywhere in the world during the past 5000 years, and none can be expected in the future. Some parts of the world, such as Australia and sub-Saharan Africa, had very few plants or animals suitable for domestication. Agriculture began in those areas only after domesticated plants and animals were brought from other places.

human population history

Why did humans wait so long to develop agriculture? The effort that people must expend to form and maintain agricultural ecosystems – preparing the land, planting a crop, caring for the crop, and protecting it from weeds, insects and other animals that want to consume it – requires much more human labour than hunting and gathering. People were probably content to live without agriculture as long as they did not need it. It was convenient to have nature do the work of producing food. However, inhabitants of the Middle East may have felt a strong need to find new ways to procure more food about 12,000 years ago, when rapid change to a drier climate reduced the biological production and human carrying capacity of the Middle Eastern ecosystem.

Over a period of several thousand years agriculture spread through the Middle East to Asia, North Africa and Europe, and arose independently in China, North America, Meso-America, South America and New Guinea. Human populations increased in the areas with agriculture (2 AD in Figure 3.2). New improvements in food production happened in different places at different times, so the human carrying capacity at any one place increased in steps (see Figure 3.3). Any significant new improvement in agricultural technology generated a rapid increase in carrying capacity, and the human population of that region increased to the new carrying capacity over a period of centuries. Once population growth was no longer possible, people felt the stress of limited food supply. This stress, known as **population pressure**, motivated people to develop additional improvements in agricultural technology, or adopt more productive agricultural practices from neighbouring people. This made the carrying capacity higher, and the upward cycle of human population continued as a positive feedback loop between population and technology.

The progressive increases in agricultural production generally required more effort to structure ecosystems so that a larger share of their biological production was channelled to human

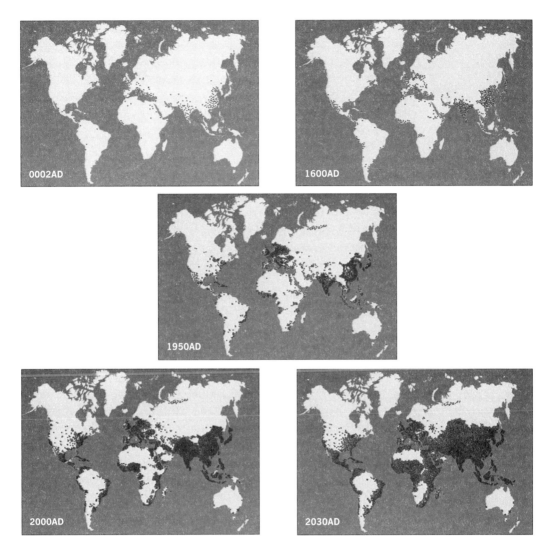

consumption (see Figure 3.4). This is the principle of 'no free lunch'. Every choice has advantages and disadvantages. Every gain has its costs. One of the costs of more food is more work.

The human population of the planet increased gradually for more than 10,000 years after the Agricultural Revolution (see Figure 3.5A). The largest populations were in the great river valleys of India and China. There was a substantial increase in Middle Eastern and European populations during this period. The world population declined by 25 per cent when the plague known as the Black Death swept across Asia and Europe during the 14th century, but it quickly returned to its former numbers during the following century. People in Europe were feeling the stress of a population at the limits of its carrying capacity, but the situation changed as

Figure 3.2
Growth and geographic distribution of the human population during the past 2000 years
Source: 'World Population' video, Zero Population Growth, Washington, DC
Note: Each dot represents one million people.

Figure 3.3
Periodic
increases in
human
population and
carrying capacity

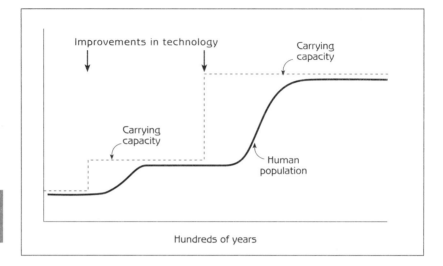

Figure 3.3
Periodic
increases in
human
population and
carrying capacity

**human
population
history**

the more powerful European nations embarked on worldwide colonialism and trade during the 16th century. The supply of resources increased Europe's carrying capacity, and the European population began to grow. Carrying capacity increased even further as the **Industrial Revolution** gained momentum during the 18th century.

The Industrial Revolution

The Industrial Revolution had a major impact on agriculture. Highly productive crops such as wheat, corn, potatoes, sweet potatoes and rice, which were previously restricted to particular

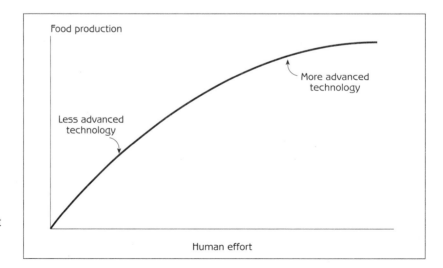

Figure 3.4
Human effort
required for
technologies that
provide higher
food production

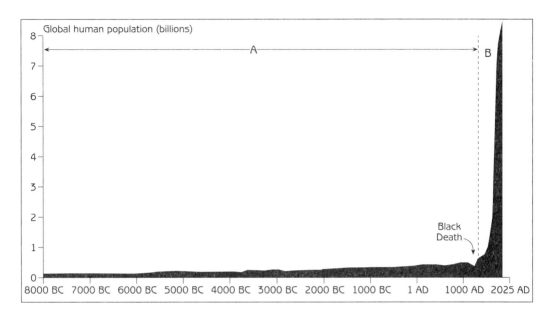

Figure 3.5
Ten thousand
years of human
population
growth
Source: Adapted from
Population Reference
Bureau (1984) *World
Population:
Fundamentals of
Growth*, Population
Reference Bureau,
Washington, DC

regions of the world where they originated, were quickly spread around the world by European trade and colonialism, giving farmers an expanded 'menu' of highly productive crops from which to choose. Mechanization gave farmers the ability to structure ecosystems more than had been possible with only human and animal labour. The Industrial Revolution was accompanied by a scientific revolution, as well as new agricultural technologies that increased agricultural production even further. People were able to capture a much larger percentage of the ecosystem's biological production for their consumption, and carrying capacity increased. The increase in carrying capacity since the Industrial Revolution has been so large and so continuous that the planet's human population has been able to grow exponentially for the past 250 years (see Figure 3.5, B).

Birth rates were high before the Industrial Revolution. Large families helped to meet the high labour demands of farm life and ensure the survival of children in order to care for parents in their old age. Improvements in public health from the scientific revolution drastically reduced death rates in industrializing countries. Their populations increased rapidly because birth rates remained high. By the 19th century, urbanization and improved survival of children made large families less necessary. Birth rates started to decline as people adopted various methods of limiting family size. The populations of industrialized nations continued to grow rapidly through the 19th and most of the 20th centuries (see Figure 3.6; compare 1950 AD with 1600 AD in Figure 3.2). However, their internally generated population growth was nearly zero by the end of the 20th century. The populations of some industrialized nations continue to grow primarily due to migration from other countries.

Population 'ageing' has recently become a major issue in industrialized nations. There is a change from a rapidly growing population with a high percentage of young people to a population that is growing slowly or not at all with a high percentage of older people. This is reducing the number of economically productive young people compared to older retired people that they must support. 'Ageing' is well underway in Japan, it is beginning in Europe and North America, and within a few decades it will become a major issue in developing world countries that reduce their population growth. Some people in countries with an 'ageing' population have suggested that birth rates should be increased to provide more young people to support the elderly – a course of action whose short-term benefits would exacerbate the long-term overpopulation problem, resulting in more elderly people to support in the future. Many industrialized nations such as Japan already have populations and levels of consumption that are much greater than they can support with resources from within their own boundaries. They are scarcely aware of the extent to which they have exceeded their carrying capacity because their privileged economic position allows them to draw upon extensive resources from beyond their boundaries.

Developing world populations began to grow rapidly during the 20th century, when modern public health reduced deaths but births remained high. Most of the world's population growth is now in the developing world (see Figure 3.6; compare 2000 AD with 1950 AD in Figure 3.2). Large numbers are migrating from

human population history

Figure 3.6
Increase in the populations of industrialized and developing world nations from 1800 to 2000
Source: Data from Population Reference Bureau, Washington, DC

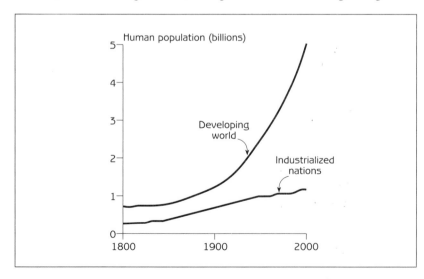

crowded parts of the developing world to seek better economic opportunities in North America, Europe and Australia. Births began to decline in some parts of the developing world about 20 years ago, but births remain high in many areas. Even if births decline drastically, the developing world population will continue to increase for several generations (2030 in Figure 3.2). Developing world populations have such a large percentage of young people that, even with smaller families, the number of births from the large number of people of reproductive age will greatly exceed the small number of elderly people who die.

The Green Revolution

human population history

The most recent increase in human carrying capacity began about 40 years ago with the **Green Revolution**, which used modern plant breeding to create **high-yield varieties** of rice, wheat, corn and other crops to increase food production for the rapidly growing developing world population (see Figure 3.7). Higher yields were only possible if the new varieties had ideal growing conditions, such as an abundance of water, optimal fertilizer applications and the use of chemical pesticides to reduce crop damage. Irrigation was expanded on a massive scale, particularly in semi-arid regions. Irrigation not only provided the water necessary for higher yields, it also allowed farmers to grow an extra crop during the dry season. Some of the new varieties were designed to mature quickly so that farmers could fit more crops into a year. More food production meant more work – 'no free lunch'. While modern agriculture uses machines with petroleum

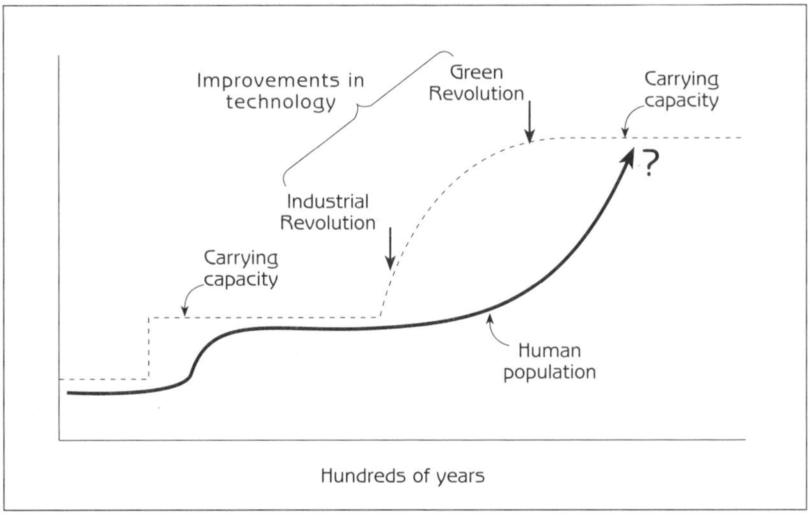

Figure 3.7 Increase in carrying capacity and human population since the Industrial Revolution

energy to do the work, many developing world families without mechanization must work long, strenuous hours to produce enough food from the small amount of land available to them.

Humans have increased their carrying capacity more than 1000-fold since the Agricultural Revolution by channelling progressively larger percentages of the Earth's biological production to human consumption. Can we expect another revolution in agricultural technology to elevate carrying capacity even higher than it is today? The answer could well be no. Moderate gains in food production will be possible through fuller implementation of the Green Revolution, particularly in Africa. Genetically modified crops and livestock could increase food production by as much as 20 per cent beyond the gains of the Green Revolution. No one knows whether unforeseen advances in agricultural technology will enable increases in food production beyond our present imagination, but the future seems to offer no further increases with the technologies now in hand.

Many of the gains during recent decades may not be sustainable. Much of the increase in food production has been due to the expansion of agriculture onto lands inappropriate for long-term agricultural use or irrigation from underground water supplies that will soon be depleted. Environmental costs of these gains could be high. Intensive inputs of chemical fertilizers and pesticides for the Green Revolution pollute the water that runs off farms. Genetically modified crops or livestock could have unanticipated detrimental effects on human health or the environment. It was recently discovered that pollen from corn that has been genetically modified to kill insect pests may drift out of cornfields and kill butterflies.

Past gains in agricultural production have been achieved primarily by increasing our share of the Earth's biological

human population history

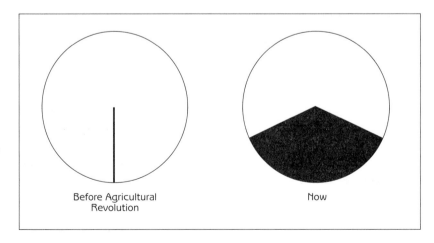

Figure 3.8
Approximate percentage of the Earth's land-based biological production controlled by humans

Before Agricultural Revolution

Now

production (see Figure 3.8), not by increasing biological production itself. It is beyond the ability of humans to significantly increase the Earth's biological production, which depends primarily on regional climates and the quantity of sunlight reaching the Earth. Nor is there much additional scope to increase the percentage for human consumption, because we already control nearly half of the planet's land-based biological production. Nobody knows exactly how many people the planet can support on a sustainable basis, but there is clearly a limit, and the human population appears to be approaching that limit.

population regulation

SOCIAL MECHANISMS OF POPULATION REGULATION

The deer population cited in Chapter 2 was limited by food supply. If animal populations are limited by their food supply, why do most wild animals look healthy and well nourished? The answer lies in the fact that many animal populations are below the carrying capacity of their environment. Carrying capacity is an upper limit that food supply places on all populations; but it is common for populations to be regulated below the limits of food supply by ecological forces other than malnutrition and starvation. Predators such as wolves and mountain lions kill deer, reducing deer populations below their carrying capacity. Where there are predators, deer have an abundance of food and they are healthy. Unfortunately, people have exterminated these predators in many regions because large predators also kill livestock. Where there are no predators, it is common for deer to be so numerous that many starve during the winter when their food supply is low.

Predation is not the only way that animal populations are regulated below the limits imposed by their food supply. Many animals have social mechanisms to prevent overpopulation. When birds select mates for reproduction, each breeding pair sets up a territory from which it excludes all other birds of the same species. As a consequence of evolution, bird territories have a size that is large enough to provide plenty of food for the breeding pair and their young. If there is not enough space to provide an adequate territory for all the birds in a population, the extra birds do not get territories and they do not reproduce. In addition, birds have physiological feedback mechanisms to reduce their egg production if food becomes scarce. Some species of birds even appear to have social displays to assess their population, with hormonal responses to the displays that reduce egg production if the population is too large.

Many other animals, including humans, have similar mechanisms to keep their populations within the limits of their food resources. The evolutionary origins of human territoriality and its function for population regulation in human societies can be seen in the social behaviour of monkeys and apes that live in groups and exclude all other individuals of the same species from their territory. Although the detailed social organization of monkeys and apes varies enormously from one species to another, it is common for males to be hostile when encountering members of another group, killing infants in the other group if they have the opportunity. When food is abundant, females with young tend to stay in the middle of their territory, where they are safe from dangerous encounters with neighbouring groups. However, if food is scarce, females can be forced to seek food near the edge of their territory, where their young are vulnerable. Moreover, females under stress frequently neglect their offspring. As a consequence, infant deaths tend to increase when there are too many individuals for food resources in the territory, and the population declines. This is a negative feedback loop that keeps the population within the limits of its food supply.

population regulation

Figure 3.9 shows how traditional human societies have used negative feedback to keep their populations below carrying capacity so that they are not regulated by starvation. When human populations grow close to their carrying capacity, it is common for land, food, irrigation water or other resources to become scarce. An increase in population leads to a reduction in resources. This leads to human actions that reduce the population by reducing births or increasing deaths (usually infant deaths). In many societies, particularly on islands, the feedback loop in Figure 3.9 has been a conscious one. In other societies the mechanisms

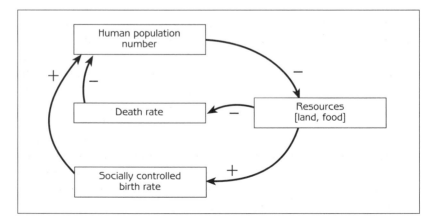

Figure 3.9
Negative
feedback loops
for social control
of human
population

for reducing births may have been part of the cultural fabric without a conscious connection to population and carrying capacity. Whatever the details, the negative feedback loop has been powerful. High death rates – based on an image that the life of primitive humans was 'short and brutish' – are not sufficient to explain the infinitesimally slow increase of human population for more than 50,000 generations.

Humans of the past survived within small-scale territories. Many traditional societies have territories of similar sizes today. Inhabitants of small-scale territories have a detailed knowledge of their area and the number of people it can support, and employ traditional birth control methods to keep their population within that limit. Breast-feeding makes a major contribution to birth control because women are generally not fertile during the period in which they are nursing a baby, and in some cultures they sleep apart from their husband during this time. The traditional custom of breast-feeding a baby for three to four years provides a natural spacing of children. Unfortunately, this custom is disappearing as modern mothers bottle-feed their babies instead of nursing them.

population explosion

Traditional population regulation is also supported by the marriage structure in some societies. For example, the husband in a polygamous society, a common form of traditional human social organization, can rotate sexual activity with his wives so that each wife becomes pregnant only once every two to three years. Traditional inheritance customs in monogamous societies can have a major effect on marriage and birth rates. For example, in some cultures it was common practice for only one son to inherit the family property. A son with inheritance could afford to marry, but the other sons without inheritance could not. This created a pool of unmarried women, who had far fewer children than married women – similar to birds that do not reproduce if they fail to secure a territory.

Traditional societies use local herbs to prevent pregnancy or induce abortion. Infanticide was common throughout the world until the 20th century, and it is still common in some regions. People kill unwanted infants in order to space their children or when they are unable to care for them because of poverty or food scarcity. Because girls have less social value than boys in many cultures, infanticide is directed primarily toward females, a practice that reduces the reproductive capacity of the subsequent generation more effectively than male infanticide. With recent advances in identifying the sex of unborn children, abortion is also directed toward females in some regions. Modern contraception methods now offer attractive alternatives to abortion and infanticide as a means of family planning.

Territorial conflict has a long-standing role in human population regulation. For example, if the population of a village is pushing the limits of its resources (for example a lack of food, land or irrigation water), it may try to use the resources of a neighbouring village or resources of disputed ownership near the village boundaries. This can set in motion a chain of effects that reduces births. Emotions can be high during village territorial conflicts. Violence is not unusual, although deaths are usually few. In all societies, traditional and modern, births often decline during periods of territorial conflict because couples wait for 'better times'. Some traditional societies prohibit sexual activity during periods of conflict.

population explosion

Territoriality remains a significant part of human behaviour in the modern world, the most important territories being nations. However, most nations are too large to provide the negative feedback loops between population and carrying capacity that smaller-scale territories provided in the past. The carrying capacity of an entire nation is obvious to no one, particularly if the nation imports large quantities of food from outside its boundaries. Instead of keeping their populations within bounds, modern nations have often encouraged population growth because of the military advantages of larger populations. Territorial behaviour becomes more perverse than functional when nations use modern weapons and well-organized armies to escalate territorial conflicts into wars that kill thousands or even millions of people without providing the ecological benefits of territoriality as in the past.

THE POPULATION EXPLOSION AND QUALITY OF LIFE

The quality of life for today's massive human population is severely limited by the finite capacity of ecosystems to provide food and other essentials for human use. The land and water resources of planet Earth are simply not enough for so many people. Rapid urban growth in recent decades has created heavy demands for materials and services from surrounding ecosystems. The consequences are particularly severe in many developing world cities, which have fallen hopelessly behind in providing housing, a safe water supply, garbage collection, sewage disposal and other basic services to their expanding populations. The prospects for a better future are diminishing rapidly as the human population continues to grow at an alarming rate.

The most serious consequence of human overpopulation is the heavy demand on ecosystems for food. There is not enough food for everyone when a population overshoots its carrying capacity (see Figure 2.11) – a problem that cannot be solved entirely by more equitable food distribution. The situation can deteriorate when overpopulation sets in motion a chain of effects through ecosystems and social systems that reduces carrying capacity instead of increasing it. This can happen when food shortages force people to produce more food by planting crops or grazing livestock on inappropriate land and with an intensity that the land cannot sustain. Erosion, depletion of soil fertility, accumulation of toxic chemicals and numerous other forms of soil damage can cause food production – and carrying capacity – to decline in a vicious cycle (positive feedback loop) of inadequate food supply and inappropriate land use.

population explosion

When this happens, it is common for people to migrate to another region where conditions are better. The developing world now has millions of **environmental refugees** migrating to cities because they can no longer survive in the rural areas where their families lived for generations. If people cannot migrate, and they lack the wealth to buy food from elsewhere, malnutrition increases deaths (particularly among young children), and the population declines much like a deer population that overshoots its carrying capacity. This grim scenario is not hypothetical. It has happened on a local scale thousands of times in the past, and it has happened more recently in North Korea and several parts of Africa. A descending spiral of hunger and land degradation is today occurring in the mountainous regions of Asia where too many people occupy land with a limited potential for food production.

Even where hunger is not a problem, the social costs of having to produce more food extend further than might be realized. High-yield varieties require higher expenses for chemical fertilizers and pesticides than locally adapted traditional varieties that farmers used before the Green Revolution. The expenses are worthwhile if yields are high enough, but high expenses can also drive farmers into debt. Economic equality has declined throughout the world as farmers lose their land due to debt, and wealthier farmers or agribusiness corporations acquire more land. Another social cost of producing large quantities of food comes from the fact that much of the increase in Green Revolution food production is achieved by means of more crop cycles in a single year. This results in correspondingly more work, with dramatic consequences for the social system. The heavy labour demands of Green Revolution agriculture leave less time for community activities. There is less time to help neighbours during peak labour periods, less time for community projects such as maintenance of terraces or irrigation ditches, or construction of homes for newlyweds (where this is still the custom), and less time for religious or other festivals that contribute to community solidarity.

Overpopulation increases competition for limited resources. Disputes over access to shared resources are now commonplace, for example irrigation water or hydroelectric power from rivers that flow through several countries, or marine resources in the 'extended economic zones' (within 320 kilometres of the shoreline) of more than one nation. Disputes over valuable natural resources have caused numerous wars in the past and can be expected to cause more in the future as competition for limited resources intensifies. However, the main source of violence at the present time is conflict within nations between different ethnic groups competing for the same resources. Wars of regional autonomy or independence have proliferated through many parts of the world in recent years. One of the main issues in these conflicts is whether resources will be controlled by majority ethnic groups or the power elite who control the nation – or by regional populations who live in the area.

population explosion

What can we do about the population explosion? The main message of this chapter has been that the Earth's human population is rapidly approaching its carrying capacity, with no major increase in the carrying capacity expected in the foreseeable future. Although people would do best to keep their population comfortably within the limits of the present carrying capacity, the momentum of the population explosion rules out that choice for now. The best that we can hope for is to slow down the increase in population as quickly as possible. Because most of the world's population growth is now in the developing world, the key to stopping the population explosion lies in that region.

There is a common belief that economic development must precede a decline in births in the developing world, as appeared to happen with the economic development of industrialized countries. However, recent studies have shown that the decline in European birth rates was associated more with access to birth control and changing attitudes about family size and the social acceptability of using birth control. Recent trends in some developing world countries have shown the same. While economic development and education, particularly for women, can contribute to lower birth rates, it is not necessary to wait for them. Many developing world women, rich and poor, want small families through immediate access to family planning. The main thing they need is access to modern birth control methods and sound information on how to use them.

THINGS TO THINK ABOUT

1. Find out the human population of your nation 100 years ago. What is the present population? What are the birth and death rates? How do the present birth and death rates compare with 100 years ago?
2. How many people do you think your local area (or your nation) can support? Do you think your local community has too few people? Too many? Just about right? What about your nation? What are the advantages and disadvantages of having more or less people? What are the connections between the number of people and quality of life?
3. Ageing populations are a major concern of industrialized nations today. There is a trend toward a larger number of retired people who are supported by a smaller number of working-age people. Some nations are considering policies to encourage a higher birth rate so that they will have a larger work force. Do you think that this is a good idea? Can you think of other ways to deal with the ageing problem?
4. What happens when human populations overshoot their carrying capacity? Can you think of concrete examples?
5. Millions of 'economic refugees' move from poor nations to wealthy nations every year. Some citizens of the wealthy nations think that immigration should be strictly controlled. Other people believe that there should be free movement of people throughout the world. What do you think? What are the advantages and disadvantages of each policy?
6. Should wealthy nations that have controlled their population growth provide food assistance to poor nations that have a high population growth rate? Should wealthy nations provide other kinds of assistance to nations that do not have enough food?

things to
think about

ECOSYSTEMS AND SOCIAL SYSTEMS AS COMPLEX ADAPTIVE SYSTEMS

Ecosystems and social systems are **complex adaptive systems**: complex because they have many parts and many connections between the parts; adaptive because their feedback structure gives them the ability to change in ways that promote survival in a fluctuating environment.

How can we understand human–ecosystem interaction when social systems and ecosystems are so overwhelmingly complex? The answer lies in **emergent properties**: the distinctive features and behaviour that 'emerge' from the way that complex adaptive systems are organized. Once aware of emergent properties, it is easier to 'see' what is really happening. Emergent properties are cornerstones for comprehending human–ecosystem interactions in ways that provide insights for sustainable development.

This chapter will begin by explaining the concept of emergent properties. It will then describe three significant examples of emergent properties in detail:

1. Self-organization.
2. Stability domains.
3. Complex system cycles.

Later chapters will describe additional emergent properties of ecosystems and social systems.

HIERARCHICAL ORGANIZATION AND EMERGENT PROPERTIES

Biological systems have a **hierarchy** of organizational levels that extends from molecules and cells to individual organisms, populations and ecosystems. Every individual plant and animal is a collection of cells; every population is a collection of individual organisms of the same species; and every ecosystem consists of populations of different species. The most important levels of biological organization for human ecology are populations and ecosystems.

hierarchical organization

Each level of biological organization from molecules to ecosystems has characteristic behaviours which emerge at that level. These distinct behaviours, called **emergent properties**, function synergistically at each level of organization to give that level a life of its own which is greater than the sum of its parts. This happens because all the parts fit together in ways that allow the system as a whole to function in a manner that promotes its survival. Because the parts are interconnected, the behaviour of every part is shaped by feedback loops through the rest of the system. A mixture of positive and negative feedback promotes growth and change in the system as a whole.

Emergent properties are easiest to perceive in individual organisms. In simple organisms such as jellyfish, we can identify basic emergent properties such as growth, development of different tissues and organs, homeostasis, reproduction and death. The richness of expression of emergent properties increases with the complexity of the organism. For example, 'vision' is an emergent property, and so is the perception of colour. Visual images are not a property of the component cells in organisms; the experience of visual images emerges at the level of an entire organism. Emotions such as fear, anger, anxiety, hate, happiness and love are also emergent properties.

Populations and ecosystems are not organisms, but some of their emergent properties are analogous to the emergent properties of organisms because they can be described by words such as 'growth', 'regulation' or 'development'. The sigmoid curve for population growth, population regulation, genetic evolution and social organization are examples of emergent properties at the population level of organization. They are not properties of the individuals in a population. They emerge as special properties of populations because every individual in a population is affected by what happens in the population as a whole. Taking population regulation as an example, individual plants and animals have the potential to live a long life, producing a large number of offspring. However, the actual survival and reproduction of each individual depends on how many other individuals are in the population and how this number compares to carrying capacity. If the total population overshoots carrying capacity, some individuals in the population are compelled to die from lack of food. The result is population regulation within the limits of carrying capacity – an emergent property of populations.

What about emergent properties of ecosystems? The component parts of ecosystems are all limited by their connections to other parts of the ecosystem. The carrying capacities for all the species together in an ecosystem's biological community are an emergent property of the ecosystem as a whole because the food supply for each species is a consequence of what happens in other parts of the ecosystem. The food supply for each species depends, firstly, on the ecosystem's **biological production** and, secondly, on the amount of the ecosystem's biological production that the **food web** channels to that particular species. More emergent properties of ecosystems will be described in later chapters.

Components at one level of organization interact primarily with other components at the same level. They do so by responding to information that emerges from those components. Protein molecules in the cell interact with other molecules in ways that respond to the structure and behaviour of the molecules, not the atoms of which they are composed. Proteins have an intricate three-dimensional structure that emerges at the level of the molecule and provides the basis for interaction with other molecules. When cats hunt mice, they do not process information on all the parts of a mouse in order to detect it. Instead, they respond to key features that emerge at the level of the whole mouse: body size; large ears; long thin tail, etc. They do not process information about the cellular structure of these features. Mice respond to cats in a similar way.

One emergent property of ecosystems and social systems is **counterintuitive** behaviour. They sometimes do the opposite of what we expect. The construction of public housing in the United States during the decades after World War II is an example. The purpose of public housing was to reduce poverty by providing decent housing to low-income people at a price they could afford. However, cheap housing encouraged unskilled people to move from rural areas to cities even when there were no jobs. The large number of unemployed people turned public housing into ghettos of poverty. The effect of public housing was the opposite of its intended

hierarchical organization

purpose because what happened depended not only on the housing but also on feedback loops through other parts of the social system.

The story of forest fire protection provides an example of counterintuitive behaviour in ecosystems. Forest managers tried to reduce fire damage by putting out fires. The result was even more fire damage. Details of this story are in Chapter 6.

Ecosystems and social systems are sometimes counterintuitive because they are not easily understood by people whose main existence is at a different level of organization – the level of an individual inside the ecosystem and social system. This difference is one important reason why people find it difficult to predict the ultimate consequences of their actions on ecosystems. Emergent properties of our own individual level of organization – our bodies, our consciousness and our direct interactions with people and other parts of the ecosystem – are obvious to us, but emergent properties at higher levels of organization are not so obvious. The difficulties in perceiving emergent properties at a higher level of organization can be illustrated by imagining a 'thinking' red blood cell in a person's blood stream. From its travels around the body, the red blood cell is quite familiar with the different parts of the body – the brain, the eye and so on – but it is very difficult for it to comprehend vision, thoughts, emotions and activities that come from the body as a whole. People, as a small part of ecosystems and social systems, have the same difficulty comprehending ecosystems and social systems.

hierarchical organization

Emergent properties of social systems

Emergent properties of the human social system are important for human ecology because they shape the ways in which people interact with ecosystems. One emergent property is distortion of information when errors accumulate as information passes through a social network. This emergent property underlies the party game of 'telephone', which starts by giving a secret message to one person in a group. That person whispers the message to a second person, and the message is whispered from one person to another. After everyone has been told the message, the first person and last person tell everyone the message as they understood it. To everyone's amusement, the last person's version of the message is typically incorrect in many ways, even though the last person is not a liar.

Another emergent property is **denial**, refusal to recognize or accept the truth when it conflicts with existing beliefs. Selective filtering of information helps to protect existing belief systems of individuals and shared belief systems of society. For example, European nations with global empires were blind to the oppression and exploitation of colonialism. They preferred to see colonialism in terms of a belief system that ascribed nobler motives to colonialism – dissemination of 'superior' European culture, science and technology, economic progress and religious salvation for subjected peoples. In a similar fashion, it is not unusual for governments and powerful people who profit from unsustainable logging of tropical forests to believe that small-scale peasant farmers are primarily to blame for deforestation, even though local farmers generally use forest resources in an ecologically sound fashion.

hierarchical organization

During the 1950s and 1960s, some ecologists tried to warn the public about the impending dangers of the human population explosion and environmental degradation. Most people, including government officials and business leaders with considerable power, would not believe it, even though the facts were clear. Society's belief system at that time had great confidence in the ability of science, technology and the free market economy to ensure continuous progress. Most people considered warnings about impending environmental problems to be extremist. It took several decades and numerous environmental disasters for people to start accepting that the problems were real. This denial had a major effect on social system–ecosystem interaction because so much time was lost before people started to take the environment seriously. This costly form of denial continues as some people, including influential politicians, persist in doubting the reality of global warming despite overwhelming evidence.

Bureaucracies provide examples of emergent properties in human social systems. One emergent property is that bureaucracies are not very effective at dealing with unusual situations. This is because bureaucracies use standard operating procedures to operate efficiently on a large scale. Bureaucracies may be effective for routine matters, but they may not do so well with unusual situations because their procedures are not designed for those situations. Another emergent property of bureaucracies is that they often do things that are contrary to their mission. Competition between different parts of a bureaucracy causes each part to do whatever is necessary for its own survival (for example, maintaining its share of the budget) in competition with other parts of the bureaucracy, even if the actions are useless or counterproductive for the agency's objectives. These are characteristics of a bureaucracy as a whole. They do not derive from the characteristics of individuals in the bureaucracy, who are usually conscientious workers. Their jobs may compel them to do things that make no sense to them personally.

SELF-ORGANIZATION

Why do all the different parts of an ecosystem fit together so well? What is responsible for organizing all the parts, their functional connections and resulting feedback loops, in a way that allows everything to function together? The amazing answer is that ecosystems organize themselves, and the same is true for social systems. They organize themselves by means of an **assembly process** resembling the well-known process of natural selection in biological evolution.

self-
organization

Self-organization of biological communities

The core of ecosystem organization resides in an ecosystem's **biological community** – all the plants, animals and microorganisms living in an ecosystem. The particular species in the biological community at a particular place are drawn from a larger pool of species living in the surrounding area. Selection of those species, and their organization into a food web, happens by a process known as **community assembly**. Assembly in this context means 'joining or fitting parts together'. The community assembly process is an emergent property of ecosystems.

The biological community at any particular place is a consequence of past arrivals of various species of plants, animals and microorganisms. Whenever a new species arrives at a site, it will survive and establish a population only if births are initially greater than deaths. Its population will not survive if deaths are greater than births. If the newly arriving species survives, its population will grow exponentially until it reaches carrying capacity as shown in Figure 2.9. In this way, the new species joins the biological community at the site.

There are three community assembly rules that determine whether the population of a newly arriving species will survive at a site. To survive and become part of the ecosystem, a newly arriving species must satisfy the following conditions:

1. It is adapted to the physical conditions at the site and can survive throughout the year.
2. The site has the right kind of food, and there is enough food and water for the newly arriving plant or animal species to grow and reproduce. (Births must exceed deaths when the population is small.) For plants, the food is water and mineral nutrients in the soil, plus sunshine. For animals, the food is

Figure 4.1
Initial food chain
in the island
story

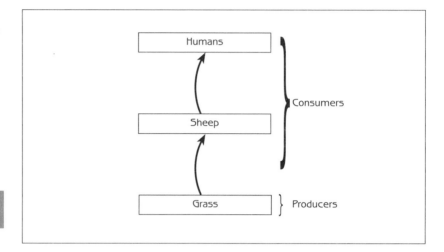

self-
organization

particular species of plants or animals that they can eat. A
newly arriving species will not survive if its food supply is
reduced too much by competing plants or animals already at
the site and utilizing the same food sources.

3. If the site already has animals that can eat the newly arriving
    species, the newly arriving species must have the ability to
    avoid being eaten too much. Deaths cannot exceed births.

The following story shows how community assembly works.
Imagine a coastal island, 1 kilometre in diameter, where all the
plants and animals are killed by a fire. Only grass survives. Soon
grass is growing everywhere on the island. The farmer who owns
the island decides that he wants to raise sheep there. The carrying
capacity of the island for sheep is 50 sheep, so the farmer puts 50
sheep on the island.

Figure 4.1 shows the simple food chain on the island after the
farmer stocks the island with the sheep.

The island is 1 kilometre from the mainland coast, where there
are hundreds of species of plants and animals that can
occasionally float to the island on, for example, a log. Different
species of plants and animals are transported to the island at
various times during the first few years after the fire. Each species
is added to the food web if it meets the three rules for population
survival listed earlier. It is best to follow this story by sketching the
new food web whenever another species is added.

1. Tree seeds arrive on the island. Sheep love to eat emerging
    seedlings and saplings. Will the trees survive?
2. Weed seeds arrive on the island. The weeds are unpalatable to
    the sheep. Will the weeds survive? What happens to the

quantity of grass on the island? What happens to the carrying capacity for sheep?

3. Mice arrive on the island. The mice eat grass and weeds. Will the mice survive on the island? What happens to the quantity of grass and the carrying capacity for sheep?

4. Rabbits arrive on the island. The rabbits eat grass. Will they survive? What happens to the carrying capacity for sheep?

5. Foxes arrive on the island. They eat mice. They cannot eat all of the mice because mice are small enough to hide. Foxes love to eat rabbits. They quickly kill all of the rabbits because rabbits are too large to hide. Will the foxes survive? What happens to the number of mice? What happens to the rabbits? What happens to the grass and the carrying capacity for sheep?

6. An insect that eats the leaves of trees arrives on the island. Will it survive?

7. Cats arrive on the island. The cats, which are better at catching mice than foxes, reduce the number of mice to such an extent that the foxes do not have enough food. However, even a small number of mice is enough for the cats to survive. What happens to the foxes? What happens to the carrying capacity for sheep?

8. Cat fleas arrive on the island. Will they survive?

self-organization

Figure 4.2 shows the biological community after all of these plants and animals arrived on the island. The biological community is organized as a food web. Food webs are another emergent property of ecosystems. Each species of plant, animal or microorganism has a particular role in the food web – its **ecological niche** – defined primarily by its position in the web (ie, other species in the

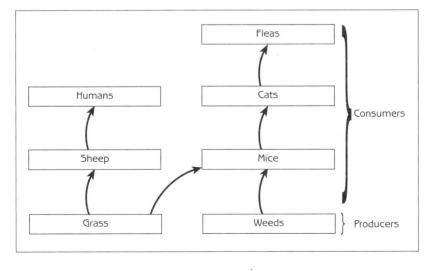

Figure 4.2
Final food web in the island story

biological community that it uses as food and other species that use it as food). Ecological niches are also defined by physical conditions such as the annual cycle of temperature and moisture in the microhabitat in which a species lives.

It is possible to see that some of the plants and animals that came to the island are not in the diagram because they did not survive. They did not fit in with the biological community that existed at the time of arrival. This is why biological communities always have plants and animals that fit together with each change in the food web. The rules that decide whether a new species survives also apply to species that are already in the biological community. Rabbits disappeared from the island when **predators** (foxes) arrived that killed too many rabbits for the population to survive. The foxes disappeared with the arrival of cats, which were superior **competitors** in the food web existing at that time. Finally, the share of the island's biological production for the farmer (ie, grass for his sheep) changed as the story progressed. This story will continue for many years as new plants and animals arrive at the island and the number of species in the food web gradually increases.

self-organization

This simple example was only about plants and animals, but microorganisms such as bacteria and fungi, though less conspicuous, are equally significant in real ecosystems. Every plant and animal provides habitat and sustenance for millions of bacteria. Some of the bacteria are harmful, but most are harmless or even essential for the plant or animal's survival. Microorganisms are also major actors in soil food webs. A typical litre of soil contains billions of bacteria whose central role in ecological cycles makes them essential for the survival of the ecosystem as a whole.

The biological community created by the assembly process is partly a matter of chance. It depends, in part, on what species arrive on the island and when they arrive. If we imagine ten islands with the same mainland source of plants and animals, the progression of biological communities on each island can be very different. Some of the communities are similar to one another, though not exactly the same. Others may be completely different. However, the chance element in community assembly does not mean that every combination of plants and animals is possible. In fact, all of the biological communities that can be created are a minuscule subset of all possible combinations because community assembly will only admit those plants and animals that fit together in a functional food web.

The community assembly process is not restricted to islands. It happens everywhere all of the time. Every place in the world is an 'island' on which plants and animals continually arrive from nearby areas. Biological communities in most regions in the world contain hundreds of species of plants and animals, and all the plants and animals in each region fit together functionally.

Self-organization of social systems

All complex adaptive systems are self-organizing. The assembly process that was illustrated by the island story is one of the main ways that complex systems, including social systems, organize themselves.

self-organization

The way the assembly process works in social systems can be illustrated by commercial activities. When someone starts a new business, the survival of the business can depend upon rules such as the following.

- The business is adapted to the community.
- There is demand for the products or services of the business.
- The business can generate enough customers to produce a profit. There are not competing businesses that provide the same product or service to such an extent that there are insufficient customers or the price of the product or service is too low to make a profit.
- The business has a good supply source of what it needs to make its products or provide its services. The cost of these inputs is not larger than the income of the business.

If you compare these rules with the assembly rules for biological communities at the beginning of this chapter, it is possible to see the similarity between the two sets of rules and how the same process that organizes ecosystems can also apply to social systems.

The assembly process for ecosystems and social systems is similar to biological evolution. Biological evolution is based on genetic mutations, which may or may not survive the process of natural selection. (Each genetic mutation is a 'new arrival'.) Biological evolution is slow because genetic mutations are random changes that are usually detrimental. Only occasionally are mutations beneficial enough to survive natural selection.

Human cultures also evolve. The mutations for cultures are new ideas. New ideas survive if they fit with the rest of the culture and prove useful. Whether or not an idea survives can depend on the situation. A new idea may survive successfully in one particular culture at one particular time and place, but the same idea may fail to survive in a different culture at a different time and place because it does not fit. Human cultural evolution can be much faster than biological evolution because cultural mutations are not random events like biological mutations. Cultural mutations are ideas that people develop to solve problems, so cultural mutations frequently fit the culture well enough, and function well enough, to survive and become part of the culture.

STABILITY DOMAINS

stability
domains

Ecosystems and social systems have a tension between forces that resist change (negative feedback) and forces that promote change (positive feedback). Negative feedback keeps essential parts of the system within the limits required for them to function together, while positive feedback provides the capacity to make large changes if necessary. Negative feedback may dominate at some times and positive feedback may dominate at other times, depending on the situation. As a result, ecosystems and social systems may stay more or less the same for long periods, but they can also change very suddenly. The changes can be like a 'switch'. 'Switching' is an emergent property of all complex adaptive systems, including ecosystems and social systems.

Figure 4.3 shows the switch of a human body from life to death. **Homeostasis**, in the form of hundreds of negative feedback loops normally keeps every part of a healthy body more or less as it should be, but the body's **state** changes when a person is sick or injured. State is everything about the body's condition at a particular moment – temperature, blood pressure, blood sugar concentration, hormone concentrations, breathing rate and hundreds of other things. The horizontal axis of the diagram represents the body's state. Each point along the horizontal axis represents a person's condition (ie, everything about his body) at a particular moment. Points that are close together represent similar states, and points that are further apart represent states that are very different from each other.

The location of the ball represents the body's state at a particular time, and movement of the ball represents a change in the body's state from one time to another. A short distance of movement represents a small change, and a longer distance represents a larger change. In this metaphor, the gravitational force on the ball represents natural forces of change in the complex system. Movement of the ball down the 'hill' represents change due to the homeostatic mechanisms that keep the body in a healthy state. The ball moves back and forth a bit as random events change the condition of the body, but the ball usually stays near the bottom of the hill (*A*). If a healthy person experiences an external disturbance such as disease or injury, the disturbance forces the ball up the hill to an unhealthy state (*B*). The body usually eliminates the infection or repairs the injury and everything returns to normal. The ball rolls back to the bottom of the hill, and the body is again healthy as in *A*. Whether sick or healthy, the body remains in the 'alive' part of the diagram (the 'alive' stability domain) because homeostasis keeps it that way.

The diagram has another stability domain: 'dead'. A severe illness or injury can change the body so much that the ball is pushed over the top of the hill from the 'alive' stability domain to the 'dead' domain (*C*). The body no longer functions as before; new feedback

stability domains

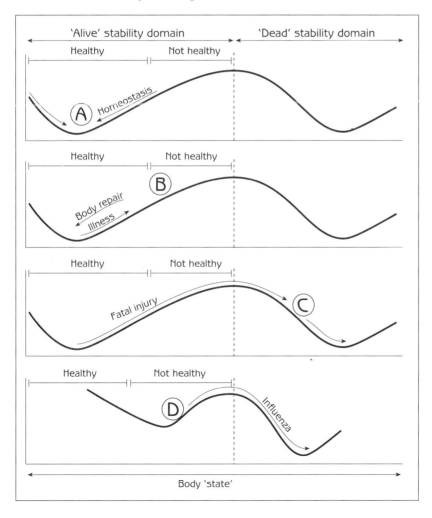

Figure 4.3
Body state of 'alive' and 'dead' to illustrate stability domains

loops change it to a very different state. Body temperature drops to the temperature of the surrounding environment, muscles become rigid and hundreds of internal processes come to a stop. As the body is changed by natural processes following death, the ball rolls to the bottom of the hill in the 'dead' stability domain. There are no natural forces to push the ball back to the 'alive' domain. The body does not return to life, even when the outside disturbance has passed.

Traumatic events such as illness or injury are not the only way that a body can change. A body can change gradually because of internal processes such as ageing. As a person's health declines with age, the shape of the hill changes so the bottom of the hill moves closer to the boundary between 'alive' and 'dead' (*D*). As homeostatic mechanisms weaken, the hill becomes less steep, so it is easier for a disturbance to push the ball the short distance over the top of the hill and into the 'dead' domain. Hip injuries and diseases such as influenza or pneumonia, which seldom kill young people, can be fatal to the elderly.

A simple puzzle illustrates how stability domains are a consequence of a system's design, that is, the organization of its component parts. The challenge is to balance six nails on the head of a vertical nail. The solution gives a simple and stable arrangement of the nails that is far from obvious (see Figure 4.4A). This represents one stability domain. If any of the six nails is moved out of its relationship with the other nails, the entire configuration collapses and changes to a different stability domain, such as in Figure 4.4B. Just as the arrangement in Figure 4.4A may be the only viable solution to the puzzle, the ways that the potential component parts of a biological community can fit together to form

stability domains

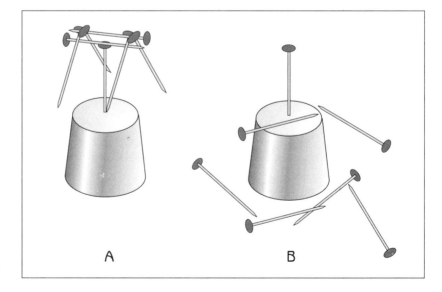

Figure 4.4
Alternative stability domains with nails. Try it!

A   B

a functional and viable ecosystem are also relatively few compared to the enormous number of possibilities.

What is the state of a social system? What are its stability domains? Social-system state is everything about a society at a particular place and time – culture, knowledge, technology, perceptions, values and social organization. It is constantly fluctuating in some ways, while remaining more or less the same in other ways. Negative feedback loops keep social systems within stability domains imposed by particular cultural, political and economic systems while processes such as cultural evolution gradually change the shape of the domains. Social systems sometimes experience major switches from one stability domain to another. The breakup of the former Soviet Union is a notable example. Glasnost and Perestroika were 'disturbances' that set in motion a multitude of feedback loops that propelled the Soviet Union from a 'single nation' stability domain to a 'separate nations' domain. There are numerous social-system switches underway in the developing world as diffusion of the global economy stimulates drastic social and cultural changes.

stability domains

What is the state of an ecosystem? **Ecosystem state** is the sum total of every part of an ecosystem: the population number of every species of plant, animal and microorganism; the quantity or concentration of every substance in the air, soil and water; and every structure built by people. Ecosystem state changes as any of these parts alter with the passage of time. The 'hillsides' in an ecosystem stability diagram represent natural ecological processes that maintain the integrity of an ecosystem by keeping it in the same stability domain. The 'hillsides' also represent processes such as community assembly, which systematically change ecosystems (see ecological succession in Chapter 6).

External disturbances for ecosystems are traumatic events, such as hurricanes, fire and the introduction of exotic animals or plants (such as the water hyacinth introduced to Lake Victoria in Chapter 1), which completely change an ecosystem, moving it from one stability domain to another. The impacts of human activities can also be an external disturbance for ecosystems. Ecosystem stability domains will have a role in the next chapter and will appear throughout the rest of this book. They are important for sustainable development because human activities can set in motion changes that switch an ecosystem irreversibly from a desirable stability domain to an undesirable one.

COMPLEX SYSTEM CYCLES

Ecosystems and social systems change in two ways:

1. Progressive change due to internal self-organizing assembly processes (biological community assembly and cultural evolution).
2. Sudden change from one stability domain to another because of external disturbance (ie 'switch').

complex system cycles

The progressive and sudden changes combine to form a complex system cycle (see Figure 4.5). '*Growth*' is a time dominated by positive feedback and self-organizing assembly processes. It is a time of expansion and increasing complexity. '*Equilibrium*' is a time of stability. The system has reached a high level of complexity and connection between its parts. Negative feedback predominates. The system may become rigid and seemingly indestructible, but stagnation and a lack of flexibility may eventually make the system vulnerable to destruction by an external disturbance. '*Dissolution*' is when the system is destroyed by an external disturbance. Positive feedback generates dramatic change, and the system falls apart. It is pushed out of its stability domain. '*Reorganization*' is a time when the system begins to recover from falling apart. It is a creative time when change can take a variety of possible directions; that is, the system has the possibility of moving into a variety of new stability domains. 'Chance' can be important to the way a system reorganizes, determining which new stability domain it enters. The growth stage that follows reorganization depends on the course initiated during reorganization.

Figure 4.6 shows how an ecosystem or social system changes from one stability domain to another in the course of a complex system cycle.

Populations have complex system cycles. The growth stage of a population is a time of exponential increase. A population is

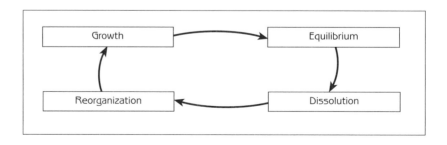

Figure 4.5
The complex system cycle

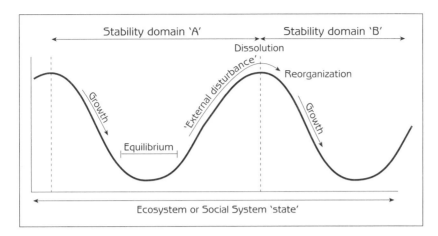

Stability domain 'A'   Stability domain 'B'

Dissolution

'External disturbance'   Reorganization

Growth   Growth

Equilibrium

Ecosystem or Social System 'state'

Figure 4.6
Complex system cycles from the perspective of stability domains

complex system cycles

regulated at or below carrying capacity during the equilibrium stage. Populations of many species of plants and animals can stay in the equilibrium stage for a long time, but the populations of other species experience frequent 'crashes' because they overshoot their carrying capacity. Population crashes are the dissolution stage. For example, an insect population that feeds on a plant may multiply rapidly (growth), spreading over the plant and eventually killing it. The insects fly away when the plant dies (dissolution). Most of them die of starvation because they fail to find another suitable host, but a few find a plant on which they can start a new population (reorganization). In the case of humans, people typically reorganize by moving to a new place if their population overshoots local carrying capacity.

Ecosystems also have complex system cycles because community assembly follows a complex cycle. The island story began with dissolution when fire destroyed the previous biological community, a forest. Survival of the grass and the farmer's herd of sheep on the island were 'reorganization' that set the course for subsequent growth of the biological community as various plants and animals came to the island. Growth will continue as more plants and animals arrive, and some are added to the biological community. Eventually, when nearly all possible niches in the food web are occupied, it will be difficult for newly arriving species to survive; the biological community will stay the same (equilibrium) until a new disturbance, such as fire or a developer's bulldozer, causes a dramatic change (dissolution). Complex system cycles in ecosystems will be described in greater detail as **ecological succession** in Chapter 6.

Social systems have complex system cycles that range in scale from a small part of society (for example, a club) to entire nations. Just as the scale varies, the time period of a cycle can vary from a few months to years or centuries. Historical periods of nations provide examples of long-term cycles. The Meiji Restoration in 19th-century Japan was a time of dissolution of the Tokugawa shogunate and reorganization to restore power to the emperor. There was then a period of growth (acquiring new political institutions and industrialization), followed by equilibrium (the military government of Imperial Japan). The defeat of Japan at the end of World War II led to dissolution of the military government, which was followed quickly by reorganization as Japan adopted new social institutions such as Western democratic processes. Japan started to rebuild its economy and became a world economic power (growth). The 'bubble economy' that Japan experienced with economic growth faded away as Japan's economy moved into equilibrium. Some of Japan's economic and political institutions were discarded (dissolution) as Japan reorganized its international economic strategy in response to industrialization and entry into the global market by other Asian countries.

complex system cycles

Policies can change dramatically during social system cycles. Policies are well developed and often rigid during equilibrium. During dissolution, people question existing policies and reject them as inadequate. New policies, even radically new frameworks, are formulated during reorganization. Details of the new policies are worked out and filled in during growth.

People and governments often make the mistake of assuming that the existing situation will last a long time. If they are in a growth stage, they think that they can continue to grow forever, and they are surprised and disappointed when growth is no longer possible. If they are in an equilibrium stage, they suppose that the stability and control of that stage will last forever, and they are surprised when an unexpected disaster makes things fall apart. When things fall apart (dissolution), they may think 'it is the end of the world', but reorganization will put them once again on a path toward normalcy.

An effective society has the ability to function during all four stages of the complex system cycle. An effective society is not only able to function well in the present stage, it is also ready to deal with very different conditions that will come with the next stage. Effective societies have the capacity to grow when the opportunity arises, and they have the capacity to function on a sustainable basis when growth is no longer possible. When things fall apart, as sooner or later they always do, effective societies have the ability to move quickly to reorganization and new growth.

THINGS TO THINK ABOUT

1. With 'switches', something stays the same because of negative feedback, and then it changes quickly to something else because of positive feedback. Think of examples of switches at various levels in your social system (family, neighbourhood, national, international).

2. Think of examples of complex system cycles in your family, your neighbourhood, your nation's history and world history. Be explicit about each stage of the cycle (growth, equilibrium, dissolution, reorganization).

3. Consider the story of the island. Beginning with Figure 4.1, draw a series of food web diagrams to show the new food chain whenever a new species is added to the island's biological community. You should finish with a diagram like the food web in Figure 4.2.

    things to
    think about

4. What are some emergent properties of your:
    *   family social system;
    *   neighbourhood social system;
    *   school or workplace social system; and
    *   national social system?

    Keep in mind that emergent properties arise from the whole system. They do not come simply from the parts; they derive from the way that the parts are organized together.

5. Think of examples of denial in your personal life. What are some examples of denial in the society in which you live?

ECOSYSTEM ORGANIZATION

Self-organizing processes in ecosystems make them awesomely complex. The organizing processes are a mixture of randomness and ordered selectivity. The resultant complexity is highly functional for ecosystem survival.

The plants, animals and microorganisms in an ecosystem are organized as a **food web** in which they all fit together functionally. There are two main reasons that they fit together:

1. The community assembly process is able to select from a pool of species with the potential to fit together because species that have lived together in the same ecosystem for thousands of years have coadapted to each other through biological evolution.
2. As the community assembly process forms a food web, it selects only species that fit into the existing web. (This is the island story in Chapter 4.)

This chapter starts by enumerating some of the ways that the living components of ecosystems are coadapted to one another. It then explains nature's design of ecosystems – how everything fits together to form an ongoing and functionally integrated whole – and goes on to describe three major kinds of ecosystems and how they differ with respect to **ecosystem inputs** and **ecosystem outputs**:

1. Natural ecosystems.
2. Agricultural ecosystems.
3. Urban ecosystems.

In addition to having their biological communities organized as food webs, ecosystems are organized across landscapes as a hierarchical patchwork of smaller ecosystems – a **landscape**

mosaic. This chapter will conclude by describing how the patchwork of biological communities in a landscape mosaic is associated with the underlying patchwork of topography and physical conditions in the same landscape – and how the patches connect together through inputs and outputs to form the landscape mosaic as a functional whole.

COADAPTATION

Coadaptation and **coevolution** are emergent properties of ecosystems. Coadaptation (fitting together) is a consequence of coevolution (changing together). While adaptation can take any form that enhances survival, the most conspicuous forms of coadaptation are associated with the ways in which animals and microorganisms obtain nutrition from other living organisms in the food web. On the one hand, animals are adapted to finding and eating the particular plants or animals that they use as food. On the other hand, they have the ability to hide or flee from animals that use them as food, and they can develop immunity against **parasites** and **pathogens** that use them as food. Coadaptation between predator and prey is an evolutionary game that never ends. Predators evolve more effective ways to capture their prey, and the prey respond by evolving ways to avoid capture. Cats evolve sensitive hearing to detect mice in the dark, and mice evolve the ability to move quietly so that cats will not hear them.

Plants cannot run or hide, but they have evolved other ways to avoid being eaten. Many plants have such low nutritional value that they are not worth consuming. Some species of plants contain chemicals that interfere with digestion by animals; other species are poisonous or are protected by defences such as thorns. Some species of animals overcome this problem by specialising in eating one particular kind of plant after evolving the ability to neutralize the poison or other defence of that plant species. This game of coadaptation gives every plant and animal species in the ecosystem the ability to obtain the food it requires for survival. It also endows every species with the ability to survive despite being consumed by other animals that use it as food. Coexistence is built into the game. It is typical for pathogens and parasites to evolve the ability to live in their hosts without killing them, a strategy that ensures a more continuous food supply.

Completely cooperative relationships – **symbiosis** – are also common. Some species of acacia trees have special structures that

coadaptation

provide food and microhabitats for ants that protect the trees from insects that eat their leaves. **Nitrogen-fixing bacteria** live in the roots of plants such as **legumes**. The bacteria convert atmospheric nitrogen to a form that plants can use, and the plants provide nutrition for the bacteria. Similar cooperation exists with fungi (**mycorrhizae**) that assist plant roots to take up phosphorous from the soil. The mycorrhizae receive nutrition from the plants. Honey bees distribute pollen that fertilizes flowers while they collect pollen and nectar as food. Nature contains thousands of symbiotic relationships such as these. The consequence of coadaptation is a group of plants, animals and microorganisms from which the community assembly process can form viable ecosystems.

ecosystem design

ECOSYSTEM DESIGN

Coadaptation and community assembly are the source of nature's design for ecosystems, a design that can be summarized by comparing ecosystems to another kind of system – a television set. Ecosystems and television sets are similar in some ways because both are systems; they are different in other ways because ecosystems are designed by nature and television sets are designed by people for a very specific purpose. One of the main ways in which ecosystems and television sets are similar is that they both have a selection of parts that function together. A television has a large number of electronic components, each precisely suited to the other components in the set. A television set would not work if its electronic components were selected and connected to one another at random. There would certainly be no picture, and the television would probably blow up when plugged in. Ecosystems also have a selection of components which are able to fit together precisely because they are coadapted by biological evolution. The component species in an ecosystem survive because they fit together in a way that enables the whole ecosystem to provide the necessary resources for each species. This happens through ecosystem processes such as material cycling and energy flow, which are explained in Chapter 8.

Television sets and ecosystems derive their whole system behaviour from the fact that the behaviour of each system component is limited by the actions of other components. Although every electronic component in a television set could theoretically have a wide range of electric currents, the current at each component depends upon currents that come from other components. As a result, electric currents throughout the television set are constrained by its design to orderly patterns that generate a picture. The picture is an emergent property of the television set.

The same kinds of limitation apply to ecosystems. Although all the plants, animals and microorganisms have the reproductive capacity to multiply to enormous numbers, their populations are constrained by food supply, natural enemies and other ecological forces. Uncontrolled populations could damage other parts of the ecosystem, destroying themselves and the system. The ecosystem ensures its survival by feedback mechanisms that regulate the biological populations within it.

ecosystem design

There are, however, some important differences between ecosystems and television sets. Ecosystems have a higher level of **redundancy** (duplication) than television sets, and this gives them greater reliability and **resilience** (see Chapter 11 for a detailed discussion of resilience). Because television sets are designed to be constructed as economically as possible, there is only one component for every function. If a component is removed, a television set ceases to function. In the case of ecosystems, there is considerable duplication of function among different organisms. Each important function in an ecosystem is normally performed by several different species – sometimes by dozens of species.

Ecosystems and television sets are different in another important way. The biological components of ecosystems are themselves complex adaptive systems with the ability to change as circumstance demands. Once a television set is put together, each component has the same operating characteristics regardless of what happens in the rest of the circuit. And once soldered into place, no component can change its connection with the other components. Ecosystems are very different because, depending upon what is happening at a particular time, plants and animals can change the way in which they interact with other species. For example, animals with the ability to eat several different kinds of food can switch from one food source to another whenever one becomes scarce and another becomes abundant.

ECOSYSTEM HOMEOSTASIS

Population regulation keeps every population in an ecosystem's biological community within limits that are imposed by the functioning of the ecosystem as a whole. The carrying capacity for each species of plant, animal and microorganism depends upon what happens in other parts of the ecosystem. Ecosystems also keep their physical conditions within limits. For example, biological and physical processes regulate the quantity of water in the soil. Plants function best when there is neither too much nor too little water. Too much water can push out air needed by microorganisms and plant roots; too little water restricts plant growth. If there is too much water in the soil after heavy rain, plants consume large quantities, and excess water percolates downward through the soil. If there is too little water during periods of lesser rainfall, plants reduce their water consumption, and clay and soil organic matter store water for use by plants and soil microorganisms.

ecosystem homeostasis

Ecosystem homeostasis is not as exacting as the homeostasis of individual organisms, but it is quite real – particularly in natural ecosystems and the natural part of agricultural and urban ecosystems. Random factors such as weather fluctuations can cause small changes in an ecosystem's biological community and physical environment from one year to the next. But as long as the ecosystem is not drastically altered by a severe outside disturbance, ecosystem homeostasis keeps the biological community and physical environment within functional bounds. If something detrimental happens to one particular species in an ecosystem, other species with the same function increase in abundance and the function continues. **Ecosystem state** may fluctuate with the passage of time, but it usually remains within the stability domain appropriate for that kind of ecosystem. It is not necessary to ascribe 'consciousness' or 'purpose' to the impressive effectiveness with which hundreds of negative feedback loops keep everything in ecosystems within the limits necessary for all to function together. Ecosystems organize themselves through coadaptation and community assembly in such a way that the ecosystem as a whole continues to function on a sustainable basis.

The Gaia hypothesis expresses the concept of ecosystem homeostasis for the global ecosystem of planet Earth. Gaia is the name of the Greek goddess Mother Earth. The Gaia hypothesis states that 'Life on Earth maintains the Earth's climate and atmospheric composition at an optimum for life'. For example, the carbon cycle maintains atmospheric oxygen and carbon dioxide at concentrations required by the plants and animals in the global ecosystem. This is accomplished by a variety of processes including photosynthesis, respiration and the carbonic acid–bicarbonate–carbonate buffer system in the ocean. Global ecosystem homeostasis is a consequence of homeostasis in the large number of local but mutually interacting ecosystems on the planet.

An imaginary planet called Daisy World illustrates the basic idea of the Gaia hypothesis. It shows how vegetation can contribute to regulating the Earth's temperature by adjusting the Earth's reflection and absorption of sunlight ('albedo'). Daisy World has three kinds of flowers. One flower is white, the second is intermediate coloured (grey) and the third is dark. Dark flowers absorb most of the sunlight that comes to them, converting the sunlight to heat, so dark flowers heat Daisy World the most. White flowers reflect most of the sunlight, so they heat Daisy World the least. Dark flowers survive best at cooler temperatures, white flowers survive best at warmer temperatures and intermediate-coloured flowers survive best at intermediate temperatures.

> **ecosystem homeostasis**

The temperature of Daisy World is regulated by a negative feedback loop that changes the numbers of light and dark coloured flowers. If sunlight increases and the temperature starts to go up, it becomes too warm for dark flowers to survive and some are replaced by lighter flowers (see the top panel of Figure 5.1). Because the lighter flowers absorb less sunlight, the temperature goes down. If sunlight intensity decreases and the temperature goes down too far, it becomes too cold for white flowers to survive, and some of the white flowers are replaced by darker flowers. Because darker flowers absorb more sunlight, the temperature goes up.

The solid line in the bottom panel of Figure 5.1 shows the temperature of Daisy World at different sunlight intensities. Over a wide range of sunlight intensity (from 0.6–1.2), the temperature in Daisy World stays around 22.5° Celsius, which is the optimum (ie, best) temperature for flowers. The dashed line in the bottom panel shows what happens in a world without different coloured daisies, where temperature has a straight line relationship with sunlight intensity (ie, there is no temperature regulation).

COMPARISON OF NATURAL, AGRICULTURAL AND URBAN ECOSYSTEMS

It is useful to distinguish three major kinds of ecosystems. **Natural ecosystems** organize themselves. Their outputs for human use include **renewable natural resources** such as wood, fish and water. **Agricultural** and **urban ecosystems** are

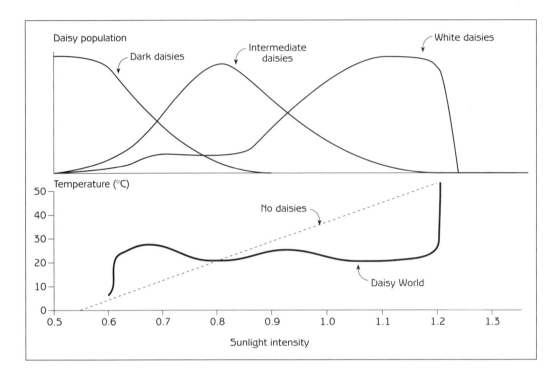

Figure 5.1
Change in daisy
populations that
keeps the
temperature of
Daisy World the
same over a
broad range of
sunlight
intensities
Source: Adapted from
Lovelock, J (1979)
Gaia: A New Look at
Life on Earth, Oxford
University Press,
Oxford

organized in part by human inputs of materials, energy and information. The rest of their organization comes from the same self-organizing processes that form natural ecosystems. Agricultural ecosystems provide outputs of food, fibre or other renewable resources. Urban ecosystems provide human habitation and industrial outputs. Agricultural and urban ecosystems that differ more from natural ecosystems require more intensive human inputs to make them and keep them that way.

The following descriptions are generalized for each major type of ecosystem. Some ecosystems, depending upon the spatial scale, are a combination of two or even three of the major types.

Natural ecosystems

Natural processes are entirely responsible for structuring natural ecosystems, which contain only wild plants and animals. Their biological communities are formed entirely by coevolution, coadaptation and community assembly. Natural ecosystems are self-organizing, self-sufficient and self-sustaining. They survive with only natural inputs such as sunlight and water. Most inputs and outputs of natural ecosystems are exchanges with adjacent ecosystems when materials which also contain energy and information are transported by wind, water, gravity or animals (see

Figure 5.2). Inputs and outputs are small because most natural ecosystems have evolved numerous mechanisms for holding onto materials. For example, natural ecosystems prevent soil loss due to rain or wind erosion by covering the soil with grass or leaves. Where soils have a low natural fertility, ecosystems keep mineral nutrients for plants inside the ecosystem by holding minerals in the bodies of plants, animals and microorganisms.

Agricultural ecosystems

Agricultural ecosystems are farm ecosystems. They use domesticated plants or animals to produce food, fibre or fuel for human consumption. The island in the community assembly story in Chapter 4 was an agricultural ecosystem because it had sheep. Agricultural ecosystems are a combination of design by people and design by nature. People provide crops or livestock, and nature supplies wild plants and animals through the usual process of community assembly. Many of the wild plants and animals are essential for the agricultural functioning of these ecosystems. Earthworms and other soil animals maintain soil fertility by breaking dead plant and animal materials into small pieces that expose them to decomposition by bacteria. Bacteria consume dead plants and animals, moving the minerals in their bodies into the soil in a form that plants can use as nutrients. Other plants and animals compete with people for the consumption of an agricultural ecosystem's production and are often regarded as weeds or pests to be excluded from the ecosystem if possible. In addition to living plants and animals, agricultural ecosystems contain non-living things made by people such as irrigation ditches

ecosystems compared

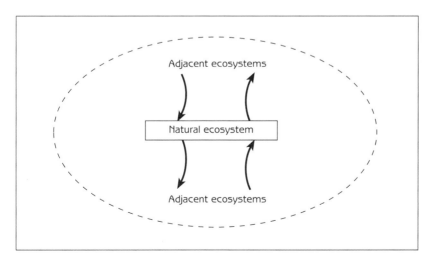

Figure 5.2
Input–output exchanges of materials, energy and information between adjacent ecosystems

and farm equipment. Agricultural ecosystems are not self-sustaining. They require human inputs to make them different from natural ecosystems in ways that farmers desire (see Figure 5.3).

Some agricultural ecosystems differ greatly from natural ecosystems; others do not. Pasture ecosystems with grazing animals such as sheep or cattle usually require less human inputs than crop ecosystems because pasture is more like a natural ecosystem. Modern agricultural ecosystems need the most inputs – farm machinery, chemical fertilizers, pesticides and irrigation – because they differ the most from natural ecosystems. Intensive inputs increase the conversion of sunlight energy to human food energy in two important ways:

ecosystems compared

1. They provide favourable conditions for crop growth, such as ample water and mineral nutrients.
2. They exclude plants and animals that compete with people for the ecosystem's biological production.

Intensive inputs to modern agricultural ecosystems depend heavily upon petroleum. Large quantities of petroleum energy are required to manufacture fertilizers and pesticides, transport these agricultural chemicals to the farm and apply them on the field. Petroleum is the source of materials and energy for manufacturing plastics that cover the ground to prevent evaporative water loss. It is the source of energy for manufacturing and operating farm machinery, pumping irrigation water and transporting the harvest to distant markets. Because it is typical to use ten calories of petroleum energy for every calorie of food production, modern agricultural ecosystems do not simply convert sun energy to food energy. They also convert petroleum energy to food energy. In effect, people are 'eating' petroleum.

Water is another intensive input, agricultural use competing with supplies for natural and urban ecosystems. Modern irrigation

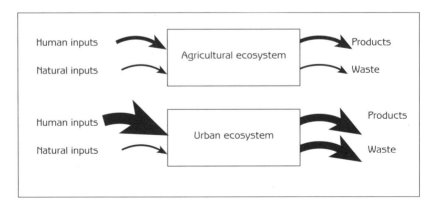

Figure 5.3
Inputs and outputs of materials, energy and information with agricultural and urban ecosystems

often requires large amounts of water, sometimes from sources hundreds of kilometres away. Conflicts over water will become an increasing part of the world scene.

The payoff from high inputs is high outputs – high levels of crop or animal production. However, intended products are not the only outputs of modern agricultural ecosystems. Wastes that can damage nearby ecosystems are other outputs. Fertilizers and pesticides carried out of agricultural ecosystems as runoff from fields can pollute streams, rivers and groundwater in the surrounding region.

Traditional agricultural ecosystems comprise the type of agriculture that people engaged in before modern technology. Traditional agriculture was developed over many centuries by a cultural assembly process of trial and error. Many parts of the developing world that have not yet been modernized still rely on traditional agriculture. Many traditional agricultural ecosystems are similar to natural ecosystems because traditional farmers have designed their agricultural ecosystems to take advantage of natural processes instead of fighting nature. For example, it is common for traditional agriculture to have a mixture of many crops in the same field, just as natural ecosystems have a mixture of different plant species. This style of agriculture is called 'mixed cropping' or **polyculture**. Traditional agriculture requires less inputs than modern agriculture, so it is more self-sustaining. Traditional agriculture also has less outputs than modern agriculture – less crop production and less pollution. Modern **organic farming**, which strives to be in harmony with nature while providing food that is free of toxic chemicals, is similar to traditional agriculture.

ecosystems
compared

Urban ecosystems

Cities are **urban ecosystems**. They are organized almost entirely by people. They are usually dominated by human-made structures such as buildings and streets. Many of the plants and animals in urban ecosystems are domesticated, such as garden plants and pets, but there are also wild plants and animals, such as weeds, birds and rats. Urban ecosystems are not self-sustaining. Urban ecosystems require large quantities of inputs and produce substantial outputs in the form of wastes (see Figures 5.3 and 5.4).

Cities are the basis of human civilization. The first cities appeared about 6000 years ago. Although half of the world's human population now lives in cities, most people in the past lived in smaller and simpler urban ecosystems such as villages. The growth of cities accelerated greatly after the Industrial Revolution, but the predominance of cities that we know today is even more

Figure 5.4
Inputs and
outputs of
materials, energy
and information
with urban
ecosystems

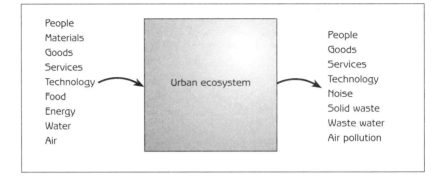

People		People
Materials		Goods
Goods		Services
Services	Urban ecosystem	Technology
Technology		Noise
Food		Solid waste
Energy		Waste water
Water		Air pollution
Air		

**ecosystems
compared**

recent. Only 14 per cent of the human population lived in cities at the beginning of the 20th century. Now, 75 per cent of people in industrialized nations live in cities. Although only 35 per cent of the developing world population lives in cities today, the actual number of people in developing world cities is already greater than the number in the cities of industrialized nations.

Figure 5.5
Expected growth
of human
population in
cities during the
next 20 years
Source: Data from the
Population Reference
Bureau, Washington,
DC

The urban population of industrialized nations is now increasing very slowly, but developing world cities continue to grow at a rapid rate (see Figure 5.5). Within 25 years, developing world cities will have three times as many people as the cities of industrialized nations. Many developing world cities are growing so fast that they cannot provide basic services such as water, waste collection, electricity, education and basic health services to a significant percentage of their population.

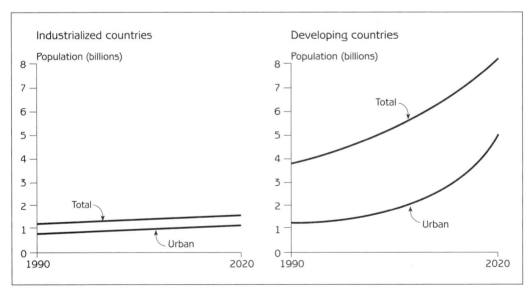

LANDSCAPE MOSAICS

Every landscape is a patchwork of different sites with different biological communities and therefore different ecosystems. This happens because:

1. Different sites have different physical conditions. These distinct conditions may be partly a consequence of natural variation in the landscape and partly a consequence of human activities.
2. The community assembly process produces different biological communities where physical conditions are different.
3. People make agricultural and urban ecosystems where conditions are suitable.

landscape mosaics

This patchwork is a **landscape mosaic**. It is an emergent property of ecosystems.

Figure 5.6 shows a typical landscape mosaic in the Kansai region of western Japan. The same kinds of ecosystems are repeated across the landscape. This happens because similar physical conditions are repeated in different parts of the landscape. Sites with similar physical conditions can have biological communities that are nearly the same. They therefore have similar ecosystems. People make similar agricultural or urban ecosystems where conditions are similar.

A particular kind of ecosystem is a grouping of similar ecosystems that are given the same name based on the most abundant and conspicuous plants in the biological community. The common forest ecosystems in western Japan are:

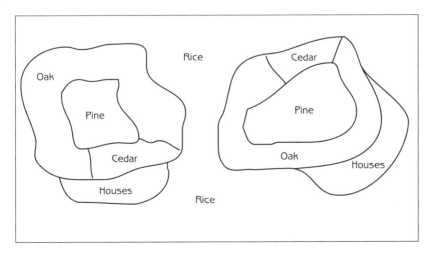

Figure 5.6
Map view of a typical landscape mosaic in western Japan

- pine (*matsu*);
- oak (*donguri*);
- Japanese cedar (*sugi*);
- Japanese cypress (*hinoki*).

Pine and oak forests occur naturally. Pine forests are common on the upper parts of hills where the soil is shallow due to **soil erosion** because soil is generally moved by rainwater from hilltops and hillsides to the valleys below (see Figure 5.7). Oak forests are common around the lower parts of hills, where the soil is deeper. Cedar and cypress forests may look superficially like natural ecosystems, but they are agricultural ecosystems planted by people to provide high-quality timber for construction. People plant cedar and cypress in orderly rows near the bottom of hills, where deeper soil holds a greater quantity of moisture and plant nutrients to support rapid tree growth. Japan has other agricultural ecosystems, mainly rice fields and vegetable fields, which people locate in the lowest and flattest parts of the valleys or on terraces at the edge of the valleys. Urban ecosystems such as village houses are usually at the base of the hills, just above the rice fields.

Every ecosystem provides habitats for the plant and animal species in its biological community. A pine ecosystem has plants that can live under pine trees, microorganisms that can decompose pine leaves, animals that eat pine bark, leaves or roots, and parasites and pathogens adapted to each of the plants and animals. All the plants, animals and microorganisms in each kind of ecosystem form a discrete group coadapted to each other.

Every ecosystem is an ecological 'island' because it is surrounded by other ecosystems which do not provide habitats for all the same species of plants and animals. Plants and animals sometimes move from sites where they already live to other sites with suitable habitats. This is **dispersal**. It is a source of newly arriving species for community assembly. Plants cannot move like animals, but their seeds are carried to new sites by wind and

landscape mosaics

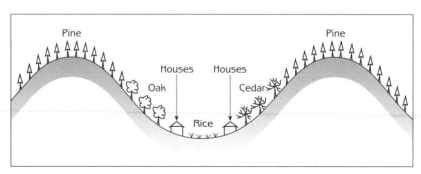

Figure 5.7
Typical landscape profile in western Japan

animals. This process of dispersal and community assembly, which is occuring everywhere all of the time, is responsible for the biological communities that we see in a landscape. Materials that are carried from one ecosystem to another by animals, wind or the flow of water are output from one ecosystem and input to another. This is a transfer not only of materials but also of the energy and information contained in the materials themselves. A plant seed that blows from one ecosystem to another contains energy in its carbon chains and genetic information in its DNA.

Landscape mosaics have their own self-organizing process, which adjusts the kinds of ecosystems in a landscape and the areas they occupy in a way that balances inputs and outputs over the landscape as a whole. For example, in a landscape with forested hill slopes and rice fields in the valley below, streams are an output of water from the forest ecosystems and an input of water to the rice field ecosystems. Farmers can extend rice fields up hill slopes by building terraces, but the consumption of water by rice fields places a limit on the quantity of land they can occupy. If there are too many rice fields, there is not enough forest to provide water for all of them. This kind of adjustment is happening constantly between all kinds of ecosystems – natural, agricultural and urban. Urban ecosystems need an appropriate area of agricultural ecosystems to provide food and other resources, and they also need natural ecosystems as a source of water.

landscape mosaics

The balance of natural, urban and agricultural ecosystems in the landscape mosaic is a major ecological issue of our time. There seems to be a progression from urban to agricultural to natural ecosystems in their ability to displace each other. Agricultural ecosystems expanded and displaced large areas of natural ecosystems in industrialized nations during previous centuries. The same process took longer to gain momentum in

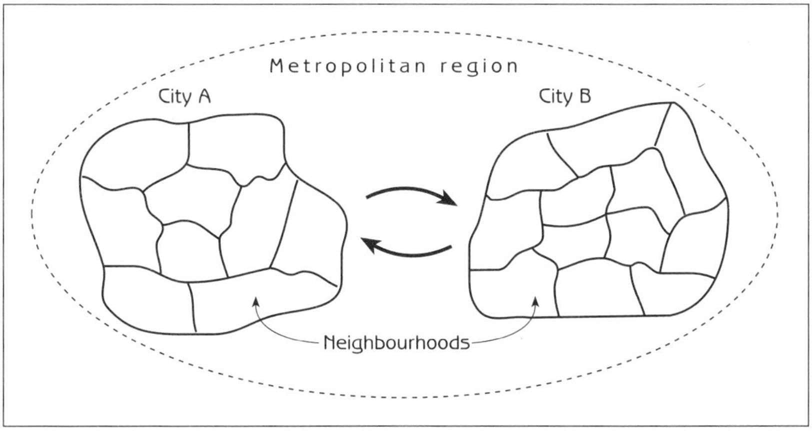

Figure 5.8
Spatial hierarchy of ecosystems in an urban metropolitan area

developing world countries but is now actively underway. Urban ecosystems are now expanding and displacing both agricultural and natural ecosystems everywhere in the world, a process that cannot continue for long because urban ecosystems depend upon agricultural and natural ecosystems for resources such as food and water.

Spatial hierarchies

landscape
mosaics

Ecosystems are **hierarchical** in space. All of the small ecosystems at one locality combine to form a larger ecosystem for that locality. All of the larger ecosystems in the various localities combine to form an even larger ecosystem for the entire region. Expanding the scale, all of the ecosystems in a major climatic zone form a **biome** ecosystem, and all the biome ecosystems combine to form the Earth ecosystem. Smaller ecosystems are more uniform within, while larger ecosystems are more variable.

Urban ecosystems also form a landscape mosaic that is hierarchical in space (see Figure 5.8). Every city is divided into neighbourhoods, and every neighbourhood contains smaller ecosystems such as residential areas, shopping centres, schools, parks, industrial sites and reservoirs. Each of these small urban ecosystems has its own structure: buildings, roads, other human-made structures and a biological community. Each neighbourhood has its own history and social system, which includes the ethnic and socioeconomic characteristics of the people who live and work there, their organizations, life style, occupations and other activities.

A city may be linked to other cities to form a **metropolitan region**. The ecosystems and social systems of each city interact with the ecosystems and social systems of the surrounding area, creating the city's **zone of influence** which serves as a source of labour, fuel, food, water and building materials for the city. In the past, a city's zone of influence was a discrete area surrounding the city. Since the Industrial Revolution, with colonialism and international trade, a city's zone of influence can extend to many parts of the world.

THINGS TO THINK ABOUT

1. What are the different kinds of natural ecosystems (as in Figure 5.6) in the landscape mosaic of your region? What is the typical position of each kind of ecosystem in a landscape profile as in Figure 5.7?

2. Talk to a farmer to learn about agricultural ecosystems in your region. What are the main kinds of agriculture? What is the typical position of each type of agricultural ecosystem in a landscape profile? What are important natural parts of their biological communities (ie, living organisms that are not crops or livestock)? How are the biological communities of different kinds of agricultural ecosystems different from one another? What are the inputs to each kind of agricultural ecosystem, and what is the function of each input? What organization or structure (ie, information inputs) do farmers impose on their agricultural ecosystem? In what ways do farmers use energy inputs to realize the organization and structure?

3. What are significant input–output exchanges of materials, energy and information between agricultural and natural ecosystems in your region?

4. Make a map for a 1-kilometre radius around your family home showing different kinds of urban ecosystems, such as residential neighbourhoods, shopping areas, parks, office buildings or industrial areas. If there are natural or agricultural ecosystems, show them too.

5. List important inputs and outputs of your city or town.

things to
think about

6

ECOLOGICAL SUCCESSION

Natural processes continually change ecosystems. The changes can take years or even centuries, working so slowly that they are scarcely noticed. They have a systematic pattern generated by community assembly, following an orderly progression know as **ecological succession**, another emergent property of ecosystems.

Ecosystems change themselves and people change ecosystems. People change ecosystems to serve their needs. Intentional changes by people can set in motion chains of effects that lead to further changes – **human-induced succession**. Sometimes changes are unintended. They can be unwanted and they can be irreversible. This chapter will give three examples of human-induced succession:

1. Overgrazing and pasture degradation.
2. Overfishing and replacement of commercially valuable fish by **trash fish**.
3. Severe forest fires when forests are protected from fires.

Since ecological succession can be of immense practical consequence, humans have responded by developing a variety of ways in which to integrate their use of ecosystems with the natural processes of succession. Modern society uses intensive inputs to maintain agricultural and urban ecosystems by opposing the natural processes of ecological succession. Many traditional societies have drawn on centuries of experimentation and experience to develop strategies that take advantage of ecological succession in ways that allow them to use fewer inputs. This chapter will describe examples from traditional management of village forests and traditional agriculture.

ECOLOGICAL SUCCESSION

Do places with the same physical conditions always have exactly the same ecosystems? The answer is 'no'. Firstly, random elements in biological community assembly can lead to different ecosystems. Secondly, ecosystems experience slow but systematic changes as community assembly proceeds. A single site has different biological communities, and therefore different ecosystems, at different times. The slow but orderly sequence of different biological communities at the same site is **ecological succession**. Each biological community is a stage of ecological succession.

ecological
succession

Change from one biological community to another can happen because:

- Smaller species of plants and animals generally grow and reproduce rapidly. Larger plants and animals take more time to grow, and their population growth is slower. As a result, the rapidly growing plants and animals populate a site first, and the slower ones take over later. For example, if a fire or logging destroys a forest, there will be many species of grass growing on the site within months because grasses grow quickly. Later, shrubs grow over the grasses, and after that trees grow over the shrubs.
- A biological community can create conditions that lead to its own destruction. For example, as trees grow older, they become weak and vulnerable to destruction by insects or diseases. When this happens, a biological community 'grows old' and 'dies', and another biological community takes its place.
- One biological community can create conditions that are more suitable for another biological community. A biological community can change the physical or biological conditions of a site, making it more favourable for another biological community. One biological community therefore leads to another.
- A biological community can be destroyed by natural or human-generated 'disturbances' and replaced by another biological community. Fires, storms and floods are examples of natural disturbances. Human activities such as logging or clearing land to make agricultural or urban ecosystems can also destroy a biological community. Activities such as excessive fishing or livestock grazing can change a biological community so much that it is replaced by a different community.

Earlier stages of ecological succession are known as 'immature'. They are simpler, with fewer species of plants and animals. As community assembly progresses, the biological community becomes more complex. It accumulates more species, many of them more specialized with regard to diet and the way they interact with other plants and animals in the food web. The ecosystem consequently becomes more 'mature'. The last stage of succession is a **climax community**. Climax communities do not change to another stage by themselves. The progression from immature biological communities to mature and climax communities is ecological succession.

ecological
succession

An example of ecological succession

Ecological succession typically begins when the existing biological community has been cleared away by human activity or natural disturbance such as a fire or severe storm. This may happen over a large area, but succession can also begin in a small patch of forest that is opened up where an old tree has fallen. In western Japan, short grasses and small **annual** flowering plants generally mark the first stage of succession (Figure 6.1A). After a few years, they may be outgrown by taller grasses. Eventually, young trees and shrubs grow up through the grasses to form a mixture of tree saplings and shrubs that is dense enough to shade out most of the grass (Figure 6.1B). Some of the saplings ultimately grow above the shrubs to form a forest. Some of the shrubs disappear, while others survive between the trees.

If the soil is deep, the first forest is typically a mixture of deciduous oaks with other trees and shrubs (Figure 6.1C). The oaks and most of the other trees are eventually replaced by *shii* and *kashi* trees to form a climax forest (Figure 6.1E). (*Shii* and *kashi* are broadleaf evergreen trees in the beech family.) As the plant species in the biological community change, the animal species also change because particular species of animals use particular species of plants for food or shelter.

Why does oak forest appear first in ecological succession, and why do *shii* and *kashi* eventually replace it? *Shii* and *kashi* grow slowly, but they live for hundreds of years. With time they can grow to a great height. Oak trees grow rapidly if they have plenty of sunlight, but they do not grow as tall. When *shii*, *kashi* and oak seedlings grow together in an open immature ecosystem (Figure 6.1B), the large amount of sunlight favours oaks, which grow faster than the *shii* and *kashi*. The first forest in the ecological succession is therefore oak trees with shrubs and small *shii* and

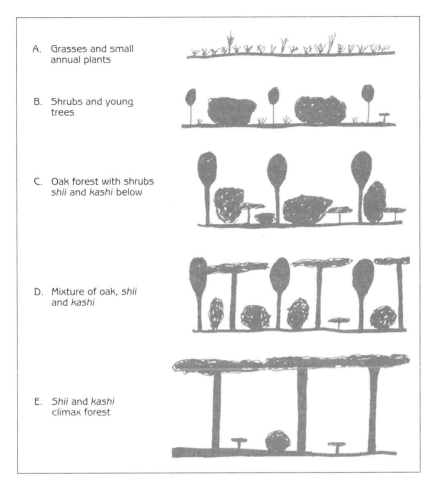

A. Grasses and small annual plants

B. Shrubs and young trees

C. Oak forest with shrubs *shii* and *kashi* below

D. Mixture of oak, *shii* and *kashi*

E. *Shii* and *kashi* climax forest

Figure 6.1
Typical ecological succession on deep soil in western Japan

ecological
succession

kashi trees beneath them (Figure 6.1C). *Shii* and *kashi* can survive in the shade of oak trees, and they slowly increase in height. After about 50 years the forest is a mixture of oaks with *shii* and *kashi* all about the same height (Figure 6.1D). By this time some of the oak trees are old and senile and some may be covered with vines that 'smother' them. The oaks begin to decline.

Eventually the *shii* and *kashi* grow above the oaks to form a dense leaf canopy that shades everything below. Oaks cannot survive in the shade of *shii* and *kashi*, so the biological community changes to a climax forest of tall shii and kashi with a scattering of young *shii* and *kashi* and shade-tolerant shrubs below (Figure 6.1E). The entire progression from a grass ecosystem to a mature *shii* and *kashi* forest takes 150 years or more. Because younger *shii* and *kashi* trees grow into the space that opens up when an old tree falls down, the climax forest stays more or less the same unless it is destroyed by human activity, fire or some other severe disturbance.

Figure 6.2
Ecological
succession in
western Japan
Note: Sites with
shallow soils have a
different sequence of
biological
communities
compared to sites
with deep soils.

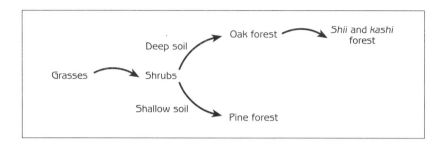

ecological
succession

The ecological succession on shallow soil in western Japan is different from the succession on deep soil (Figure 6.2). Oaks, *shii* and *kashi* require deep soil to grow tall, but pine trees do well even if the soil is shallow, provided they have plenty of sunlight. The climax ecosystem on shallow soil is pine forest. Pine saplings may also thrive in open sunny areas with deep soil, but other trees eventually predominate on deep soil because pines cannot tolerate their shade.

It is evident then that a landscape mosaic contains different biological communities at different places not only because of spatial variation in physical conditions but also because of ecological succession. Sites with similar physical conditions have similar ecological successions, but sites with similar physical conditions can have very different ecosystems because they are in different stages of the same succession.

Because climax communities stay more or less the same for many years, one might expect a lot of *shii* and *kashi* forest in western Japan. The regional landscape was dominated by *shii* and *kashi* climax forest in the distant past, but people cut down most of the *shii* and *kashi* forests many centuries ago. *Shii* and *kashi*, including some very old and large trees, are scattered across the landscape today, but fully developed *shii* and *kashii* climax forests are unusual. Remnants of the climax forests remain primarily in sacred groves around temples and shrines.

Ecological succession as a complex system cycle

Ecological succession is cyclic (see Figure 6.3). It follows the four stages of the complex systems cycle described in Chapter 4: growth; equilibrium; dissolution; and reorganization. Immature biological communities such as grasses or shrubs are the *growth* stages of ecological succession. Because immature communities have relatively few species, newly arriving species do not face strong competition from species already in the community. Most new arrivals survive the community assembly process, and the

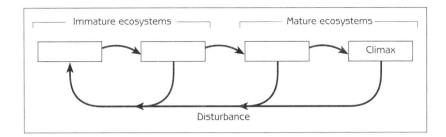

Figure 6.3
Ecological
succession as a
complex system
cycle

number of plant and animal species in the community increases
rapidly. The most successful species in immature ecosystems are
ones that can grow and reproduce quickly with an abundance of
resources.

ecological
succession

Ecosystems mature as additional species of plants and animals
become established over the years through the community
assembly process. It becomes increasingly difficult for newly
arriving species to join the mature ecosystem because it has so
many species, which already occupy all potential ecological
niches. Newly arriving species can survive in the mature
ecosystem only if they can outcompete and displace species that
are already there. Eventually the biological community changes
little. This is the **climax community** (*equilibrium*). It has the
largest number of species, and they are all efficient competitors,
good at surviving with limited resources. A climax ecosystem may
last for centuries, provided outside disturbances such as fire or
severe storms are not too damaging.

However, sooner or later, the climax community is destroyed
by some kind of disturbance. This is *dissolution*. Most plant and
animal species disappear from the site. Then comes the
reorganization stage. Because many niches are empty at this time,
competition is low and survival is easy for newly arriving species
if the site has suitable physical conditions and the biological
community has an appropriate food source. The reorganization
stage is a time when the community might acquire one group of
plants and animals, or a very different group, depending upon
which species happen to arrive at the site by chance during this
critical time. Ecological succession then proceeds from immature
to mature communities (*growth*) until there is another disturbance
or succession once again reaches the climax community.

The disturbances that cause mature communities to be
replaced by earlier stages of succession vary in scale. As a result,
landscape mosaics have patches of many different sizes. For
example, lightning can strike one tree in a forest. The tree dies and
falls over, opening up a small gap in the forest, which is occupied
by early successional species. At the other extreme, a severe

typhoon or fire, or large-scale logging, can tear down hundreds of square kilometres of forest.

Interaction of positive and negative feedback in ecological succession

This section examines the tension between positive and negative feedback in ecological succession. **Negative feedback** tends to keep ecosystems the same (ecosystem **homeostasis**) but they change from one stage to another as **positive feedback** takes effect.

We will look once again at the succession of an ecosystem from grass to shrub community, beginning with an ecosystem in which the ground is carpeted with grasses (see Figure 6.4A). Shrubs may be present, but they are young and scattered. The ecosystem may stay this way for 5 to 10 years, or even longer, because shrub seedlings grow very slowly. They grow slowly because grass roots are located in the top soil, while most of the shrub roots are lower down. Grasses intercept most of the rainwater before it reaches the roots of the shrubs. Because the grasses limit the supply of water to the shrub seedlings, they maintain the integrity of the ecosystem as a grass ecosystem. At this stage, **negative feedback** acts to keep the biological community the same.

However, after a number of years, some of the trees and shrubs, which have been growing slowly, are finally tall enough to shade the grasses below them (see Figure 6.4B). The grasses then have less sunlight for photosynthesis, and their growth is restricted. This results in more water for the shrubs, which grow

ecological succession

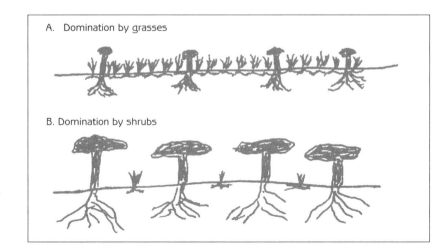

A. Domination by grasses

B. Domination by shrubs

Figure 6.4
Competition between shrubs and grasses for sunlight and water

faster and shade the grasses even more. This process of positive feedback allows the shrubs to take over. They now dominate the available sunlight and water, and the grasses decrease dramatically.

This example shows how negative feedback can keep an ecosystem in one stage of ecological succession until there is enough change in some part of the ecosystem to trigger a positive feedback loop that changes the ecosystem to the next stage of succession. This example is about much more than grasses, shrubs and trees. The same kind of interplay between positive and negative feedback is responsible not only for ecological succession but also for much of the behaviour of all complex adaptive systems. Ecosystems, social systems and other complex adaptive systems stay more or less the same for long periods because negative feedback predominates until a small change triggers a powerful positive feedback loop to change the system rapidly. Negative feedback then takes over to hold the system in its new form.

human-induced succession

Urban succession

Urban ecosystems and their social systems change in ways that are similar to ecological succession. As a city grows, every neighbourhood within it experiences changes in its social system. A neighbourhood can change drastically over a period of 25 to 100 years. It may be primarily residential during one time and become commercial or industrial during another. Neighbourhoods experience growth, vitality and progress during certain times, and at other times they deteriorate as the focus of growth and vitality shifts to other neighbourhoods. The same is true for entire cities. Cities grow and decline as the focus of growth and vitality shifts from one city to another.

HUMAN-INDUCED SUCCESSION

Human activities can have a powerful effect on ecosystems and the way they change. This is known as **human-induced succession**, which can lead to changes that are often unexpected and sometimes seriously detrimental to the benefits that people derive from ecosystems. Pollution of the lagoons that surround small South Pacific islands provides a striking example. Many South

Pacific communities now consume imported packaged and canned foods, disposing of the empty cans and other waste in dumps. Rainwater runoff from the dumps pollutes the lagoons, reducing the quantity of fish and other seafood. With less seafood, people are forced to buy more and more cheap canned food, the pollution becomes worse and the lagoon has fewer fish. This positive feedback loop changes the lagoon ecosystem while also degrading the people's diet.

Pasture degradation due to overgrazing

human-induced succession

Another example of human-induced succession is the effect of **overgrazing** on pasture ecosystems. Overgrazing occurs when a pasture ecosystem has more grazing animals such as sheep or cattle than its carrying capacity for those animals will support.

Pastures usually have a mixture of different grass species that differ in their nutritional value. Many species of grass are not nutritious as a defence against being eaten by animals. Some species of grass are even poisonous. Because grazing animals know which grasses are best to eat and which are not, they select the nutritious species and leave the rest uneaten. Different species of grass in the same pasture compete with each other for **mineral nutrients** in the soil (mainly nitrogen, phosphorus and potassium), water and sunlight (see Figure 6.5). A mixture of different grass species can coexist in the same ecosystem as long as no species has an advantage. However, if some species have a disadvantage, they will disappear and the other species will take over.

What happens when too many cattle graze for a prolonged period of time? Because cattle select nutritious grasses, these species have a disadvantage in their competition with grasses that are not nutritious. The population of nutritious grasses decreases, leaving more resources for other species to grow and increase in abundance. A positive feedback loop is set in motion for grasses

Figure 6.5
Competition between grasses that are nutritious or not nutritious for sunlight, water and mineral nutrients

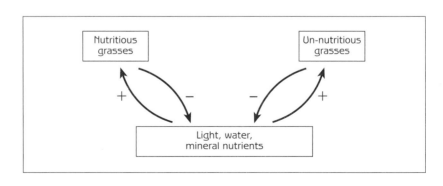

that are not nutritious to replace nutritious grasses. By tracing the arrows through the diagram in Figure 6.5, it is possible to see that each species of grass has a positive feedback loop that passes first through its 'food' in the soil and then through the other species of grass. This replacement process can take years, but when it is finished, the pasture has changed from an ecosystem with a mixture of grasses to an ecosystem dominated by grasses of low nutritional value. As a result, the carrying capacity for cattle is much lower than it was before.

Desertification

human-induced succession

Grass ecosystems are an early stage of succession in regions where the mature ecosystems are forests. However, grass ecosystems are **climax ecosystems** in grassland regions, where there is not enough rainfall to support a forest. Desert ecosystems are climax ecosystems where there is not enough rainfall even for grassland. **Desertification** is the change from a grassland ecosystem to a desert ecosystem in a region where the climate is suitable for grassland. There is enough rainfall for grass, but overgrazing can change the grassland to desert.

In a healthy grassland ecosystem, all of the ground is covered by grasses, which protect the soil from erosion due to wind or rain. If there are too many cattle, grass cover is reduced. Bit by bit, wind and rain carry away the fertile topsoil from ground that is no longer protected by grasses. When topsoil is lost, the soil becomes less fertile and its capacity to hold water declines. Grasses then grow more slowly and are replaced by shrubs whose roots can reach water deeper in the soil. Because the shrubs are not nutritious for cattle, the carrying capacity for cattle declines. People may then use goats instead of cattle because goats can eat shrubs that cattle cannot. Goats can also eat grass, which they pull out by the roots. If there are too many goats, they destroy the remaining grasses, and more ground is left without its protective cover. There is more erosion, and eventually the soil is so badly degraded that grass can no longer grow at all. The grassland has changed to a desert with scattered shrubs (see Figure 6.6)

These changes are slow. It can take 50 years or more for a grassland ecosystem to become a desert ecosystem that provides very little food for people. The entire ecosystem changes. Desert shrubs replace grasses and the rest of the biological community changes because it depends upon the plants. Physical conditions change as well, often irreversibly. Because degraded soil cannot hold enough water to support the growth of grasses, a desert ecosystem may not change back to a grassland ecosystem, even if all the grazing animals are removed.

Worldwide, about 50,000 square kilometres of grassland change to desert every year. The causes are complex and varied, but overgrazing is often a major factor. Why do people put too many grazing animals on grasslands when the consequences are so disastrous? The main reason is human overpopulation. The human population in many grassland areas already exceeds the carrying capacity of the local ecosystem. People use too many grazing animals because they need the animals to feed themselves now, even if it means less food in the future. Desertification has contributed to famine in places such as the African Sahel. This is an example of population **overshoot** that can cause the human population and its ecosystem to crash together.

human-induced succession

Fisheries succession

Commercial fishing can have far-reaching effects on fish populations in oceans and lakes. If fishermen focus heavy fishing on a few species of high commercial value, those species have a higher death rate than other species of fish with which they compete for food resources. The populations of commercially valuable fish decline and are replaced by **trash fish** or other aquatic animals of little or no commercial value. This is known as **fisheries succession**. It is basically the same ecological process as replacement of nutritious grasses by species that are not nutritious because of overgrazing. During the 1940s and 1950s, the sardine population off the California coast declined and was replaced by anchovies. While recognizing that long-term climatic or biological cycles may have a role in this story, it appears the change was primarily due to overfishing. In a similar fashion,

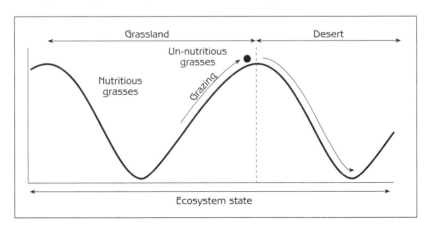

Figure 6.6
Human-induced succession from grassland to desert caused by overgrazing

sardines replaced anchovetas off the coast of Peru and Chile when there was heavy fishing during the 1960s and 1970s, and similar stories have occurred numerous times with other species of fish in oceans and lakes throughout the world.

When this happens, a decline in the population of a particular fish species can set in motion a chain of effects through the aquatic ecosystem that alters the biological community in many other ways. Physical conditions sometimes change as well. The fish that disappeared may not be able to return even after overfishing has ceased. When people damage part of an ecosystem, it adapts by changing to a different kind of ecosystem – one that may not serve human needs as well as before. A multitude of changes through the ecosystem have 'locked' it into a new biological community (see Figure 6.7).

**human-
induced
succession**

The 'okay/not okay' principle of human-induced succession

Desertification and fisheries succession are examples of a more general emergent property of ecosystems. Human-induced succession can make ecosystems switch from a stability domain that serves human needs ('okay') to another stability domain that does not ('not okay').

Ecosystems continue to be 'okay' as long as people do not change them too much. If an ecosystem is altered drastically, natural and social forces can transform it even more to a different stability domain that may be okay but often is not.

Ecosystems are impressively resilient in their capacity to continue functioning and providing services over a range of uses and even moderate abuse. Moderate levels of fishing, grazing, logging or other uses may alter the state of a natural ecosystem,

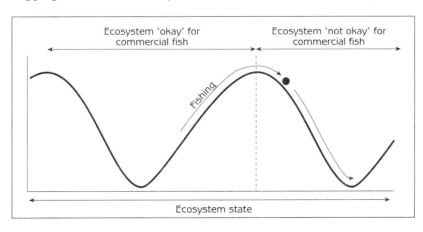

Figure 6.7
Disappearance of commercial fish due to overfishing

but the ecosystem remains in the same stability domain and continues to provide fish, forage or wood (see Figure 6.8). The same is true for agricultural and urban ecosystems that include a healthy natural biological community, such as animals and microorganisms that maintain soil fertility on a farm, or trees that remove pollution from the air in a city. However, if an ecosystem is transformed too much, a chain of effects can be set in motion through ecosystems and social systems that changes the ecosystem even more. Fish, forage, forests, soil animals or urban trees can disappear. The **ecosystem state** passes from one stability domain to another, and the new ecosystem may not serve people's needs as it did before.

managing
succession

MANAGING SUCCESSION

Traditional forest management in Japan

Human-induced succession is not always detrimental. People who know how to interact with ecosystems on a sustainable basis can encourage ecosystems to change – or not change – in ways that best serve their needs. They can use natural processes to change ecosystems to a stage of ecological succession that they want. People can also structure their activities in the ecosystem so that the biological community remains at a desired stage of succession instead of developing into a stage that they do not want.

Figure 6.8
The okay/not okay principle of human-induced succession

The traditional Japanese *satoyama* system (literally 'village/mountain') is an example of sustainable landscape

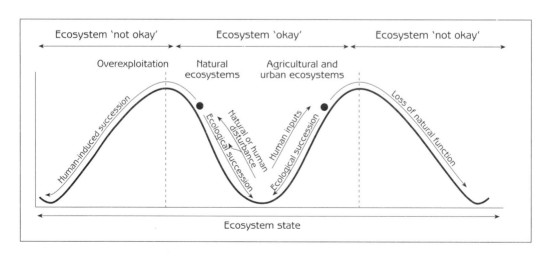

management that for many centuries provided essential materials for village life. The villagers maintained young oak forests and patches of a tall **perennial** grass (*susuki*) as a major part of their landscape because of the valuable products they provided. The long tough stems of *susuki* grass were used as thatch for houses and as mulch or compost on the farmers' fields. Villagers prevented their *susuki* grass areas from changing to forest by setting them on fire after cutting the grass stems for use. The fire killed young trees and shrubs but the underground roots of the grass survived to sprout soon after the fire.

Village forests were the main source of construction materials, charcoal for cooking food and heating houses, and leaf litter for application as mulch to agricultural fields. Oak forests were more useful than the more mature *shii* and *kashi* forests because oaks grow faster. The villagers used a very simple procedure to ensure that they had enough oak forest to meet their needs. Each year they cut all the oaks in a small area, doing so in a way that allowed new oak trees to sprout from the stumps of the cut trees. Because the new oaks could use the large root systems of the cut trees, the new oaks could grow so fast that within 20 to 25 years they were once again ready for cutting. Once the 20–25-year-old trees were cut, the same process was repeated, with new trees sprouting from the cut stumps; more oak trees were then ready for cutting in another 20 to 25 years. Because different parts of the forest were cut at different times, the landscape had a mosaic of oak forests of different ages that provided a diversity of forest products and a diversity of habitat for many species of plants, insects, birds and other animals.

Every year the villagers cut all young *shii* and *kashi* trees so that they could not grow above the oak trees. In this way they retained oak forest as a major part of their landscape mosaic for centuries. It was essential to cut the oaks every 20–25 years. If they waited too long and did not remove *shii* and *kashi*, the oaks would eventually be replaced by *shii* and *kashi*. If they cut too soon, the oaks would never grow large enough to produce the seeds necessary for new trees. Without new trees the oak forest would eventually disappear and be replaced by other kinds of trees or an earlier stage of succession with grasses and shrubs.

The situation is very different today. For the past 40 years, Japan has imported petroleum and gas instead of using charcoal. Moreover, Japan has imported large quantities of timber from other countries for construction while using less wood from its own forests. Most farmers apply large quantities of chemical fertilizers to their fields instead of mulch from the forest. Oak forests are no longer cut on a regular basis, the trees are becoming

managing succession

senile, and some are starting to die. Oak forests may eventually be replaced by *shii* and *kashi* forests.

Forest fire protection

Frequent fires – started mainly by lightning – are a natural part of many forest ecosystems. The seeds of some plants germinate only when stimulated by fire. Dead tree leaves accumulate on the ground to form **leaf litter**, which provides fuel for fires that are usually started by lightning. When the quantity of litter is small, there is not much fuel, fires burn slowly and are not excessively hot. Most of the leaf litter burns away and some of the leaves on the trees may be burned; however, few trees are killed. If fires kill any trees (usually old trees), young trees quickly grow to fill the canopy gaps.

managing
succession

Fires have an important function for forests. Fallen leaves contain minerals such as phosphorous and potassium that the ashes from a fire return to the soil as **mineral nutrients** for trees and other forest plants. However, if a forest has too much leaf litter on the ground, a fire can burn at extremely hot temperatures because the large amount of litter provides so much fuel. A fire with too much leaf litter can spread over a large area and burn with such intensity that it destroys all of the trees and buried tree seeds in the soil. When this happens, the forest is destroyed and a grass ecosystem emerges from the ashes. It can take many years before there is forest again, particularly if there is no longer any woodland close by to provide a seed source.

Frequent fires are a negative feedback mechanism that prevents excessive accumulation of leaf litter in forest ecosystems (see Figure 6.9A). Because frequent fires seldom result in serious damage, they are nature's way of protecting forests from severe

Figure 6.9
Natural regulation of forest litter by fire (no fire protection) and accumulation of litter with fire protection

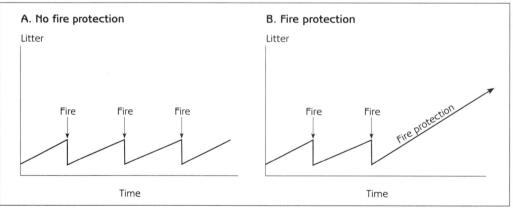

A. No fire protection

Litter

Fire   Fire   Fire

Time

B. Fire protection

Litter

Fire   Fire

Fire protection

Time

fires that could destroy them. This is 'ecosystem homeostasis'. A forest landscape with frequent natural fires is a mosaic of mature forest with grass and shrub ecosystems, and less mature forest in areas where there were fires in recent years (see Figure 6.10). The kind of ecosystem in each patch depends upon how many years have passed since a fire occurred and how severe it was. People generally consider a varied landscape, punctuated with different kinds of forest and open areas, to be more pleasant than a landscape that is solid forest.

Around 1900, the United States Forest Service initiated a policy of protecting forests from fire because foresters did not understand the value of frequent forest fires. They did not want any tree damage due to fire. For 80 years they put out all forest fires as quickly as possible. More and more leaf litter accumulated on the ground because so much time passed without frequent small fires to get rid of the leaf litter (see Figure 6.9B). By 1980, leaf litter had accumulated within forests to the extent that they were increasingly susceptible to fire. New forest fires became very difficult to control, particularly in the extensive dry areas of Western United States.

managing succession

The more the forest service tried to protect forests from fires, the worse the problem became because every fire was more difficult to extinguish and could destroy such large areas of natural habitat. Forest protection became increasingly costly because it was necessary to use large numbers of fire fighters, fire trucks and airplanes to drop water. Despite this effort, thousands of square kilometres of forest were sometimes destroyed by a single fire.

This example shows how human interference with fire as a natural part of 'ecosystem homeostasis' caused fires to become a

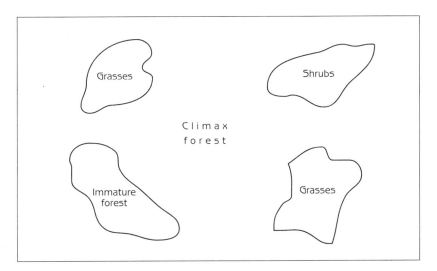

Figure 6.10
Landscape mosaic of a forest without fire protection

disturbance that could destroy mature ecosystems and transform them to an earlier stage of succession (grass ecosystems). The solution to the problem is **controlled burning** to get rid of the leaf litter and **selective logging** to reduce the number of trees that provide fuel for a fire. This is what the forest service does now. Even a large quantity of leaf litter does not burn at high temperatures if it is wet, so there are times (for example, after rainfall) when foresters can start a fire and burn away the accumulated leaf litter without destroying the trees. These new forest management practices are working in harmony with the natural feedback loops in ecosystems instead of fighting them. However, it has not been easy to correct the situation. Many forests still have excessive quantities of combustible material such as decaying trees, litter or shrubs, and the United States government still spends many millions of dollars combating destructive forest fires. Moreover, controlled burning occasionally escapes control, leading to serious and unexpected destruction of forests, millions of dollars worth of property damage and considerable political controversy.

managing
succession

The forest fire example shows how the response of ecosystems to human activities can be counterintuitive – the opposite of what we expect. Our actions can have not only the direct effects that we intend; they can also generate a chain of effects through other parts of the ecosystem that come back in unexpected ways.

Ecological succession and agriculture

Agricultural ecosystems such as farms and pastures contain few species of plants and animals compared to mature natural ecosystems. People make agricultural ecosystems simple because simple ecosystems channel a large percentage of their biological production to human use. Agricultural ecosystems are immature ecosystems, and like all immature ecosystems they are continually subject to natural processes of ecological succession that change them in the direction of mature natural ecosystems. Weeds invade fields. Insects and other animals that eat crops join the ecosystem. The basic strategy of modern agriculture is to counteract these forces of ecological succession. Modern society uses intensive human inputs in the form of materials, energy and information to prevent ecological succession from altering its agricultural ecosystems.

It is typical for traditional agriculture to follow a different strategy. It reduces the need for intensive inputs by harmonizing agriculture with the natural cycles of ecological succession. For example, **swidden** agriculture, which is also known as **slash-and-burn** agriculture or **shifting cultivation**, is common in tropical areas where the soil is unsuitable for permanent agriculture. Swidden agricultural is particularly useful on:

* forested hillsides that are susceptible to erosion when a forest is cleared for agriculture;
* infertile forest soils that are vulnerable to leaching of plant nutrients to soil depths beyond the reach of crop roots.

A typical swidden procedure is to clear a patch of forest by cutting and burning the trees and shrubs. Fire is a means that swidden farmers employ to use a large supply of natural energy to prepare their fields for crops. Fire converts trees and shrubs to ash that serves as natural fertilizer, and fires kill pests in the soil. The ash provides natural liming to ensure suitable soil pH for crops. A farmer can grow crops in the cleared patch for one or two years. After that, soil fertility declines and crop pests increase, so that harvests are too small to justify the effort. The farmer abandons the patch before these problems materialize, moving to another part of the forest where he clears a new patch for crops. The abandoned patch is left in **fallow** for at least ten years.

managing succession

Once a patch is left in fallow, numerous plants and animals invade from the surrounding forest, generating a sequence of biological communities that follows the usual progression of ecological succession from grasses and shrubs to trees. Natural vegetation and a covering of leaf litter protect the soil from erosion. Fertility is eventually restored to the soil surface by the forest's **nutrient pump**, as deeply rooted trees bring plant nutrients to their leaves and deposit the leaves on the ground. Crop pests disappear because they cannot survive in a natural ecosystem without crops as food. The farmer can return to the same place after about ten years of fallow, repeating the process of cutting and burning trees and shrubs and planting a crop. A landscape in swidden agriculture has a mosaic of patches, some of them agricultural fields with crops, but most of them different stages of ecological succession in the course of forest fallow.

Swidden agriculture is a highly efficient and ecologically sustainable way to use fragile lands when the human population is small enough for farmers to leave the land in fallow for the required time. Unfortunately, swidden does not work if the human population is too large. When land is in short supply, farmers are compelled to clear the forest and plant crops before the fallow has had enough time to fully restore the land. The result is a vicious cycle of soil degradation and declining harvests. Population explosion in the developing world has changed swidden agriculture from ecologically sustainable to unsustainable in many places. One solution to the problem is **agroforestry**, which mixes shrub or tree crops such as coffee or fruit trees with conventional food crops to create an agricultural ecosystem that mimics a natural forest ecosystem.

The human population of Java in Indonesia is too large for swidden agriculture with a natural forest fallow. Most Javanese farmers are quite poor because they must meet all of their family needs with only one or two hectares of land, but they make the best of this difficult situation with traditional agriculture that simulates the natural cycle of ecological succession. They start by planting a polyculture of crops such as sweet potatoes, beans, corn and several dozen other food crops that grow quickly. They plant a scattering of bamboo or trees in the same field. The fast-growing crops predominate during the first few years (*kebun* agricultural ecosystem in Figure 6.11), and the trees or bamboo take over later (*talun* in Figure 6.11). As soon as the trees and bamboo are large enough, they harvest them for use as construction material and fuel, clear the field, burn unused plant materials, and once again plant a polyculture of food crops and trees. Much of the Javanese landscape looks like natural forest but is, in fact, carefully cultured agroforestry – 'forest' stages of an agricultural cycle that takes full advantage of ecological succession. Each family manages a small landscape mosaic of different fields in different stages of the cycle, so they have a continuous supply of the various foods and other materials that they need.

managing succession

Figure 6.11
Succession of a Javanese polyculture field from domination by annual field crops to domination by tree crops
Source: Christanty, L, Abdoellah, O, Marten, G and Iskandar, J (1986) 'Traditional agroforestry in West Java: The *pekerangan* (homegarden) and *kebun–talun* (annual–perennial rotation) cropping systems' in Marten, G, *Traditional Agriculture in Southeast Asia: A Human Ecology Perspective*, Westview, Boulder, Colorado

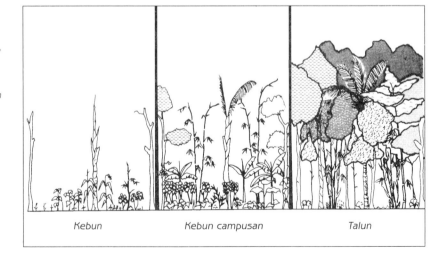

Kebun   Kebun campusan   Talun

THINGS TO THINK ABOUT

1. What are the typical sequences of natural succession in your region (as in Figures 6.1 and 6.2)? Do sites with different physical conditions have different sequences? What role does chance seem to have in the sequences that actually occur?

2. Have there been examples of human-induced succession in your region? What were the human activities that made them happen? Were they reversible?

3. Talk to your grandparents or other relatives or friends that have lived in the vicinity of your family home for a long time. How have natural, agricultural, and urban ecosystems changed? Make a map showing the landscape mosaic over a radius of 1 kilometre around your family home 50 years ago. Compare the map of 50 years ago with the map from 'Things to think about' in Chapter 5 (ie, a map of the ecosystems today). How has the landscape mosaic changed during the past 50 years? (If there were no houses in your area 50 years go, make the map for a more recent time such as 30–40 years ago.) If possible, make a series of maps that show progressive change in the landscape mosaic over time.

things to think about

COEVOLUTION AND COADAPTATION OF HUMAN SOCIAL SYSTEMS AND ECOSYSTEMS

The last several chapters introduced some of the emergent properties of social systems and ecosystems. This chapter is about two closely related emergent properties of the interacting social system and ecosystem:

1. **Coevolution** (changing together).
2. **Coadaptation** (fitting together).

Chapter 5 introduced coevolution and coadaptation as an integral part of the biological evolution of plants, animals and microorganisms that live together in the same ecosystem. Coevolution and coadaptation are a game of mutual adjustment and change that never ends.

The same thing happens between humans and the rest of the ecosystem (see Figure 7.1). Human social systems adapt to their environment, the ecosystem, and ecosystems adapt to human social systems. Natural ecosystems, and the natural parts of agricultural and urban ecosystems, respond to human interventions by making adjustments that promote survival. Agricultural and urban ecosystems also evolve and adapt to the social system as people change them to fit with their changing society.

This chapter begins with two examples of coadaptation between social systems and ecosystems. It ends with the story of coadaptive changes that the Industrial Revolution stimulated between the modernizing social system and agricultural ecosystems.

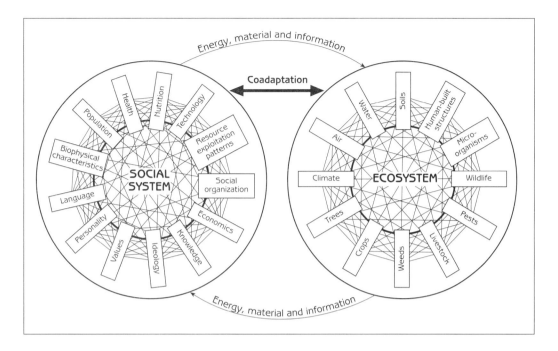

COADAPTATION IN TRADITIONAL SOCIAL SYSTEMS

Figure 7.1
Interaction, coevolution and coadaptation of the human social system with the ecosystem
Source: Adapted from Rambo, A and Sajise, T (1985) *An Introduction to Human Ecology Research on Agricultural Systems in Southeast Asia*, University of the Philippines, Los Banos, Philippines

Traditional societies are a rich source of examples to illustrate coadaptation between social systems and ecosystems. Centuries of trial-and-error cultural evolution have fine-tuned many aspects of traditional social systems to their environment. The following passage contains two stories of coadaptation between social systems and disease-transmitting mosquitoes. The first story concerns the adaptation of one part of the human social system, house design, to one aspect of the ecosystem, mosquitoes and malaria. The second story is about adaptation of one component of the ecosystem, mosquitoes, to one aspect of the social system, pesticide technology. The example in the subsequent passage concerns the use of fire by Native Americans to modify their landscape mosaic.

Coadaptation of people and mosquitoes

Approximately 100 years ago, the French moved large numbers of people in colonial Vietnam from the lowlands to the mountains. They wanted more people in the mountains to cut forests, work on rubber plantations and work at tin mines. Unfortunately, many lowland people died of malaria when they were forced to live in the mountains. This was surprising, because malaria had not been a serious problem in Vietnam. Malaria is transmitted by mosquitoes but, fortunately for lowland people, the species of mosquito that breed in the vast rice fields of the lowlands do not transmit malaria. Although the mountains have malaria-transmitting mosquito species, the disease was never a serious problem for the mountain people, who lived there for many generations. Because of malaria, the French never succeeded at moving large numbers of lowland people to the mountains.

coadaptation

Why did lowland people get malaria when mountain people did not? The reason was a difference in culture. Mountain people build their houses raised above the ground, keep their animals such as water buffalo below the house and have their cooking fire inside the house (see Figure 7.2). Mosquitoes fly close to the ground, prefer to bite animals instead of people and are repelled by smoke, so they seldom enter the raised, smoke-containing houses of the mountain people, and bite the animals beneath the houses instead of the people.

Lowland people build their houses right on the ground, keep their animals away from the house and cook outside (see Figure 7.2). When lowland people moved to the mountains, they continued to build their houses and cook in the traditional way. Mosquitoes easily entered the ground-level, smoke-free houses and bit the people within the houses because there were no animals to attract them away. The lowland house design worked well in the lowlands but was not adapted to the mountain ecosystem.

The mountain people were protected from malaria without realizing that mosquitoes transmit the disease. At that time, before scientists discovered the role of mosquitoes in malaria

Figure 7.2
Traditional house design of mountain people and lowland people in Vietnam

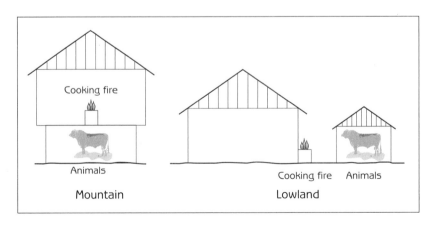

transmission, people everywhere in the world believed that malaria was caused by spirits or contaminated water. If mountain people were asked why they built their houses in a specific way, they would say it is tradition. Their house design was a product of centuries of cultural evolution that adapted their buildings to all of their needs, including health.

In 1940, scientists invented DDT, an effective insecticide against mosquitoes that transmit malaria. Because malarial mosquitoes rest on house walls, and because DDT stays on surfaces for months after it is first applied, it was possible to kill almost all of the mosquitoes by spraying house walls with DDT just a few times a year. The World Health Organization mounted a global DDT campaign against malaria in the 1950s, and at first it worked perfectly. Malaria almost disappeared by the end of the 1960s. However, the mosquitoes came back during the 1970s, and so did malaria. About 500 million people now suffer from malaria worldwide each year, and several million of them die.

coadaptation

Mosquitoes returned because they evolved a resistance to DDT. A few mosquitoes had a genetic mutation that protected them from DDT. After DDT went into heavy use, this DDT-resistant gene spread quickly through the mosquito populations because mosquitoes with the resistant gene survived when other mosquitoes were killed. There was also a behavioural mutation in some regions. The mosquitoes started to rest on vegetation outside of houses instead of on house walls sprayed with DDT. DDT was not a sustainable technology for malaria control. But what about other insecticides? DDT is very inexpensive; however, all other insecticides are too costly for large-scale use against malarial mosquitoes. Most countries gave up on controlling the disease, and there has been little progress in controlling malaria since then. The use of anti-malarial drugs has reduced fatalities in some areas, but many of these drugs no longer work because the malarial parasite has evolved a resistance to them.

A detailed account of the coadaptation of people and mosquitoes is found in Chapter 12.

Controlled burning by Native Americans

The example of forest fire protection in Chapter 6 explained how the United States Forest Service learned the value of controlled burning for forest management. This is something that Native Americans knew long before Europeans came to North America. Because Native Americans coevolved with North American ecosystems for thousands of years, their social system and their technology for using the land were highly adapted to a sustainable relationship with the environment. Controlled burning was an integral part of their forest management. They started fires because they knew that frequent fires were a way to maintain healthy forest ecosystems. They also used controlled burning to create small patches of other ecosystems, such as grassy meadows. A landscape mosaic comprising different stages of ecological succession provided more wild plants and animals as food sources than a landscape with only forest. When Europeans came to North America, they made numerous mistakes because their social system was not adapted to North American ecosystems. (Chapter 10 provides some examples of environmental consequences due to cultural differences between Europeans and Native Americans in North America.)

coevolution

COEVOLUTION OF THE SOCIAL SYSTEM AND ECOSYSTEM FROM TRADITIONAL TO MODERN AGRICULTURE

Ecosystems adapt to human social systems in two ways:

1. Ecosystems reorganize themselves in response to human actions.
2. People change ecosystems to fit their social system.

The mosquito example illustrated how natural ecosystems reorganize themselves. Mosquitoes evolved DDT resistance in response to a high death rate imposed by DDT. The natural components of agricultural and urban ecosystems also adapt to human actions by reorganizing themselves. The parts of agricultural and urban ecosystems that are organized by people change with the social system because people change them. People make agricultural and urban ecosystems to fit their social system, and people adjust their social system to fit with their agricultural and urban ecosystems. The modernization of agriculture after the Industrial Revolution illustrates coevolution of the social system with agricultural ecosystems.

Before the Industrial Revolution, people were very much aware of environmental limitations. Their culture, values, knowledge, technology, social organization and other parts of their social system were by necessity closely adapted to nature. Most people were small-scale **subsistence** farmers; most of the agricultural production was for home consumption. Most families had a variety of farm animals and cultivated many different crops to meet the family's needs for food and clothing. Agricultural techniques were adapted to local environmental conditions. The amount of land that each family could cultivate was limited by the large amount of human or animal labour that was necessary for agriculture. Most farmers used **polyculture** – a mixture of several crops together in the same field. The agricultural ecosystems in Figure 6.11 are polycultures.

Polyculture had a number of advantages:

coevolution

- It protects the soil from erosion, and can maintain soil fertility without the use of chemical fertilizers. The mixture of different crop species in a polyculture creates a large quantity of vegetation, which covers the ground completely. In contrast, it is common for a **monoculture** (one crop) field to have a lot of bare ground. The large quantity of vegetation in polyculture protects the soil from falling rain, thereby reducing soil erosion. The vegetation also provides substantial amounts of organic fertilizer when the unused part of the crop is ploughed back into the soil. If some of the plants in the field are legumes (for example, beans or peas), bacteria in the roots of the legumes convert atmospheric nitrogen to forms that plants can use.
- It provides natural pest control. Agricultural pests are usually specific to a particular kind of crop. For example, if a field is 100 per cent corn monoculture, corn pests multiply to large numbers and inflict a lot of damage if pesticides are not used. However, if a field has many different crops, with only a few corn plants, the corn pests have trouble finding their host; as a result, they are unable to multiply to large numbers and the damage is limited. Polyculture also provides good **habitat** for animals such as birds and predatory insects that eat insect pests. Predators provide natural control of the pests. When chemical pesticides are used in modern agriculture, many of the predators are killed, and much of the natural pest control is lost.
- It allows farmers to diversify their risks. If the weather during one year is bad for some kinds of crops, it will probably not be bad for all crops. If market prices are low for some crops, the prices will probably be better for other crops.

Agriculture changed in Europe when the Industrial Revolution made it possible to use machines instead of human and animal labour for work such as ploughing fields and harvesting crops. Starting with mechanization, the chain of effects can be traced through Figure 7.3. Machines gave farmers the ability to cultivate larger areas of land. Farm sizes increased dramatically because mechanized agriculture is more efficient on a larger scale (economy of scale). These initial changes in the social system and the ecosystem set in motion a series of changes through interconnected positive feedback loops in the ecosystem and social system.

When farm sizes increased, farmers were able to produce more than they needed for their own families, so they changed from subsistence farming to a market economy. Larger farm size also meant that there was surplus production to support cities. Many people got out of farming and moved to cities, where economic opportunities were better.

coevolution

One of the main changes in the ecosystem was from polyculture agriculture to monoculture. With mechanization, farmers stopped mixing crops together because farm machines work best with single crops. The market economy also provided an incentive to change from polyculture to monoculture because producing and marketing a single crop was more convenient for farmers. The change from polyculture to monoculture led to many other changes. Monoculture did not protect the soil from erosion or maintain soil fertility as well as polyculture did. Risks of crop failure due to bad weather or pest attacks were also greater with monoculture because 'all the eggs were in one basket'. As a result,

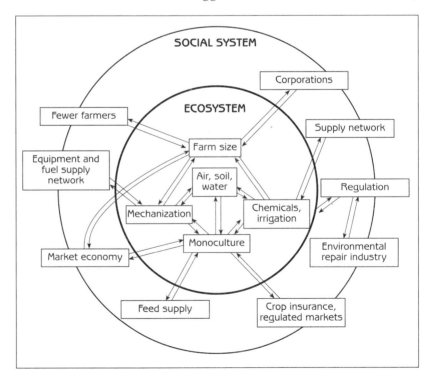

Figure 7.3
Interaction of the social system with agricultural ecosystems after the Industrial Revolution

it was important to make agriculture more independent of the environment by means of irrigation, chemical fertilizers and pesticides – all of which were possible with new developments in science and energy from fossil fuels.

Governments gradually became involved in research to provide better technology for the new style of agriculture: improved crop varieties to provide higher yields with high inputs (chemical fertilizers, pesticides, etc), as well as better techniques for using the inputs. Commercial networks were set up to provide machines, chemicals and high-yield crop seeds to farmers. Government crop insurance and market regulation, including government subsidies, were developed because of the higher risks associated with monocultures.

coevolution

The improvements in technology made monoculture even more advantageous compared to polyculture. Because different plants have different growth requirements, conditions in a polyculture field cannot be optimal for all of the different species of plants that grow together. Specialization through monoculture made it easier for a farmer to use high inputs to provide optimal conditions to attain the highest yields with one particular crop.

Farmers changed their belief system – their **worldview**. Once the Industrial Revolution was underway, technology, machines and fossil fuels seemed to free people from many environmental limitations. People began to think of agriculture more in economic terms, as a business enterprise, and less in environmental terms. Everyone believed that the future was going to provide advances in science and technology that offered endless possibilities for capital accumulation and economic development. Eventually, many farms were taken over by large corporations, and agriculture became more and more 'vertically integrated'. Today many of the same corporations that own supermarkets also own the farms and food processing factories that supply their supermarkets with food.

People eventually had to make changes to their beliefs as the environmental and human health implications of pesticides and chemical fertilizers became apparent in recent years. Governments began to regulate the use of chemicals, and they conducted research on how to deal with the consequences of applying chemicals. A new environmental industry arose in the private sector to deal with pollution from agriculture and other sources.

Throughout history, social systems and agricultural ecosystems have changed in ways that have allowed them to continue functioning well together. The same is generally true today. Modern social systems and agricultural ecosystems continue to change together and they are strongly coadapted (see Figure 7.4). The problem today is that modern agricultural

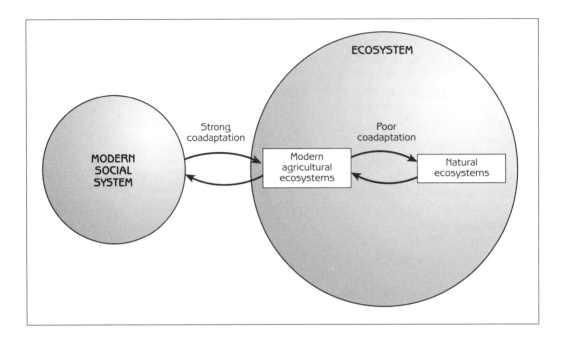

Figure 7.4
Coadaptation of modern social sytems and ecosystems

ecosystems have lost their coadaptation with the natural ecosystems that surround them – natural ecosystems upon which the agricultural ecosystems depend for their long-term viability. Modern agricultural ecosystems rely on large-scale fertilizer and pesticide inputs from natural sources that may not be sustainable on such a scale, and they pollute surrounding ecosystems with fertilizer and pesticide runoff from fields. Modern agricultural ecosystems also depend upon natural ecosystems for massive inputs of energy and, in many instances, irrigation water, which may not be possible to sustain.

The recent popularity of organically grown foods is stimulating a return to agricultural ecosystems that are more compatible with natural ecosystems. Organic farmers are returning selectively to traditional farming methods while employing organic fertilizers and environmentally benign methods of pest control. Their agricultural ecosystems are not dependent on chemical inputs, and the pollution of surrounding ecosystems is minimal. As the market for organically grown foods continues to expand, agricultural scientists and farmers will be stimulated to develop new and ecologically sound agricultural technologies.

THINGS TO THINK ABOUT

1. Consider the example of the coevolution of social systems and natural ecosystems from traditional to modern agriculture, presented in this chapter. List what happened for each arrow in Figure 7.3.
2. Talk to a farmer about how agricultural ecosystems in your region have changed during the past 50 years. Ask the farmer about:
   - material inputs 50 years ago and how the material inputs have changed since then;
   - changes in the organization and structure of the agricultural ecosystems and how cultivation methods and energy inputs have changed during the past 50 years;
   - associated changes in the social system (such as changes in farming life styles, organization of the local community, farm ownership, agricultural associations and marketing of farm products, food imports, the role of government).
3. Think about input–output exchanges and other interactions of agricultural and natural ecosystems in your region. Do the agricultural ecosystems seem to be well coadapted to the natural ecosystems? Do they have a sustainable relationship with the natural ecosystems?
4. In what ways is your neighbourhood (or town) social system coadapted with the local environment? In what ways is your national social system coadapted with the environment? List the ways in which these social systems are poorly coadapted with their environments.

things to think about

ECOSYSTEM SERVICES

We all depend upon ecosystems for the food and natural resources that sustain our lives. Most of the resources are **renewable** because ecosystems supply them on a continual basis. People use the resources and return them to the ecosystem as waste such as sewage, rubbish or industrial effluent. Ecosystems renew the resources by processing the waste so it is once again available for use by people (see Figure 8.1). A continuous supply of energy from the sun is required to do this. Solar energy fuels the cyclic movement of materials through the ecosystem providing all animals, including humans, a supply of renewable natural resources and a repository for their wastes.

The provision of renewable natural resources is a major part of ecosystem services. These services depend not only on sunlight but also on a healthy biological community to pass materials and energy to humans in a form they can use. The ability of ecosystems to provide these services derives from two important emergent properties: **material cycling** and **energy flow**. As we shall see, materials cycle, but energy does not cycle because energy passes out of the ecosystem as it flows through it.

Figure 8.1
Human use of renewable resources and return to the ecosystem as waste

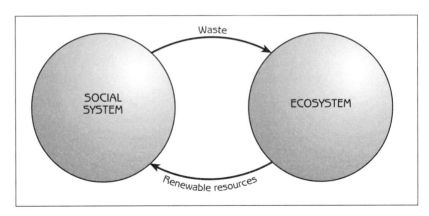

The human population explosion and increasing levels of consumption with economic development have recently generated increasing demands on ecosystems for these services. When people try to take too much from ecosystems – when they overexploit ecosystem services – they get less because they damage the ecosystem's capacity to provide the services. If people persist with excessive demands, the ecosystem can be changed so much that the services disappear entirely. The loss of services can be irreversible. As we saw with overfishing and desertification of grasslands through overgrazing in Chapter 6, **overexploitation** can switch an ecosystem to a new stability domain so that the service does not return even when demand is reduced.

material
cycling and
energy flow

MATERIAL CYCLING AND ENERGY FLOW

Material cycling and **energy flow** are emergent properties of ecosystems that result from ecosystem **production** and **consumption** (see Figure 8.2).

Production

Using energy from sunlight, photosynthesis joins carbon from carbon dioxide into the carbon chains that form the living tissues of plants. **Biological production** (also called net **primary production**) is the growth of the plants. In addition to providing the structural material for all living organisms, carbon chains store a large quantity of energy that they can use for metabolic 'work'.

Consumption

Animals and microorganisms eat plants, animals or microorganisms and use the carbon chains in their food as:

- building blocks for their own growth;
- a source of energy for metabolic activities (physiological processes that living organisms use to put carbon-chain building blocks together to make their bodies).

To get energy from carbon chains, the carbon chains are broken apart and released to the atmosphere as carbon dioxide. This is known as **respiration**.

Material cycling

The movement of materials in an ecosystem is **material cycling**, also called mineral cycling or nutrient cycling because elements such as nitrogen, phosphorous and potassium are minerals that provide nutrition for plants. Materials move through ecosystems in a cycle of production and consumption. The most important elements are carbon, hydrogen and oxygen which are required for photosynthesis, and nitrogen, phosphorous, sulphur, calcium and magnesium which are required for the construction of proteins and other structural compounds in the bodies of living organisms. Potassium and some minor elements (iron, copper, boron, zinc, manganese) are also necessary for plant growth. These elements are transferred from soil and water to green plants when the plants grow (ie, production). They are returned to soil and water whenever carbon chains are broken apart during consumption.

Animals and some microorganisms are **consumers**. Different species have different ecological roles such as:

- herbivores (animals that eat plants);
- predators (animals that kill and eat other animals);
- scavengers (animals that eat dead plants or animals);
- parasites (animals that live inside plants or animals which act as their hosts);

material cycling and energy flow

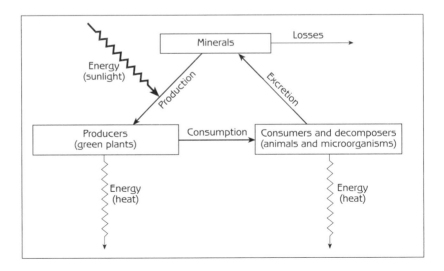

Figure 8.2
Material cycling and energy flow through the ecosystem

- pathogens (microorganisms that live inside plants or animals and cause disease).

Consumers use the carbon chains in their food as building blocks for their bodies. When consumers derive more mineral nutrients from their food than they need for their own bodies, they release the extra minerals into their environment. For example, nitrogen is excreted as ammonia or urea. The minerals return to the soil, where they serve as nutrients for plants.

Most microorganisms are **decomposers**, which consume the bodies of dead plants, animals and other microorganisms to obtain the carbon chain building blocks that they need for their growth. They release any surplus mineral nutrients from their food into the environment, where the mineral nutrients are available for use by plants. The basic function of decomposers in the ecosystem is in many ways similar to consumers.

material cycling and energy flow

The laws of thermodynamics

Energy has six basic forms:

1. Radiation (sunlight, radio waves, X-rays, infrared radiation).
2. Chemical (such as batteries, carbon chains).
3. Mechanical (movement).
4. Electrical (movement of electrons).
5. Nuclear (energy inside atoms).
6. Heat (movement of atoms and molecules).

The first law of thermodynamics concerns the conservation of energy. It states that energy can never be created or destroyed, but it can be transformed from one form into another. This means there is always the same amount of energy before and after transformation of energy from one form to another.

The second law of thermodynamics states that whenever energy is converted from one form to another, some of the energy becomes low-level heat. This means that conversion of energy from one form to another is never 100 per cent efficient (see Figure 8.3). Some of the energy is lost as heat. The 'lost' energy is still energy but is no longer high-level energy that can be used for work, such as moving things or fuelling metabolic processes in plants and animals.

An important consequence of the second law of thermodynamics is that all systems in the universe, both physical and biological, need energy input to continue functioning. The

Figure 8.3
The second law
of
thermodynamics:
conversion of
energy to heat
when energy is
transformed from
one form to
another

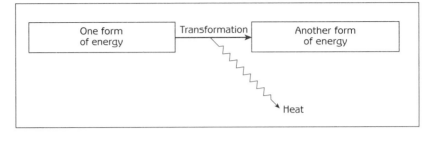

Figure 8.3
The second law of thermodynamics: conversion of energy to heat when energy is transformed from one form to another

**material
cycling and
energy flow**

functioning of physical and biological systems involves numerous energy transformations. Every time energy is transformed from one form to another for physical or metabolic 'work', some of the energy is converted to low-level heat, which can no longer be used. In other words, the system loses useful (high-level) energy as it uses it. If there is no energy input to a system, all of the system's useful energy is eventually lost as low-level heat, and no high-level energy remains for the system to continue functioning. The main energy input to ecosystems is sunlight. The biological community uses the energy for physical work such as the movement of animals and microorganisms, metabolic work and other work that ecosystems require to continue organizing themselves and to function properly (see Figure 8.4).

A metaphor for material cycling and energy flow in ecosystems

A pot of water on a stove illustrates how materials and energy move through an ecosystem (see Figure 8.5). A fire heats the water at the bottom of the pot, changing it to a higher energy level (hot objects have a higher energy level than cold objects). Because warmer water is lighter in weight than colder water, the heated water rises to the top of the pot. While the heated water is at the

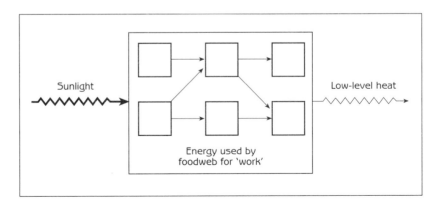

Figure 8.4
Flow of energy through an ecosystem food web

top of the pot, it becomes cooler as heat energy moves from the heated water to the cooler air above. After losing heat, the water (which is now cooler and heavier) sinks to the bottom of the pot to replace newly heated water that is rising. The result is water circulation – a physical cycle. The fire is the energy input to the system, and the heat loss from the water at the top of the pot is the energy output of the system.

Because of the energy input (the fire), the water in the pot is self-organizing. It makes its own structure (different temperatures in different parts of the pot). The water in the pot forms a material cycle, but the energy does not cycle. Energy enters the pot from the fire, moves from the bottom of the pot to the top with the heated water, and leaves the pot as low-level heat. This is known as energy flow. If the fire (the energy input) is turned off, the water in the pot stops cycling, energy stops flowing and the water loses its self-organizing structure.

material cycling and energy flow

Energy flow in ecosystems

Like the pot of water, the movement of materials in ecosystems is cyclic, and the movement of energy is not cyclic. Energy enters ecosystems as sunlight (like the fire under the pot). The energy is bound by photosynthesis into carbon chains that green plants use for the growth of their bodies. Carbon chains are similar to the hot water in the pot and contain a high level of energy. Plants break down some of the carbon chains in their body (respiration) to get the energy they need for their own metabolism, and some of the energy is released into the environment as heat. The carbon chains that are left (ie, photosynthesis minus plant respiration) are the

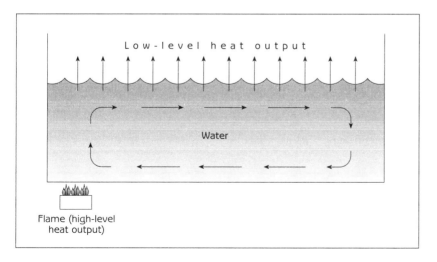

Figure 8.5
A pot of water as a metaphor for material cycling and energy flow in ecosystems

carbon chains that plants have for growth. The growth of all the plants in an ecosystem is the ecosystem's net **primary production**. Primary production is the source of living material and energy (in the form of carbon chains) for ecosystems.

When consumers (animals and microorganisms) use the carbon chains in their food as building blocks for their bodies, they break down some of the carbon chains to release energy for their metabolic needs. This is respiration, and the energy is used for movement – firstly, movement and reorganization of molecules required for growth and metabolic activities essential to survival; secondly, movement of the entire body. After consumers use the energy from respiration, the energy is released to the environment as heat. As one consumer eats another, there is a flow of high-level energy in carbon chains along a food chain through the food web, and there is a loss of energy as heat when the energy is used at each step for metabolic work (respiration). The percentage of energy at one step of a **food chain** that is available for consumption by the next step is called **food chain efficiency**. It is calculated as the energy in the food minus the energy used for respiration. It is typically 10 per cent to 50 per cent. Figure 8.6 shows energy flow from one step of a food chain to another.

As they pass through the food web, carbon chains are broken apart bit by bit for energy until they disappear (see Figure 8.7). When consumers respire carbon dioxide and water and excrete other minerals, such as nitrogen, phosphorous, potassium, magnesium and calcium, these minerals are in the form of plant nutrients, exactly the same as when they entered the biological system. They cycle back to plants. Waste from consumers is food for producers. Energy does not cycle back to plants because energy leaves consumers as low-level heat, which plants cannot use; plants can only use sunlight. On a global scale, the sunlight

material cycling and energy flow

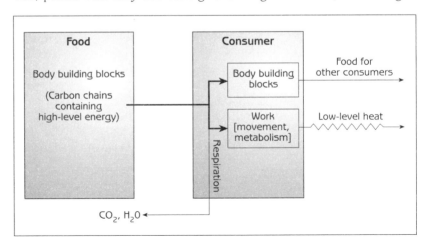

Figure 8.6
Energy flow from one step of a food chain to another

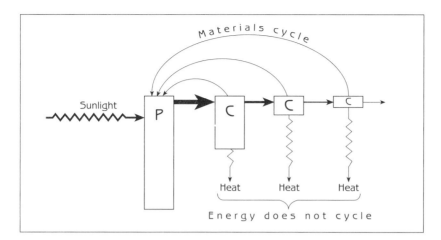

Figure 8.7
Energy flow
through an entire
food chain
P=producers
C=consumers

material
cycling and
energy flow

energy that reaches the Earth is eventually converted to low-level heat, leaving the Earth as infrared radiation (see Figure 8.8).

In agricultural ecosystems, the number of steps in a food chain that leads to people determines how efficiently the primary production of an agricultural ecosystem is channelled to people. Longer food chains mean less food for people. People obtain more food from the same amount of land when they eat plants.

Sunlight is the only major source of energy input to most natural ecosystems, but human energy inputs are important in agricultural and urban ecosystems. Human energy inputs include human labour, animal labour, mechanized energy inputs, such as tractors and other machines, and the energy contents of materials

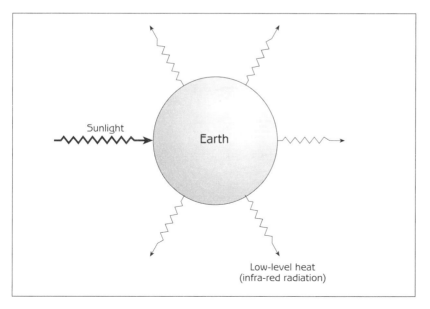

Figure 8.8
Energy
input–output of
planet Earth

that people bring into ecosystems. Human energy inputs do not become part of the biological energy flow as sunlight does. Human energy inputs are used to organize ecosystems by changing the biological community and adding man-made physical structures. This in turn affects biological energy flows and material cycling by changing primary production and the food web. With modern agriculture, most of the human energy inputs come from petroleum energy.

ecosystem
services

ECOSYSTEM SERVICES

Figure 8.9 shows how dependent humans are on the functioning of other parts of the ecosystem. Humans are consumers – just one among all the consumers in an ecosystem. Almost everything that people require for survival comes from material cycling and energy flow as two essential services:

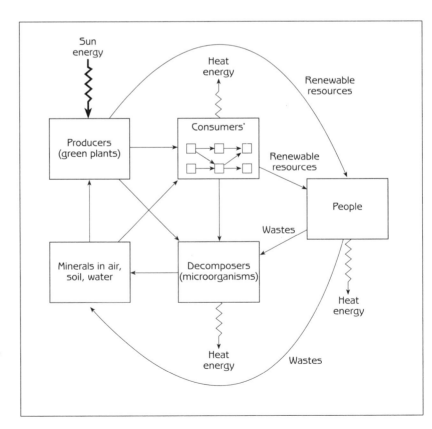

Figure 8.9
Ecosystem services as material cycling in the ecosystem
Note: * Consumers are animals (herbivores, predators, parasites) and pathogenic microorganisms (diseases), arranged in a food web.

1. Supply of renewable resources (plants, animals and microorganisms as food; plant and animal fibres for clothing; timber for construction; and water).
2. Absorption of pollution and wastes (consumption and decomposition of organic wastes by bacteria, removal of mineral nutrients from water by aquatic plants, dilution of toxic materials by rivers, oceans and the atmosphere).

THE RELATION BETWEEN ECOSYSTEM SERVICES AND INTENSITY OF USE

intensity of use

An important emergent property of ecosystems is that ecosystem services decline if they are used so intensively that the ecosystem's ability to provide services is damaged (see Figure 8.10).

Using fisheries as an example, if fishing intensity (the number of nets or hooks in the water) in a particular aquatic ecosystem is minimal, greater fishing intensity leads to a higher fish catch. However, if fishing intensity is greater than the optimum, then more fishing leads to a lower fish catch. This is because the fish population is depleted to such an extent that there are insufficient adult fish to produce an adequate number of new fish for the next generation to sustain the same fish catch. **Overexploitation** has depleted the ecosystem's **natural capital**.

The same thing happens with forests, pastures and agriculture. When logging is not very frequent, more logging yields more

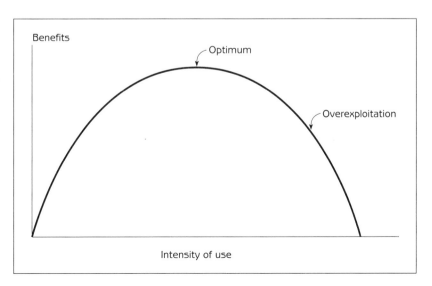

Figure 8.10
The relation between ecosystem services and intensity of use

wood; when there are not many animals grazing on a pasture, more animals yield more production of meat or milk; and more intensive agriculture generates higher yields if the agriculture is not already too intense. However, if trees are felled too often, forests are unable to mature; as a result, the quantity of wood extracted soon becomes unsustainable. If pasture is grazed too heavily, grasses become less abundant. The food supply for grazing animals is therefore reduced, and production yields (ie, growth of the animals) are less. Excessive use of chemical fertilizers or pesticides to increase crop production can pollute the soil and reduce production. Large quantities of fertilizers or pesticides can be toxic to plants; pesticides can also kill soil animals and microorganisms that maintain soil fertility. The exploitation of natural areas for recreation can damage natural ecosystems and impact on the visual beauty that draws people to these areas in the first place.

intensity
of use

An emergent property of ecosystems: ecosystem services may disappear if the intensity of use is excessive

This typically happens when **human-induced succession** changes an ecosystem from a stability domain that is 'okay' to one that is 'not okay' (see Figure 6.8). Fisheries succession – when commercially valuable fish disappear because fishermen focus their fishing on particular species of fish – is an example (see Figure 6.7). The ecosystem switches from providing commercially valuable fish to not providing them. Desertification due to overgrazing is another example (see Figure 6.6). The relation between intensity of use and benefits can change from that in Figure 8.10 to the relation in Figure 8.11.

Another example is the intensification of food production by extending inappropriate agriculture to hillsides – a common practice in the developing world today. When crops are grown year after year on hillsides, soil erosion can remove all of the topsoil, leaving the land unsuitable for further cultivation. Similarly, inappropriate intensification of food production by means of irrigation can render the land unsuitable for food production. The use of irrigation in arid regions where there is insufficient water can lead to **salinization** that makes the soil toxic for crops. When irrigation water evaporates from the soil, it leaves behind minerals that can accumulate to concentrations that are toxic for crops unless the field is flushed with extra water to carry away the salts. If extra water is not available, the salts accumulate until crop

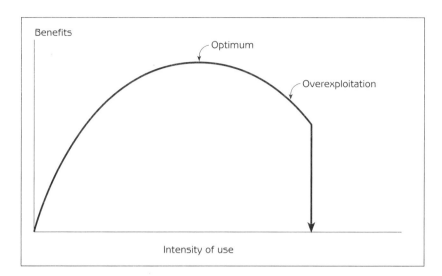

Figure 8.11
Disappearance of an ecosystem service due to overexploitation

yields are so low that agricultural production is not worth the effort. Large areas of land in southern Asia that were put into agricultural production as part of the Green Revolution several decades ago are now waste lands due to salinization.

The same thing happens with absorption of wastes by rivers, lakes, the ocean and other aquatic ecosystems. Dumping too much waste into an aquatic ecosystem can reduce its capacity to absorb wastes. Ecosystems absorb organic wastes, for example, when decomposers such as bacteria use the wastes as food. The decomposers use oxygen from the water for respiration, and they release partly broken-up carbon chains into the water as by-products of decomposition. Increasing amounts of waste that must be absorbed means more respiration and more by-products. If too much organic waste is dumped into the water, decomposers use all of the oxygen in the water, and by-products released by the decomposers reach toxic concentrations. The chemical condition of the water changes so much that even the waste-consuming decomposers can no longer survive. The waste-consuming decomposers are replaced by other kinds of bacteria, which do not purify the water, and the natural capacity of the aquatic ecosystem to absorb organic wastes is reduced.

Before the Industrial Revolution, when the human population was relatively small and demands on ecosystem services were correspondingly minimal, the use of ecosystem services was in the 'ascending' portion of the curve in Figure 8.11. Now, with overpopulation and a massive worldwide industrial machine that consumes large quantities of natural resources, human use of ecosystem services is increasingly in the 'descending' overexploitation portion of the curve.

How do we know what intensity of use is best? How can we know if we are overexploiting ecosystem services? Our social system has not developed effective means of answering this question because overexploitation was not a major problem in the past, when the human population was smaller and people did not place heavy demands on ecosystems. A practical approach to avoiding overexploitation is to increase intensity of resource use in relatively small increments, watching carefully how the benefits change as intensity of use increases. Relevant parts of the social system and ecosystem can be monitored simultaneously for signs of unintended consequences. Intensity of use is okay if benefits increase when intensity increases (see Figure 8.10). A decrease in benefits indicates overexploitation.

intensity of use

Simple as this approach may be in principle, its implementation is far from simple in practice. Operational procedures for evaluating ecosystem services are sometimes not at all obvious. Data collection and tabulation can be expensive, and the results may be less than conclusive. Human activities include so many different actions that affect ecosystems, and ecosystem responses can involve so many services, it can be virtually impossible to sort out specific causes and effects. Moreover, the response of ecosystem services to changes in human activities can take years or decades, a time frame that in many instances does not fit the pace of change in the human activities. When in doubt about overexploitation, it is prudent to follow the **precautionary principle** that is described in Chapter 10.

THE FALLACY THAT ECONOMIC SUPPLY AND DEMAND PROTECT NATURAL RESOURCES FROM OVEREXPLOITATION

Some people assume that the invisible hand of supply and demand protects renewable resources from overexploitation (see Figure 8.12). This belief is based on the idea that excessive use of a resource is prevented by higher prices when the resource becomes scarce. The protection comes from a negative feedback loop. For example, if too many fish are caught, fish become scarce, the price of fish increases, there is less demand for fish, fewer fish are caught, and the fish population increases again.

The negative feedback loop for supply and demand is real, but the belief that market forces protect renewable resources from

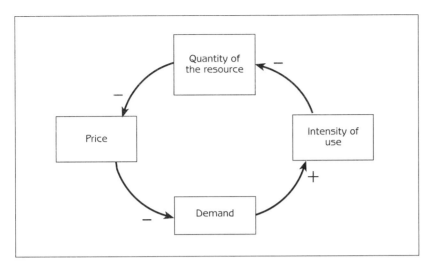

Figure 8.12
The control of resource use by supply and demand
Note: Negative arrows represent negative effects: if the quantity of resource increases, price decreases; if quantity of resource decreases, price increases. Positive arrows represent positive effects: if demand increases, intensity of use increases; if demand decreases, intensity of use decreases.

overexploitation is based on a simplistic view of ecosystems that ignores irreversible human-induced successions. There can be a switch from one stability domain to another (see Figure 6.6). When commercially valuable fish are replaced by 'trash fish' because of overfishing, the valuable fish may not return even if fishing is stopped completely.

Forests provide another example. If trees are cut too frequently, the biological community may change from forest to grass or shrub dominated ecosystems. If forests are clear-cut over a large area, they may not regenerate at all because there are no seeds from mature trees to generate new trees. In addition, without trees to provide leaf litter, the soil can lose the cover of leaves that protects it from erosion, and erosion can reduce soil fertility to such an extent that trees can no longer survive. There are social as well as ecological reasons for irreversible loss of forest after excessive logging. The same roads that logging companies build to remove trees from a developing world forest can also provide a way for land-hungry people to reach recently logged areas in order to plant crops. The forest never regenerates if people continue to use the land for farming.

THINGS TO THINK ABOUT

1. List some of the most important plant, animal and microorganism products that you use. These products correspond to the arrows from producers, consumers and decomposers to humans, as shown in Figure 8.9. What kinds of ecosystems do the different products come from? Where are those ecosystems located? In the case of animal and microorganism products, how many steps are there in the food chain leading to a product? What significant products or other services come from an ecosystem as a whole?

2. Think of some important renewable resources that you consume directly or indirectly. Do you think the intensity of use of those resources is optimal in the sense of Figure 8.10? Is it less than or more than the optimum (ie, overexploitation)? For resources that seem to be overexploited, how can use be reduced? What are significant practical or social obstacles to reducing the use? Has overexploitation led to irreversible changes in some of the resources?

3. Think of some non-renewable resources. Are they being used in a way that will allow them to last for as long as people need them? For resources that are being rapidly depleted, what can be done to reduce the rate of consumption? What are significant obstacles to reducing consumption?

4. People make demands on ecosystems to provide services that improve the quality of their lives. Because the capacity of ecosystems to satisfy human demands is limited, we need to be aware of what we really want from life and what we really need from ecosystems. List the things that are most important for your quality of life. How much of your list is about consumer goods? What are the implications of your list for demands on ecosystems?

PERCEPTIONS OF NATURE

People make sense of the complexity that surrounds them by carrying hundreds of images and 'stories' in their minds about themselves, their society and their biophysical environment – how each of these is structured, how each functions and interrelationships among them. Each image or story encapsulates a piece of their reality in a simplified form. Together, the images and stories form a person's **worldview** – his **perception** of himself and the world around him. Shared images and stories form a society's worldview. People and societies use their worldview to interpret information and formulate actions.

The images and stories that societies have about ecosystems are the basis for their perception of nature, which has a central role in shaping social system–ecosystem interaction. ('Nature' in this chapter refers to the entire biophysical world, including agricultural and urban ecosystems as well as natural ecosystems.) Perceptions shape the interpretation of information when it enters a social system from an ecosystem, and perceptions shape the decision-making process that leads to actions affecting the ecosystem (see Figure 9.1). Different cultures – and different people in the same culture – have different perceptions of how ecosystems function and how they respond to human actions. While every perception has a basis in reality, some perceptions of nature are more useful because they embrace reality more completely or accurately. Recognizing different perceptions can help to understand why different individuals and different societies interact with the environment in such strikingly different ways.

This chapter describes five common perceptions of nature. The first two perceptions – 'everything is connected' and 'benign/ perverse' – are major concepts in human ecology, but they are not restricted to scientists. The last three perceptions of nature – 'fragile', 'durable' and 'capricious' – are special cases of the

Figure 9.1
The role of
perceptions of
nature in
decisions
affecting
ecosystems

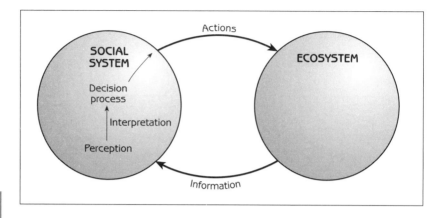

perceptions

'benign/perverse' perspective. Each of these three perspectives represents a valid part of reality. However, each is less complete than 'benign/perverse' in ways that can cause people to interact with ecosystems without taking full account of the ways that ecosystems will respond to their actions.

Religion is a powerful way in which societies organize their worldviews and shape human behaviour. Hunter-gatherer societies regarded nature with awe and respect. Their spirit religions considered people to be an integral part of nature, basically no different from other animals. Religion changed with the Agricultural and Industrial revolutions. Western religions considered humans to possess a unique character that vested them with authority over nature, as well as responsibility for its integrity. Awe for nature diminished as Western societies achieved greater dominion, and responsibility gave way to exploitation. Respect for nature revived with the appearance of environmental problems in recent years.

COMMON PERCEPTIONS OF NATURE

Everything in nature is connected

People in traditional societies typically emphasize the fact that everything in nature is connected. They believe that many events are, directly or indirectly, a consequence of human actions, beyond human understanding. It is part of their culture to treat nature with careful respect in order to avoid adverse consequences. This perception of nature is similar to the concept in human ecology that human actions generate chains of effects that reverberate through ecosystems and social systems. The main difference between human ecology and the traditional perception that everything is connected is that traditional societies do not focus on the details of connections. Human ecologists are as explicit as possible about the details so that people can better understand and predict the consequences of their actions.

Nature is benign and perverse (the 'okay/not okay' principle)

Benign means 'kind' or 'promotes well being'. Perverse is the opposite. This perception of nature states that nature is benign (ie, provides services we desire) as long as people do not radically change ecosystems from their natural condition (see Figure 9.2). In other words, the ecosystem is okay. However, nature can be perverse (ie, not provide all the services we need) if people change ecosystems to such an extent that they are unable to function properly. The ecosystem changes to a form that does not provide the services as well as before. In other words, the ecosystem is not okay. This perception of nature is the same as a switch from okay to not okay due to human-induced succession (see Chapter 6). The broad scope of the benign/perverse perspective and its confirmation by scientific observation make it particularly relevant to human ecology.

perceptions

   The following three perspectives are common special cases of the benign/perverse perspective. Each is incomplete because it emphasizes only one aspect of the broader reality captured by benign/perverse.

Nature is fragile

This view believes that nature has a delicate balance that will fall apart if people change ecosystems from their natural condition. It emphasizes the 'not okay' element of the 'okay/not okay' response of ecosystems to human actions. This perspective holds that small departures from natural conditions can lead to disastrous and irreversible consequences for ecosystems. Changing the **ecosystem state** even a little can move the ecosystem to another stability domain (see Figure 9.2). Of course 'fragile' does not mean that the ecosystem disappears. Every place always has an ecosystem, and it always will. Fragile means it is easy to change from one type of biological community to another.

Figure 9.2
Stability domain
diagrams for
different
perceptions of
nature

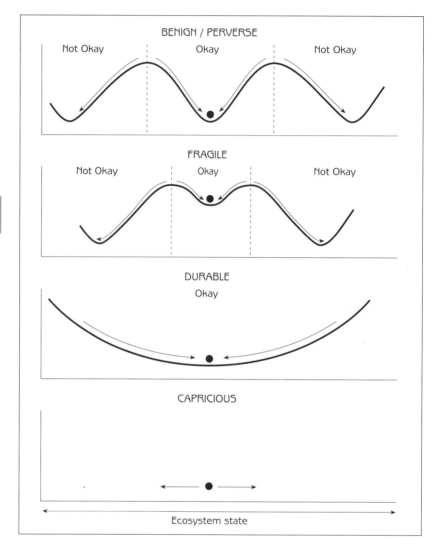

perceptions

Nature is durable

This perception of nature is the opposite of the 'fragile' point of view. It has been a common part of Western society's worldview since the Industrial Revolution. It focuses on the 'okay' element of the 'okay/not okay' response of ecosystems to human actions (see Figure 9.2). This view holds that people can use and shape nature any way they want. Nature can meet any demands that people make on it, as long as people use the proper science and technology to extract the benefits that nature has to offer. If human activities damage ecosystems, science, technology and other human inputs can repair the damage or provide viable alternatives to natural ecosystem processes. No matter what people do to ecosystems, there are natural and social forces to prevent the ecosystem from being damaged so severely that it breaks down. People with this view of nature may believe that economic supply and demand protect ecosystems from overexploitation (see Chapter 8).

Nature is capricious

Capricious means 'unpredictable'. This perspective emphasizes the random element in ecosystems. Many people, such as farmers and fishermen, who depend directly upon nature for their living, experience nature as highly variable and unpredictable. During some years the weather is good for crops; during others it is harsh and damages crops. Insect damage is severe during one year but not during another. During some years there are plentiful fish stocks; during other years there are not. People who view nature as capricious do not understand why nature is sometimes benign and sometimes perverse. Because the impacts of their activities can extend through long and imperceptible chains of effects through the ecosystem, they see little connection between what they do and the inevitable outcomes. This perception of nature supposes there are no strong natural forces to maintain ecosystems in particular way. Ecosystem state (the ball in Figure 9.2) is simply pushed around by 'fate' as nature acts at random.

religious
attitudes

ATTITUDES OF RELIGIONS TOWARD NATURE

Religion is a way in which societies use generations of accumulated wisdom to organize their values, perceptions and behaviour. It can have a major role in a society's perception of the relation that people have with one another and with nature. Religions convey a sense of awe and respect for things larger than ourselves. Religious beliefs are a source of meaning; they tell us what is important in our lives. Religions offer moral codes – guidelines about right and wrong and rules of behaviour – that are particularly effective because they are reinforced by emotionally compelling beliefs, symbols and rituals. The importance of such moral codes for human–environment interaction is the balance they promote not only between the desires of each individual and the needs of others, but also between short-term desires and longer-term considerations, such as a concern for future generations.

Different religions can have significantly different perceptions about the relation of humans to nature and significantly different moral codes to guide human interaction with the environment. The following accounts explore the attitudes of major religions towards nature, without attempting a thorough description of each religion. While it is difficult to generalize about religions because they are complex, diverse and highly changeable over time, comparisons can illustrate the different perceptions that people and cultures have about the environment.

religious
attitudes

Spirit religions (animism)

Before the development of modern science, people explained nature through the presence of spirits. Spirits are invisible beings who exert power over weather, illness and other natural phenomena of significance to people. Spirits are different from modern science because spirits have human-like personalities, whereas scientific explanation of natural phenomena is objective and technical. Nonetheless, scientific explanations are remarkably similar to spirits in many ways. While science has made the functioning of nature more 'visible' (for example, bacteria and viruses causing disease, and the role of DNA in genetics and protein production in the body), many concepts of modern science are still as invisible as spirits. Invisible theoretical constructs, such as the gravitational field, the electromagnetic field and the subatomic particle, have impressive powers of prediction; but scientists do not know what they really are or why they function as they do.

Originally, spirits were a major part of all religions. Belief in spirits continued to be common in all societies, regardless of religion, until spirits were replaced by modern science. The religions of many tribal societies are still based on spirits, and spirit religion (such as Japanese Shinto) is still important in some modern societies.

Some spirits are the souls of dead ancestors who remain with the households of their descendants. Others spirits are gods responsible for various elements in nature. Spirits typically dwell in the bodies of plants, animals and conspicuous geographic structures such as large rocks, hills, mountains or lakes. Many spirit religions have two spirits that are particularly powerful: Creator of the Universe (who can also have names such as Great Spirit, Great Mystery or Life Giver) and the Spirit who Controls the Land (also called Mother Earth). Any plant, animal or site in which a spirit dwells is sacred and worthy of great awe and respect. Particular places are often considered sacred because they were part of mythological history. It is common for spirit believers to have sacred groves, such as natural forest ecosystems that no one is allowed to disturb. Sacred groves serve a practical function of maintaining natural ecosystems and biological diversity in landscapes that people have otherwise changed to agricultural and urban ecosystems.

Spirits are more than primitive explanations for natural processes. They serve as contacts for people to maintain harmonious relations with nature. They are like invisible 'lords' who have the power to help people; but if displeased, they can also harm people. For spirit believers it is important to respect the spirits and keep them happy. Spirit believers make an effort to pursue their daily lives – the way they hunt or gather food, work their farms and maintain their homes – so that the spirits will be pleased. Spirit believers make frequent ritual offerings to please the spirits (often a small amount of food prepared in a carefully prescribed manner). Many spirit believers do not think of this as religion. To them, it is simply their way of life.

religious attitudes

The details of spirit religions vary among cultures. For example, Australian aborigines are nomadic hunters and gatherers with well-defined territories and a strong emotional and spiritual attachment to the land on which they live. Their land has a story, which began during 'Dream Time' many years ago when their spiritual ancestors shaped the land in its present form and gave rise to all living things, including people. Humans have a strong kinship with all other living things because people, plants and animals all came from the same ancestors. Aborigines believe this story continues into the present time, and every person is part of the story. The ancestors continue as spirits in hills, large rocks, plants, animals and people, and the strength and creativity that these spirits give to the land is responsible for its continuing fertility. For aborigines it is important to learn the story of their land – and the ways in which they are a part of the story – so that they can live their lives according to the story. Aborigines believe they have a responsibility to help maintain this creative process by performing rituals and making offerings to help sustain the ancestral spirits on the land. They see themselves as an integral part of the land, while continually recreating the land in their daily lives.

The traditional religion of Native Americans also includes the belief that land formations, plants and animals have spirits. All living things are equal inhabitants of the Earth. The entire world and everything in it is sacred, worthy of profound awe and respect. Animals have consciousness, feelings and personalities like

people. On reaching adulthood, a Native American who follows traditional ways selects a guardian spirit associated with a particular kind of animal. This spirit serves as a lifelong source of personal guidance. The most important thing for Native Americans is harmony and balance in their relations with nature. Animals 'give themselves' to hunters only if people show proper respect. When people take from nature, they must give in return. Plants and animals will continue to provide food, clothing and shelter for people only if people thank the plant and animal spirits by appropriate ritual. Prayers and gifts to the spirits are a regular part of daily life. When gathering plants or hunting animals, Native Americans thank them for 'giving themselves' and apologize for taking their lives. They consider it important to show respect for nature by not being wasteful. They kill or harvest only what is needed, use every possible part of the plant or animal and dispose of unused parts in a ritually respectful manner. Lack of respect can bring misfortune. Not only will plant and animal spirits withhold their benefits, but animal spirits who are angered by disrespectful treatment can provoke human illness or accidents.

religious attitudes

The Ainu are hunter-gatherers of northern Japan. While the Ainu consider humans and gods to be different in many ways, they perceive humans and gods to be similar in power and ability. Gods can provide things to humans that humans want, and humans can provide things to gods that gods want. The gods live in their own world, but they frequently visit the human world in the form of animals. The reason they visit is to trade with humans. When a hunter kills an animal, there is a god in the animal's body. The god provides the animal's body to the hunter, and the god returns to his own world. In exchange for the animal's body, the Ainu give wine and beautifully carved sticks to the gods in ceremonies that can last for several days.

Eastern religions

The major Eastern religions such as Hinduism, Buddhism and Taoism are similar to spirit religions because spirits are part of their worldview. People are part of nature and have no special status in the eyes of God. However, the major religions are different from spirit religions because the myths and dogma of major religions are preserved in written form. Spirit religions are oral traditions whose customs and stories have passed from one generation to another by word of mouth.

Hinduism is the religion of India, as well as the island of Bali in Indonesia. The Hindu name for their religion is 'the eternal essence of life'; it cannot be separated from daily life. For Hindus all life on earth is divine because it is a manifestation of their god Vishnu. Vishnu is part of everything. The universe is a cosmic person with consciousness; every part of the universe (land, plants, animals, people) has consciousness; everything is connected. All living things have souls that are exactly the same as people's souls. When people die, their souls pass by reincarnation to the bodies of plants, animals or other people.

Hinduism's 'moral law of cause and effect', karma, says that all thoughts, words and deeds of people affect everything in the world around them and come back to affect people. What we experience now is a consequence of past thoughts and deeds; present thoughts and deeds will lead to what we experience in the future. The benefits that people receive from the world are a consequence of people's spiritual behaviour. Good spiritual behaviour is not taking more than one's share and showing gratitude by giving. Hindus make daily offerings (such as small amounts of food) to God so that the Earth will be satisfied and continue to provide what they need.

religious attitudes

Nature is very important in Hindu mythology. There are many stories about demons (evil demigods) who were damaging the Earth, so Vishnu took the form of an animal with super powers and came to the Earth to save it. The most beloved Hindu god is Krishna (another form of Vishnu), who lived a simple life herding cows in the forest. Hindus consider trees and forests to be sacred because they provide so many useful things to the gods in Hindu mythology (for example, shade, fruits and a peaceful place for meditation). Many animals are considered sacred, particularly the cow because of its nurturing role for humans.

Buddhism arose from Hinduism 2500 years ago. Many Buddhist ideas about the relation of people to nature are similar to Hinduism. People and nature are as one. Negative thoughts lead to negative actions and negative consequences. Although Buddhism considers the Buddha spirit to be in everything, Buddhism has no all-powerful god from whom Buddhists can request favours, protection or forgiveness. People must look into themselves for harmonious relations with the rest of the world. Demons are not external enemies; they are part of ourselves. A central philosophical idea of Buddhism is that the main cause of unhappiness is desiring things that we cannot have. Restraining desire is the key to happiness. Use of natural resources should be limited to satisfying basic needs such as food, clothing, shelter and medicine. Another major idea of Buddhism is reverence, compassion and loving kindness for all life forms. Animals should not be killed and plants should be harvested only to meet essential food needs.

For Chinese religions the universe is harmonious and complete. The universe was not created by a superior being separate from the universe itself. The universe is like a large living creature. Everything contains a vital energy, and everything is constantly changing. Opposites (such as good and evil), which appear to be in conflict with each other, are really complementary aspects (yin-yang) of a diverse and ever changing universe. Spirits are important in Chinese religion. Feng-shui is a spirit religion of southern China that provides guidelines on how people should use the land. Activities that damage the landscape are prohibited because they injure or offend 'dragons' or other powerful spirits that live in the land.

religious attitudes

Taoism and Confucianism are two different views of the same Chinese themes. Tao ('the Way') emphasizes that nature is mysterious beyond comprehension. People do best by changing nature as little as possible, fitting in with nature's rhythms and flows and tapping into nature's energy instead of trying to dominate nature or control it. Confucianism emphasizes social relationships – the need for people to develop and refine their mutual responsibilities. For Confucianism, humans are children of nature; the proper attitude toward nature is filial piety (respect for elders). Because humans have an 'elder brother' relationship with nature's other creatures, humans have a responsibility as custodians of nature to maintain nature's harmony. Chinese culture has been a mixture of Taoism and Confucianism since these two religions originated 2500 years ago. Taoism has been dominant during certain periods of China's history, and Confucianism has been dominant during others.

Western religions

Western religion began in the Middle East with Judaism. The main difference between Judaism and other religions during this time was Judaism's belief in only one God. Other religions had numerous gods – gods who participated in creating the world and continued to be responsible for various parts of its functioning. For Jews there was only one God, with whom they had a strong historical connection because he was responsible for their survival as a people. Jews believed that 'God created Man in his own image'. They did not consider themselves to be part of nature like other animals. God was obviously different from people in many ways, but people were similar to God (and superior to other animals) because of their ability to reason. Judaism believed that God created a wondrous, orderly and harmonious world, but it rejected the worship of nature because Judaism associated nature worship in other religions with belief in many gods.

Although Judaism's God had absolute dominion over the Earth, Judaism believed that God was not involved in the everyday details of what happened in the world. Instead, God chose humans as his representatives to maintain God's wisdom (ie, his natural order) on Earth while using and managing the Earth to meet their needs. God rewarded people who obeyed his commands about how people should live, and God punished those who did not obey. Although Jews considered nature to be sacred because it was God's creation, their idea of managing the Earth for God was not to leave everything completely natural. The Agricultural Revolution dominated social change in the Middle East during the time when Judaism arose. Irrigation and cultivation of the first domesticated plants, such as wheat, barley, peas and olives, and the grazing of domesticated animals such as sheep and goats, were central to the survival strategies of Middle Eastern societies in an arid environment.

religious attitudes

Christianity grew out of Judaism and inherited Judaism's attitudes toward nature:

* Humans are superior to other animals.
* Nature is sacred because it is God's creation.
* Humans have a responsibility as custodians of the Earth to maintain God's natural order.

Early Christianity was also influenced by the ancient Greeks, who perceived nature as beautiful and harmonious, operating under its own laws with its own reality and its own power to survive. The Greek perception of nature was very different from Judaism, which perceived nature as dependent upon God.

Christ valued a simple life with a minimum of material consumption, an ideal that has continued until the present day in monastic traditions such as the teachings of Benedictine monks, who engage in a simple communal life 'close to the Earth'. Francis of Assisi, the most famous of Christian saints to embrace the sanctity of nature, saw all creation – hills, water, plants, animals and the Earth itself – as loved by God and loving God. All living creatures were his spiritual brothers and deserved the same loving kindness that Christ advocated for the brotherhood of man. However, the deep concern for nature expressed by Saint Francis of Assisi was not part of mainstream Christianity. Christianity has always emphasized the relation of humans to each other and to God – not the relation of humans or God to nature. For Christianity, only humans have souls.

The early Christian belief that nature was sacred began to diminish about 400 years ago. As modern science provided new explanations for how nature functions, Western society began to view nature as a machine created by God, but apart from God, for people to manipulate and use as they wish. The Protestant Reformation led to further departure from the attitudes of early Christianity toward nature. The extreme was expressed in Calvinism, which had a major influence on Northern European and American culture during the past 300 years and included the belief that people whom God chose for salvation and eternal life in heaven were rewarded with material wealth on Earth. Wealth acquired a positive spiritual value, even if obtained through the destructive exploitation of nature. Europeans who colonized America and exploited the land for material wealth could rationalize taking land from Native Americans because they were not 'using' the land to generate wealth as God intended.

religious attitudes

With the advent of the environmental crisis in recent years, many Christians are turning to earlier Christian values for guidance on the relationship that humans should have with nature. Once again they consider nature to be sacred because it is God's creation and a manifestation of God on Earth. Many Christians now recognize the spiritual kinship of humans with all living things. The World Council of Churches promotes the preservation and restoration of the natural environment, advocating policies which recognize human responsibilities not only to other people but also to all fellow creatures and the whole of creation.

Islam was strongly influenced by Judaism and Christianity when it was founded by the prophet Mohammed about 1300 years ago. Islam believes that a benevolent and compassionate God created an orderly universe. Nature is sacred because it is God's creation, and God's will is present in every detail. As in Judaism, God granted to humans the privilege of using all of his creations on Earth and the responsibility of caring for them. The *Koran* contains detailed instructions from God on how people should do this, instructions that were subsequently elaborated into Islamic law which every Muslim is expected to follow. The main message of Islamic law on human–environment relations is that people should not use more than they need, and they should not be wasteful of what they use. Land for grazing livestock or collecting wood should be held in common ownership for the entire community to use, and irrigation water should be shared by all. A wild animal can be killed only if it is needed for food or is a threat to crops or livestock, and when trees are cut, they should be replaced by planting more trees. However, as with Christianity, nature has never been a principal concern of Islam, which considers the afterlife and every person's relation with God to be more important than the material world and the transient life of humans on Earth.

Contemporary attitudes towards nature

Although many people in industrialized nations today do not consider themselves religious in the sense of participating actively in an organized religion, everyone, in fact, has beliefs that deal with the same matters as organized religions do, and everyone participates in social rites to reaffirm those beliefs. Self-actualization, materialism and a coherent worldview associated with capitalism, free enterprise, economic growth and the global economy have become major components of our worldview. Shopping has become a major ritual. High priests are economic advisors, multinational corporation executives and entertainment celebrities. Such developments in our modern worldview have far-reaching consequences for human–ecosystem interaction. Demands for consumer goods, and consequent demands for ecosystem services, are driven by a socially defined need for consumption that extends far beyond that required for a decent life.

romanticizing nature

On the other hand, a growing number of people feel a strong spiritual connection with the natural world independently of whether they participate in an organized religion. Some have invested their spiritual energy in green political movements. Some westerners have been attracted to exploring eastern religions, Native American spirituality or other religions that have a conspicuous focus on respect for nature. The New Age movement has also provided an outlet for those who wish to emphasize their spiritual connection to nature.

NOTES OF CAUTION ABOUT ROMANTICIZING NATURE AND TRADITIONAL SOCIAL SYSTEMS

Humans are completely dependent upon nature for their sustenance. There are good reasons to be sensitive to how nature functions and to strive for human activities that are compatible with nature. It makes sense to work with nature and have nature working for us, instead of fighting nature. However, this does not mean that everything completely natural is good for people. Nature is not designed to provide special privileges for the human species. People have always found it useful to modify ecosystems so that they function in ways which serve human needs.

In a similar manner, we should be careful not to romanticize tradition. The interaction of traditional societies with their environment is often more sustainable than the interaction of modern society because many traditional social systems have coevolved with their ecosystems for centuries. They are coadapted. Modern society can benefit from traditional wisdom, but we should appreciate traditional societies for what they really are, not what we want them to be. Not all traditional societies have healthy relationships with the environment, nor have they always had in the past. If they do have healthy relationships with the environment, it is for reasons that go beyond romantic concepts such as harmony with nature. It is for practical reasons related to dependence on their environmental support systems – landscapes and biological communities that provide essential material resources such as food and shelter along with emotional resources such as beauty.

Traditional practices are not always better. The social institutions and technology of traditional societies are a product of the environmental conditions in which those societies evolved. They may or may not be appropriate for modern circumstances. The challenge for modern society is to perceive and interact with ecosystems in ways that not only serve our needs but also do so on a sustainable basis. There are no easy recipes for sustainable development in today's rapidly changing world.

things to think about

THINGS TO THINK ABOUT

1. What was your perception of nature before reading this book? What is your perception of nature now? If it has changed, why do you think it changed? Remember that nature has a broad meaning in this context. It refers to the entire biophysical world, including natural, agricultural and urban ecosystems. Also keep in mind that you may have more than one perception of nature. It could be a combination of two or three different views.
2. Environmental issues can be highly controversial. It is not unusual for different people to have radically different opinions. Think about some issues that have received considerable public attention. In what ways does the controversy seem to come from different perceptions of nature?
3. Tell a 'story' about your nation's relationship with nature. It can be an historical account that explains how the present relationship with nature

evolved from the past, or the story could take another form such as a traditional folk tale.

4. What are the main belief systems of your society today? They may include major religions, but they may also include belief systems that are not part of established religions. Be specific about what the beliefs have to say with regard to the following.

    •   Who am I?
    •   What is the meaning of my life?
    •   What is my relation to other people and the rest of the world?
    •   What do I respect? What is important?
    •   What is good? What is right?
    •   What should I do? How do I know what I should do?
    •   What kind of relationship should people have with nature?

    What are the shared beliefs in your society? Do different people in your society have fundamentally different beliefs? Do your beliefs vary from the prevailing beliefs in your society? Think about where your society's beliefs come from. How do people acquire them? Who are the 'priests' that interpret and disseminate the beliefs?

things to think about

UNSUSTAINABLE HUMAN–ECOSYSTEM INTERACTION

Past and present experiences with human–ecosystem interaction can provide lessons about how to avoid mistakes. Environmental problems are not entirely new. Although most societies in the past have lived in harmony with the environment most of the time, there have been occasions when particular societies have had very **unsustainable** interactions with the environment. Considering the consequences, it is natural to ask: 'How could people make such serious mistakes in the past, and why does modern society continue to repeat such mistakes today?'

As a rule, human–ecosystem interaction is sustainable when social system and ecosystem are coadapted. Conversely, interaction is less sustainable when coadaptation is weak. Sudden changes in the social system or ecosystem can disrupt coadaptation, setting in motion a chain of effects that reduces an ecosystem's ability to provide essential services. This chapter will illustrate how coadaptation can be lost when people migrate to new places with completely different ecosystems – ecosystems with which they have no previous experience. It will also describe how coadaptation can decline after sudden social system changes such as new technologies.

This chapter will then turn to powerful social forces that cause unsustainable interaction between modern social systems and ecosystems. The basic source of unsustainable human–ecosystem interaction today is an expanding human population, coupled with an expanding economy that makes excessive demands on ecosystems. The chapter will describe how modern economic institutions motivate individuals to use ecosystem resources in ways that are unsustainable. It will describe the role of urbanization, which erodes social system–ecosystem coadaptation as urban populations become alienated from their environmental support system. The rise and fall of past civilizations provides insights into urbanization and economic development that are proceeding on a global scale today. The chapter will show how aggressive commercial exploitation of ecosystem resources can lead to wishful thinking about the intensity of resource use that an ecosystem can sustain. It will close with the precautionary principle as a prudent way to ensure sustainable resource use in the face of incomplete knowledge about how much resource depletion ecosystems can sustain.

HUMAN MIGRATIONS

human
migrations

Unsustainable interaction between people and ecosystems has often been associated with human migrations. When people move to a new area where the ecosystem is different, they typically have little knowledge about the new ecosystem and lack appropriate **social institutions** and technology for sustainable interaction. This appears to have occurred when the first human inhabitants of North America migrated there from Asia about 13,000 years ago. When these people arrived, North America had numerous species of large mammals similar to the impressive fauna in East Africa today. Most species of large mammals disappeared within a few centuries of the people arriving, probably due to overhunting. We do not know that the Native Americans were definitely responsible, but it appears likely. Many large animal species in Europe and Australia also disappeared soon after the first humans migrated to those continents.

During the centuries that followed, Native American social systems coevolved with their local ecosystems until the social systems and ecosystems were generally coadapted. While the cultures of different tribes and the details of their interaction with the environment were diverse, social institutions for sustainable interaction with the ecosystem were a common part of Native American cultures. Tribal territoriality was important for defining clear ownership of common property resources, such as deer and other animals that the Native Americans hunted on a sustainable basis.

Coadaptation did not mean that Native Americans left the environment in a completely natural state. In fact, they modified their ecosystem in many ways. They used fire to create small patches with early stages of ecological succession such as grass meadows in parts of North America that were mainly climax forest. A diverse mixture of different stages of ecological succession created a landscape mosaic with more favourable hunting and a greater variety of other ecosystem 'services' than was possible from one kind of ecosystem alone.

The Great Plains of North America had a deep, rich topsoil and tall, dense perennial grasses that provided food for large herds of buffalo. The perennial grasses were a mixture of native species, a natural polyculture adapted to the windy conditions of the Great Plains. Because they were perennial, the grasses covered the soil completely throughout the year, protecting it from wind erosion (see Figure 10.1). Native Americans adapted to the Great Plains ecosystem by using buffalo as their main resource (see Figure 10.2a). Because their religion emphasized respect for nature, wild animals could only be killed when required for food or other basic needs. They used almost every part of the buffalo's body for food, clothing or building materials for their houses.

human migrations

When Europeans invaded North America about 300 years ago, they exploited North American resources in an unsustainable manner because they did not have the values, knowledge, technology and other social institutions appropriate for sustainable interaction with the North American ecosystem. They perceived the vast resources of the continent as virtually unlimited, and they considered the transformation of natural ecosystems to agricultural and urban ecosystems of European design to be unequivocal progress. They considered the Native American social system to be a primitive stage of human social evolution inappropriate for modern times. Many Europeans considered the Native Americans themselves to be an inferior race destined for extinction.

When European immigrants reached the Great Plains, they saw buffalo as a source of money. Professional hunters killed buffalo by the millions, selling buffalo hides to the international leather market. Within 20 years the buffalo were reduced from a population of 60 million to almost nothing. The Native Americans living on the Plains were reduced to starvation and desperation when the buffalo – their main source of food – was destroyed and large numbers of Europeans settled on their land to farm it. The

Figure 10.1
Comparison of the natural Great Plains ecosystem (perennial grasses) with annual crops planted by Europeans

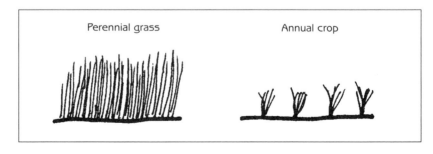

Perennial grass   Annual crop

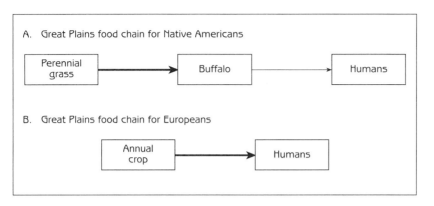

A. Great Plains food chain for Native Americans

Perennial grass → Buffalo → Humans

B. Great Plains food chain for Europeans

Annual crop → Humans

Figure 10.2
Great Plains food chain for people before and after the European invasion of North America

human migrations

Native Americans responded with war, but they lost the war and their land, and were subsequently reduced to a marginal existence.

The European farmers who replaced the Native Americans on the Great Plains grew **monocultures** of wheat, corn and other **annual crops** (see Figure 10.2b). These crops provided a shorter food chain than grass and buffalo, so the farmers were able to capture a larger percentage of the Great Plains biological production than the Native Americans had obtained from buffalo. However, unlike the natural vegetation of the Great Plains, these crops were not adapted to protect the soil from wind erosion. Annual crops are food plants that have a new generation each year. They do not cover the soil completely like perennial grass, and because annual crops are on the fields for only part of each year, the soil is not protected during the other part of the year (see Figure 10.1). This kind of farming worked well under European conditions, where wind erosion is not such a serious problem, but it could not protect the soil under weather conditions on the Great Plains. As a consequence, most of the Great Plains topsoil has been carried away by wind since Europeans began farming there 120 years ago. The soil has lost its natural fertility and now provides high crop yields only with large fertilizer inputs. The latest chapter in the Great Plains story comes from a small number of scientists who are developing new agricultural ecosystems with **polycultures** of native perennial grasses that produce enough grain to be of commercial use. Agricultural ecosystems that mimic the natural ecosystems of the Great Plains should reduce erosion because they cover the soil better.

Migrations continue to be important around the world as millions of land-hungry people move from overpopulated areas to areas with fewer people. Governments often encourage these migrations, a policy that is not ecologically wise when the population movement is to an area that has fewer people because the human carrying capacity cannot be changed readily by modern technology. Immigrants usually damage the environment and reduce the carrying capacity, not only because their large numbers force them to overexploit local resources but also because their cultural traditions do not provide the worldview, values, knowledge, technology and social institutions that are needed for sustainable interaction with their new environment.

Millions of rural people have migrated from overpopulated Asian lowlands to less crowded mountain regions in countries such as Vietnam and the Philippines during recent years. Relatively few people lived in the mountains in the past because the human carrying capacity of mountains is less than river valleys and coastal plains which have deep, flat, fertile soil. Mountain people have farmed the steep mountain land for centuries without environmental damage because their agriculture is coadapted with the mountain ecosystem. Lowland people who move to the mountains often use lowland agricultural methods that are not sustainable in the mountains because their agriculture is not designed to protect steep hillsides from erosion.

human migrations

The same thing is happening with human migrations to tropical rainforests. Millions of Brazilians have moved to the Amazon, and millions of Indonesians have moved from the overpopulated island of Java to farm Indonesia's outer islands, where lush green forests have thrived for thousands of years on some of the world's poorest soils. Rainforest ecosystems maintain the fertility of their soil with complex adaptations that prevent the loss of scarce mineral nutrients from the forest ecosystem. Until recently, only a small number of people lived in rainforests, and they used the forest in ways that did not interfere with the sustainability of the ecosystem, such as hunting and gathering and slash–burn agriculture.

Today a large number of people are cutting rainforests and replacing forest ecosystems with farms that are unsustainable on nutrient-poor rainforest soils. Their agricultural ecosystems lack the intricate mechanisms that allow rainforest ecosystems and the traditional agriculture of the region to maintain soil fertility. These inappropriate agricultural ecosystems stop producing within a few years. The land may then be used for grazing, producing beef for export to industrialized nations (the hamburger connection). Eventually even grasses may not grow, or there is grazing-induced succession to grass too tough for cattle to eat, and the land is subsequently abandoned. It is a 'tropical desert' with soil so severely damaged that it can be many years before it will once again support a rainforest or human use. Tropical forest immigrants then move to new places, where they clear-cut forests in order to farm soil that has not yet lost its fertility. Eventually, immigrant farmers will cut down all the forest and, in the end, these people will still not have a suitable place in which to live.

The story of human migrations shows us how human–ecosystem interaction can change with the passage of time. Migrating people bring a social system that is not adapted to their new environment, but with time they have the potential to reorganize and adjust their social systems to the new conditions. Problems of unsustainable activities by migrants will become increasingly common as more people in the developing world move from overpopulated areas to areas that are less populated but also less suited to accommodate a population increase. The most important lesson from this example is that people can learn and adapt. International and national policies for sustainable development need to assist migrant people to learn from people who have lived in the same area for many generations, so that migrants can adapt quickly to their new environment, doing as little damage as possible.

new
technologies

NEW TECHNOLOGIES

People often cause extensive environmental damage when they adopt a new technology. They do not know the environmental consequences of the new technology, and their social system does not have the institutions to use the technology in ways that are environmentally sustainable. For example, traditional hunting societies used weapons such as spears, bows and arrows, or blowguns with poison darts, which were not effective enough to damage the populations of their food sources. It was safe for hunters to kill as many animals as possible. However, the same resources can be overexploited when a new technology, such as guns, is introduced and hunters continue to kill as many animals as possible. The hunters' knowledge of nature may be immense, but their culture may not have evolved a conservation ethic if it was unnecessary in the past. Fishermen around the world now use monofilament nylon nets, which are much more effective than traditional fishing nets because fish cannot see them in the water. The result has been severe overfishing and decline of fish populations in many parts of the world.

Market changes can disrupt the sustainable use of natural resources because new market opportunities encourage people to use production technologies with which they have little previous experience. For example, the rapid growth of developing world cities in recent years has created expanding markets for European crops such as cabbage, stimulating large-scale commercial production of these crops in mountains where they were not cultivated in the past. Tropical mountain hillsides are very susceptible to erosion. If they are not protected from rainfall by plants covering the soil, rainwater can carry away hundreds of tonnes of soil from each hectare of hillside every year. Traditional mountain agricultural ecosystems have been sustainable for centuries because they use crops that cover the soil and protect it from erosion. Most European crops do not protect the soil as well because they come from European agricultural ecosystems that evolved under very different topographic and climatic conditions. European crops are sustainable in their places of origin, but they are not sustainable on tropical mountain hillsides where land with these crops can lose so much of its topsoil that agriculture is eventually no longer possible.

portable capital

PORTABLE CAPITAL IN A FREE MARKET ECONOMY

Economic conventions frequently encourage people to use renewable resources in unsustainable ways. A common way to use forests on a sustainable basis is to cut a small percentage of the trees each year. If too many trees are cut, the tree population will decline and the trees will eventually disappear. The percentage of a forest's trees that can be cut on a sustainable basis each year depends upon the growth rate of trees. If the trees grow fast, a larger percentage can be cut each year. A typical growth rate for temperate forests is 5 per cent each year; the quantity of wood in the forest increases by 5 per cent during a year. To use a forest on a sustainable basis, no more than 5 per cent of the wood should be cut each year.

Imagine that you own 10 hectares of forest. You have two choices. You can cut 5 per cent of the wood each year for a sustainable harvest. Or you can cut all of the trees as soon as possible, sell the wood and invest the money in another business. If you invest the money in another business, return on the investment will be 10 per cent per year. However, if you cut all of the trees, it will be at least 40 years before there are mature trees on your land that will provide more timber. Which way will enable you to obtain the most money over the long term:

- Harvest the forest sustainably?
- Cut all of the trees and invest the money from the timber in another business?

The second choice provides the most long-term income. This example illustrates the fundamental conflict between the profit motive and sustainable use of natural resources. Our modern economic system has a strong effect on the way renewable natural resources are used because capital is 'portable'. Capital is portable because money is easily moved from one business enterprise to another. If decisions about the use of renewable natural resources are based exclusively on profits, even long-term profits, renewable natural resources will be used on a sustainable basis only if their biological growth rate is greater than the expected growth rate of alternative investments. Because the growth rate of the world economy today is greater than the biological growth rate of most renewable natural resources, there are powerful economic incentives not to use renewable natural resources on a sustainable basis. If people accept the rules of the game in a free market economy, it is rational to use renewable resources unsustainably whenever biological production fails to compete with alternative forms of investment.

> tragedy of
> the commons

TRAGEDY OF THE COMMONS

Commons means common property resource, a resource that is shared by many people. The atmosphere, oceans, lakes and rivers are commons that provide natural resources and absorb pollution. Forests, grazing lands and irrigation water may also be common property resources. Many commons are the property of no one in particular. Such commons typically have 'open access'; they can be used by anyone to any extent. Open-access commons are vulnerable to overexploitation because no one is responsible for controlling the intensity of their use.

Overexploitation under these circumstances is known as the **tragedy of the commons**. What is best for each individual is not best for all resource users together. For example, the Earth's atmosphere is a common property resource that is polluted by automobile exhaust. Air pollution from a single automobile is of little consequence, but pollution from all of the automobiles in a crowded city can create a serious health hazard. Carbon dioxide from automobile emissions is contributing to the global warming that is dramatically changing the global ecosystem.

Overfishing illustrates how tragedy of the commons is a consequence of 'rational' decisions by individual resource users to get as much of the resource as possible. It is best for sustainable fishing if all fishermen limit the number of nets that they use to no more than the optimum, as in Figure 10.3 (point *A*). Too many nets will reduce the fish population to such an extent that everyone catches less fish (point *B*). Tragedy of the commons occurs because the nets of one fisherman cannot catch enough fish to have a noticeable negative effect on the fish population. Each fisherman knows that he will catch more fish if he uses more nets, regardless of the number of nets that other fishermen are using. For one fisherman, twice as many nets catch twice as many fish (A_2) because the nets of one fisherman cannot catch enough fish to have an effect on fish stocks. However, if all fishermen use more nets, they will catch so many fish that the fish population is reduced, and the long-term fish catch will decline (point *B*). Tragedy of the commons can cause fishermen to use more and more nets until fish stocks disappear, because even when overfishing is severe, each individual fisherman catches the most fish by using more nets than other fishermen (B_2). A fisherman who uses a smaller number of nets, when other fishermen are overfishing, is punished by catching almost no fish at all (B_1).

Tragedy of the commons is rational for individuals, but it is not rational for society. Preventing tragedy of the commons is almost impossible with open access to resources, but it can be prevented if a resource has clear ownership with the owner (or owners) controlling who uses the resource and how it is used. This is known

tragedy of the commons

Figure 10.3
The response of fish catches to fishing intensity as an example of tragedy of the commons
A All fishermen use fewer nets to achieve a high sustainable catch.
B All fishermen use more nets. Everyone catches less because overfishing reduces the fish population.
A_2 One fisherman uses twice as many nets when all the other fishermen use fewer nets for a high sustainable catch.
B_1 One fisherman uses fewer nets when other fishermen are overfishing.
B_2 One fisherman uses twice as many nets as fishermen who are overfishing.

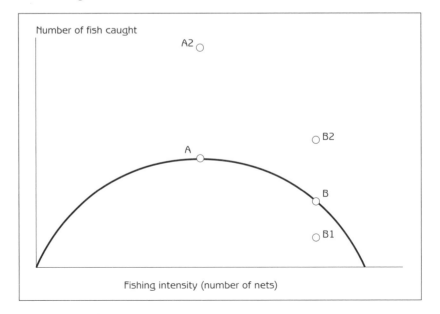

as closed access. Closed-access resources can also be overexploited, but overexploitation of these resources can be prevented if resource owners have **social institutions**, established rules for behaviour in a community, that give them the power to make sure everyone uses the resource in a sustainable manner. The next chapter will describe social institutions that prevent tragedy of the commons from occurring.

LARGE INPUTS TO AGRICULTURAL AND URBAN ECOSYSTEMS

large inputs

People create agricultural and urban ecosystems by using energy inputs of materials, energy and information to modify the structure of ecosystems so that they function in ways that better serve human needs. In the past, energy inputs came from human and animal labour. Today, most of the energy comes from fossil fuels.

There is an important relationship between inputs and sustainability: agricultural and urban ecosystems are less sustainable over the long term if large quantities of human inputs are required to keep the ecosystem functioning in the way that people want. This is because it is difficult to ensure that large inputs can be provided on a reliable basis for a long time.

The experience of ancient Middle Eastern civilizations provides a good example. Civilization in the Middle East has always depended upon irrigation agriculture because the arid climate seriously limits natural biological production. Cities such as Babylon were able to develop along the rivers of Mesopotamia because water from rivers was used to create agricultural ecosystems that produced enough food to support cities. The cities lasted for centuries, but eventually they collapsed and were buried under desert sands because their agriculture collapsed.

The reasons for agricultural breakdown in these ancient civilizations were varied and complex, but one common explanation was the failure to maintain the ditches that transported irrigation water from the river to farm fields. River water contains sediment (eroded soil suspended in the water), which settles to the bottom of irrigation ditches as water travels along the ditches. If sediment is not removed from a ditch, it continues to accumulate on the bottom until the ditch is so full of sediment that it can no longer transport water. In ancient times, human and animal labour were used to remove sediment from the ditches. Today in industrialized nations, machines do the job with petroleum energy.

Middle Eastern civilizations used large quantities of wood for the construction of their cities. The wood came from nearby mountains, as did the water in the rivers. After hundreds of years, deforestation and grazing by goats destroyed most of the vegetation that covered the mountain soil and protected it from erosion. Sediment increased in the rivers, the quantity of sediment that settled in irrigation ditches increased correspondingly, and more human and animal energy inputs were required to remove sediment from ditches. Before deforestation, nature performed the work of keeping sediment out of irrigation ditches by providing sediment-free water. After deforestation, the work shifted to people. Eventually, there was more sediment in the ditches than people could remove, particularly when the labour supply was reduced by demands from other sectors of the complex society, including emergencies such as war. The ditches filled with so much sediment that it was not possible to channel river water to the fields, irrigation agriculture collapsed and so did the civilization. Where this occurred, agriculture ecosystems were unsustainable because the social systems were not able to continue providing energy inputs large enough to maintain them.

urbanization and alienation

URBANIZATION AND ALIENATION FROM NATURE

The inborn need for humans to learn about nature is apparent when we observe the curiosity that children have for nature and the intensity with which they explore their natural environment during casual play. Childhood experience generates an emotional attachment to nature and a concrete and intimate knowledge of nature in the locale where a child lives. This emotional need for nature has been termed **biophilia**. The childhood imprinting process, so essential to the full development of biophilia, appears to be a basic part of the human psyche, but it can only happen if a child has access to nature – an opportunity denied to children who live in cities with no natural ecosystems within their reach. The result may be adults who lack the emotional attachment to nature and knowledge of nature that is necessary for sustainable interaction. It may be that no amount of international treaties, government planning and regulations, or even environmental instruction in the classroom, will be sufficient if people lack the love and respect for nature to compel them to conduct their everyday business in ways that do not destroy their environmental support system.

The potential significance of direct contact with nature during childhood can be appreciated by imagining a futuristic society in which children are separated from their families at birth and raised in dormitories. Even if the children receive daily indoctrination in school about love and respect for parents, the way that they relate to parents as adults will be fundamentally different from adults who were held in their mothers' arms and experienced the full richness of family interactions throughout childhood. Similarly, a concern for the environment that comes only from school may lack the substance and depth that is necessary for a society to be ecologically sustainable.

**complex
societies**

THE RISE AND FALL OF COMPLEX SOCIETIES

A prominent characteristic of urban social systems is their social complexity characterized by extensive differentiation and specialization of social roles and elaborate organization of human activities. The role of social complexity in the growth and decline of cities can be seen in past civilizations, such as those in Mesopotamia, Egypt and Greece, as well as Mayan and Pueblo Indian civilizations of the Western Hemisphere. These civilizations experienced cycles of growth and decline that extended over centuries. The European empires experienced a similar process of growth and decline during the past 400 years.

The growth of complex societies

Urban ecosystems were primarily simple villages before the Agricultural Revolution. They were small and nearly independent of one another. Village social systems were egalitarian; nearly everyone was of equal status. There was division of labour by sex, but the number of distinct social roles was small. Almost everyone was a jack of all trades, doing whatever was necessary for a **subsistence** way of life. Most families produced their own food, made their own clothing and built their own houses. There was some specialization, but the simplest societies had as few as 25 different occupational roles. Though very sophisticated in other ways, all human social systems before the Agricultural Revolution were relatively simple with regard to occupational roles. Pre-industrial societies in more isolated parts of the world still exist in this way.

The formation of cities as larger and more complex urban ecosystems is only possible when a society's agricultural ecosystems are productive enough to supply a surplus of food beyond the needs of the families who produce the food. The extra food allows city people to specialize in a variety of non-farming occupations – a **division of labour** that forms the core of social complexity. It is typical for modern society to have more than 10,000 different occupational roles in a single large city.

Many of these occupations work in support of the society's productive activities to make them more effective. There is also the opportunity for innovators and artists to flourish. Potters and poets, engineers and scientists, teachers and priests all add to the richness of life. However, such extensive division of labour requires that large amounts of time and energy are spent in processing information, communicating, distributing goods and keeping track of property ownership and the exchange of goods and services. This is true today and it was equally so for civilizations in the past. Records from ancient civilizations commonly feature voluminous and detailed accounts of commercial exchanges and inventories of goods.

Division of labour in complex societies is not only occupational. There is social stratification with regard to power and wealth, and there is a hierarchical authority structure in the form of government.

Past civilizations were associated with cities, or clusters of cities, that grew in size and complexity for centuries, extending their influence over a larger and larger area, their **zone of influence**. This expansion was not always peaceful and often involved the exploitation of conquered people and their resources.

complex societies

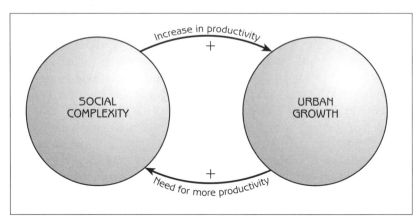

Figure 10.4
Positive feedback loop between social complexity and the growth of cities

Once started, it is typical for complexity to continue increasing. This leads to further growth and expansion, which creates a need for additional productivity by means of greater complexity (see Figure 10.4). Growth and complexity thus form a **positive feedback** loop that makes them increase exponentially. A city can eventually grow to dominate such a large area, and it can be so complex and with so many social controls that it appears the power and wealth of the city will continue forever. This is the *equilibrium* stage of the complex system cycle.

The decline of complex societies

complex
societies

Eventually the social system of a complex civilization becomes too complex to continue functioning effectively. When social complexity is greater than the optimum (see Figure 10.5), more complexity can lead to less productivity because of the following:

* Many of the benefits from social complexity have **diminishing returns**. Once a certain level of technology and organization of human activities is reached, more intensive technology and organization do not produce more results (see the benefits curve in Figure 10.5).
* Social complexity has a substantial cost in terms of the energy and effort needed to organize and maintain it (see the cost curve in Figure 10.5).
* Costs continue to increase, even when there are no additional benefits from greater complexity, so productivity (which equals benefits minus costs) declines (see the productivity curve in Figure 10.5).
* Society develops cultural values that encourage additional complexity. This can lead to a random proliferation of complexity that lacks the structure to contribute to functionality in the system as a whole.

As a result, the productivity of the society, as well as its standard of living, decline. It might appear logical for a social system with too much complexity to reduce its complexity to the optimum. However, social systems usually become even more elaborate because societies have evolved a cultural belief that more complexity is the best way in which to deal with problems.

By the time a society has exceeded optimum complexity, it is common for it to start experiencing serious environmental problems, and *dissolution* begins. Damage due to excessive demands on the ecosystem that has been building up slowly for centuries finally leads to a decline in agricultural productivity and a shortage of food and other renewable natural resources (see Figure 10.6). The society no longer has the surplus food and other resources that it needs to support a large urban population and maintain food reserves. As reserves of food and other essential resources diminish, the society loses its **resilience** to cope with further decline. (Resilience is discussed in Chapter 11.)

When the standard of living declines, communities in the city's zone of influence become dissatisfied and try to break their ties with the city (see Figure 10.6). In response, political authorities may rely on military force to compel surrounding communities to continue supporting the city. Political authorities may also channel more resources into projects such as monuments or elaborate ceremonies to glorify the image of the civilization. Because military expenditures and glorification projects are expensive but do not increase productivity, the standard of living declines even further. Greater demands are placed on people and the ecosystem in the surrounding area to increase production. There is more environmental damage, agricultural productivity declines, the standard of living declines and people are more dissatisfied. These

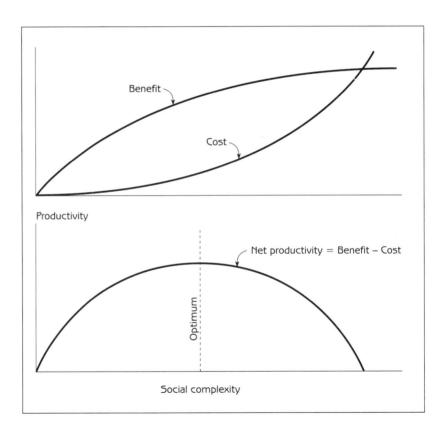

Figure 10.5
Benefits and
costs of social
complexity

downward positive feedback loops may eventually cause the city to be abandoned. The city's inhabitants migrate to places where opportunities are better (*reorganization*), and a new city begins to grow somewhere else.

The rise and fall of complex societies is not just a story of ancient civilizations. Contemporary urban ecosystems experience complex system cycles of growth and decline on a spatial scale that extends from neighbourhoods and small cities to large cities, metropolitan areas and entire civilizations. A neighbourhood grows as people or commercial activities move to it from other neighbourhoods. A few decades later, the same neighbourhood may decline as people and commercial activities move to other competing neighbourhoods. The same thing happens with whole cities on a longer time scale.

complex societies

Because this example of urban growth, collapse and reorganization is as old as human civilization, the modern world's story of population explosion and an expanding global economy is not so new, except in one very important way. Until recently, the growth and decline of urban ecosystems have been on local or regional scales. When cities or regional civilizations collapsed, people moved to new areas. Now, with global transportation and communications and a global economy, human social systems are becoming a single global social system, and the Earth's ecosystems are becoming strongly connected through human activities. For the first time in history, the growth of human population and social complexity is happening simultaneously in almost every urban ecosystem and social system over the entire planet. While growth, collapse and migration were local or regional in the past, there is now a possibility of global collapse with nowhere to move.

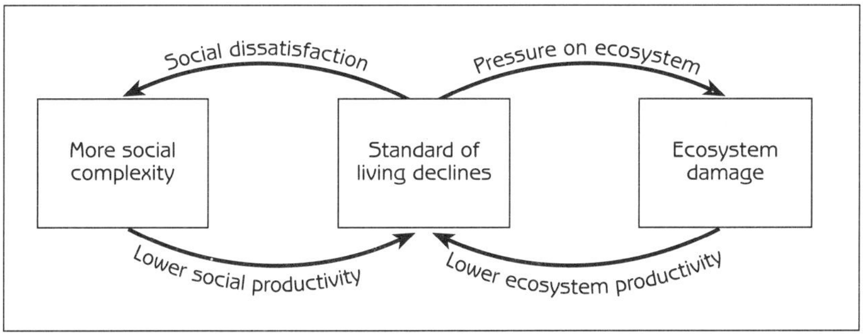

Figure 10.6
Positive feedback loops for the dissolution phase in the rise and fall of complex societies

WISHFUL THINKING AND THE PRECAUTIONARY PRINCIPLE

With the increase in environmental awareness during recent years, many governments are taking measures to prevent overexploitation and depletion of natural resources. Ironically, some renewable resources have collapsed since the effort to protect them began. In part, this has happened because population growth and economic growth have made greater demands on ecosystem services than before. However, many of the attempts to protect renewable resources from overexploitation have been unsuccessful because people were not realistic about the limits of the resources. I call this wishful thinking.

precautionary principle

The history of ocean fisheries during the past two decades illustrates the hazards of wishful thinking. About 20 years ago, coastal nations declared their ownership of the ocean and its resources to a distance of 320 kilometres from their shores. These areas are known as **extended economic zones** and cover the fish, petroleum and minerals in the zones. Governments formulated management plans and regulations to control the quantity and kind of fishing by their own fishermen and foreign fishermen in the extended economic zones. A common practice was to manage for 'maximum sustainable yield' – the largest fish catch possible on a long-term basis. Management plans were generally based on advice from scientists and representation from the fishing industry. In the years that followed, a number of commercially valuable fish populations collapsed despite the effort to protect them. Many of the management plans were not completely successful. Why did this happen?

Firstly, scientists had to work with imprecise information, and often management plans did not allow for the possibility that the estimates of fish production and the capacity of fish populations to withstand fishing might be wrong. Secondly, management plans did not take into account the way that fish populations change from year to year because of natural fluctuations in the physical and biological conditions of the oceans (ie, natural changes in ocean ecosystem state). During some years physical conditions and the supply of food in the oceans are more favourable for new generations of fish stocks; during other years young fish have difficulty surviving. As a result, fish populations can withstand more fishing during some years, while during other years stocks are seriously depleted by the same amount of fishing. Thirdly, improvements in fishing technology can increase the number of fish that fishermen catch. When this happens, it is necessary to revise the regulations to ensure that fish catches stay within sustainable bounds.

Governments accepted optimistic but risky plans because the fishing industry wanted to catch as many fish as possible. In their initial forms, management plans frequently allowed fishermen to catch the same number of fish every year, whether it was a good year for fish or a bad year. Fish populations collapsed when a plan overestimated the sustainable catch, when the allowable catch was too close to the limit or when regulations were not revised when conditions changed. Fish populations could not withstand fishing close to the limit during several years in a row of unusually low fish production (see Figure 10.7). The most spectacular collapse was the North Atlantic cod fishery, which had provided livelihoods for thousands of fishermen for several centuries. The changes may not be reversible. Commercially valuable fish populations may not return, even if fishing is reduced.

precautionary principle

The lesson from this story is that ecosystem services can be used on a truly sustainable basis only if the intensity of use is substantially less than the apparent maximum. This is the **precautionary principle**. Pushing ecosystems to the limit is risky because of imprecise estimation of the limits, as well as fluctuations in the capacity of ecosystems to provide the services. If people push the ecosystem state too close to the boundary between stability domains by using an ecosystem service too intensely, natural ecosystem fluctuations may push the ecosystem into a stability domain with diminished ecosystem services (see Figure 10.7).

The precautionary principle has become a major instrument for elaborating environmental policies. It reflects common sense. A Japanese Zen proverb says: 'The care with which a blind man crosses a log bridge is a good example of how we should live our lives.' The probing of a blind man is similar to the assessment

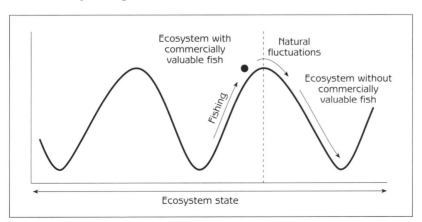

Figure 10.7
Change from one stability domain to another when fishing is too close to the boundary between stability domains in a fisheries ecosystem with natural climatic fluctuations

process in adaptive development described in Chapter 11. While the precautionary principle can contribute to ecological health and sustainability over a broad spectrum of human–ecosystem interaction, its implementation is far from straightforward in a social system strongly committed to maximum possible exploitation of ecosystem resources and services. The simple wisdom of the precautionary principle is counter to the prevailing ethos of the modern global economy, which rewards entrepreneurial boldness and portrays confidence in economic growth as an ultimate virtue.

precautionary principle

Practical implementation of the precautionary principle cannot be separated from short-term tradeoffs between ecological sustainability and other social concerns. A recent episode involving commercial fishing in Hawaii illustrates how people can have radically different opinions about where to draw the line. Several conservation organizations have initiated legal action to compel the United States government to close down long line fishing in areas where long lines kill marine mammals, seabirds, turtles and fish that are not an intended part of the catch. The consequences of this legal action are numerous. Closing long line fisheries will reduce employment for fishermen and reduce the supply of fish for consumers. Whether the fisheries are closed or not, dealing with this issue entails government expenses for litigation and research that can divert funds from other government programmes benefiting the same species (for example, protecting beaches where marine turtles lay their eggs). An answer to the question: 'To what extent is long line fishing harming these species, and how will closing the fisheries really benefit them?' is crucial to identifying appropriate restrictions on long line fisheries. However, scientific information is limited and interpretation of this information by legal adversaries can be biased. Some people believe that long lines kill few turtles and that modifications in fishing methods can protect other marine species. They prefer to modify fishing methods and see what happens, before resorting to more drastic measures such as closing an entire fishery. Other individuals, who have a lower tolerance for even potential damage to the marine ecosystem, believe that long line fishing should simply stop.

This example has far-reaching implications. Today's modern social system is vulnerable to wishful thinking not only about the magnitude of demands that ecosystems can sustain but also about the ability of modern science and technology to manipulate ecosystems to satisfy these demands. We do not have enough scientific knowledge about ecosystems to know precisely how far we can change them without risking collapse. Even with more scientific information and more powerful computers to process the information, ecosystems are so complex that we may never know precisely in advance what the consequences of our actions will be. Moreover, micromanagement of the vast ecosystems on which we depend for survival is a practical impossibility. There are not enough scientists – and there is not enough human labour and fossil fuel energy – to fix all of the problems created by misusing ecosystems, and then to fix all of the new problems created by ecological intervention.

THINGS TO THINK ABOUT

things to
think about

1. Look at the example of portable capital in a free market economy. The first alternative, harvesting the forest sustainably, provides a long-term supply of timber. The second alternative, cutting all of the trees and investing the money in another business, does not. Do you understand why the second alternative provides the highest long-term income? The second alternative explains why portable capital makes the unsustainable use of biological resources with slow growth rates a rational option from a business perspective. Think of concrete examples that illustrate unsustainable human–ecosystem interaction because of portable capital.

2. Think about sources of unsustainable human–ecosystem interactions in the social system in which you live. Think firstly about the local level, and then think about the national and international levels. Consider concrete examples that demonstrate how human–ecosystem interactions can be less sustainable because of:
   - human migration;
   - technology;
   - tragedy of the commons;
   - the economic system;
   - urbanization.

3. List specific benefits of social complexity at different levels of your social system (local community, nation, global society). What are some of the costs of social complexity at these different levels of social organization? Where do you think your social system is located on the curve in Figure 10.5? Is its social complexity near, less than or greater than the optimum?

4. Childhood contact with nature seems to be important in order to develop the knowledge and judgement that people need for sustainable interaction with ecosystems as adults. What kind of contact did you have with nature as a child? Talk to people with childhood experiences similar to your own, as well as to people with very different experiences. How did your childhood experiences influence your attitudes and actions toward ecosystems as an adult?

5. Identify ways in which agricultural and urban ecosystems in your region are dependent upon large quantities of energy or other resources,

making them vulnerable to price increases or shortfalls in supply. What can be done to reduce this vulnerability?

6.   What are the ways in which your local and national community leaders (business, government, etc) exhibit wishful thinking concerning the demands that the community or nation can safely place on ecosystems? How do their attitudes and actions compare with the precautionary principle? Why do community leaders think the way they do? Do most citizens have attitudes and actions similar to their community leaders? If there is a diversity of attitudes and actions, what are the rationales for different approaches? Are there particular ways in which you think that people should pay more attention to the precautionary principle?

things to think about

SUSTAINABLE HUMAN–
ECOSYSTEM INTERACTION

How can modern society embark on a course of ecologically sustainable development? Firstly, and most importantly, do not damage ecosystems.

- Do not damage ecosystems to such an extent that they lose their ability to provide essential services.
- Watch carefully for environmental or social side effects when using new technologies.
- Do not overexploit fisheries, forests, watersheds, farm soils or other parts of ecosystems that provide essential renewable resources. Increase the use of renewable natural resources gradually, monitoring for damage to the resource.
- Develop social institutions to protect common property resources from tragedy of the commons.
- Follow the precautionary principle when using natural resources, disposing of wastes or interacting with ecosystems in any way.

Secondly, do things nature's way so that nature does as much of the work as possible.

- Take advantage of nature's self-organizing abilities, thereby reducing the human inputs needed to organize ecosystems.
- Develop technologies that have low inputs because they are designed to let nature do the work.
- Take advantage of natural positive and negative feedback loops instead of struggling against them.
- Take advantage of natural cycles that use waste from one part of the ecosystem as a resource for another part of the ecosystem.

- Organize agricultural and urban ecosystems to mimic natural strategies. For example, organize agriculture ecosystems as polycultures that resemble natural ecosystems in the same climatic region. Recycle manufactured goods in a 'technical cycle' that keeps the wastes from manufactured goods separate from biological cycles in the ecosystem.

How can sustainable development be achieved in practice? This chapter starts with an important example – social institutions to prevent tragedy of the commons. It then examines the issue of coexistence of urban ecosystems with nature. The chapter concludes by exploring two essential and interrelated aspects of sustainable development:

human social institutions

1. **Resilience** – the ability of social systems and ecosystems to continue functioning despite severe and unexpected stresses.
2. **Adaptive development** – the ability of social systems to cope with change.

Resilience and adaptive development are important because ecologically sustainable development is not simply a matter of harmonious equilibrium with the environment. Preventing damage to ecosystems is absolutely essential for sustainable development, but it is not enough. Human society is constantly changing, and so is the environment. Sustainable development requires a capacity to deal with change. Resilience and adaptive development are the key to attaining that capacity.

HUMAN SOCIAL INSTITUTIONS AND SUSTAINABLE USE OF COMMON PROPERTY RESOURCES

How can we prevent tragedy of the commons? Where existing social institutions encourage tragedy of the commons by making the overexploitation of common property resources a rational choice for individuals, we need new institutions that make sustainable use the rational choice. Scientists have compared hundreds of societies around the world to discover what social institutions are associated with the sustainable use of resources, such as forests, fisheries, irrigation water and communal pastures. They have discovered that some societies are highly successful at preventing tragedy of the commons. While details are different in each instance, the successful cases all have the following themes in common.

1. Clear ownership and boundaries: group ownership of a clearly defined area provides the control that is necessary to prevent overexploitation. This is closed access. Territoriality is a common social institution that people use to define ownership and boundaries. Extended maritime jurisdictions that nations have declared for ownership of marine natural resources within 320 kilometres of their shores are modern examples of closed access for common property resources.

2. Commitment to the sustainable use of the resource: the owners of a common property resource must really want to use it on a sustainable basis. They must agree that:

    human social institutions

    *   individual use is damaging the resource;
    *   cooperative use of the resource will reduce the risks of damage;
    *   the future is important (ie, opportunities for their children and grandchildren are as important as their own short-term gains).

    It is best if the owners have a shared past, trust each other, expect a shared future and value their reputation in the community. It is easier if ethnic differences or economic status are not sources of conflict for the resource owners.

3. Agreement about rules for using the resource: everyone should have enough knowledge about the resource in order to understand the consequences of using it in different ways. Good rules require not only a thorough knowledge of the resource itself but also a knowledge of the behaviour of the people who are using it. Good rules are simple, so everyone knows what is expected, and good rules are fair. No one likes to sacrifice for the selfish gain of others. Good rules produce benefits that exceed the costs of cooperation, costs that include organizational overhead, the effort or expense necessary to make a group function. Good rules don't waste people's time or other valued resources.

4. Internal adaptive mechanisms: sooner or later, it is necessary to adapt the rules for using a common property resource because of changes in the social system or the ecosystem, changes that often originate from the 'outside world'. The mechanisms for adapting rules should be simple and inexpensive. Changes should usually be incremental so that large mistakes are avoided. It is important to monitor carefully what happens after new rules are put into effect, so the group can decide whether to make further changes. Trial-and-error

evolution of rules is an example of self-organization in the social system.

5. Enforcement of rules: people usually follow rules if they think that everyone else is following the rules too. The best way to prevent people from breaking the rules is by internal monitoring – resource users watch each other – supplemented by external monitoring, such as guards. Everyone must know that everyone else will know if he or she break the rules. Severe punishments are not necessary if infractions are likely to be detected. Social pressure and the embarrassment of being caught are sufficient deterrents. Punishments should be minimal because punishments are disruptive to a spirit of cooperation.

human social institutions

6. Conflict resolution: people sometimes have different perceptions about applying rules to particular situations. Conflict resolution should be simple, inexpensive and fair.

7. Minimum external interference: local autonomy – being able to function independently, without control by others – is important because external authority may impose decisions that are not appropriate for local conditions. One of the most frequent reasons for unsustainable use of common property resources is interference from government authorities or economic forces outside the area. 'Outsiders' may not care about local sustainability, and outsiders seldom know enough about the local situation to understand what rules will work under local conditions.

An example of successful common-property resource use: coastal fisheries in Turkey

Tragedy of the commons is a frequent problem when fishermen do not cooperate to prevent overfishing. Because many traditional fishing villages have territorial jurisdiction over the fishing areas near their village, they have the clear ownership that is essential for sustainable resource use. Once ownership is established, the key is the establishment of good rules to prevent overfishing. Coastal marine fishermen in Turkey provide an example of rules that work because they are adapted to local conditions. The fishery in Turkey has two important characteristics:

1. Some areas are better for fishing than others.
2. Some areas are better for fishing during particular times of the year because fish move to different waters during different times of the year.

The fishermen have devised the following rules:

- They use a map to divide the fishing area into sites that are equal in number to the number of fishermen (see Figure 11.1). They draw lots at the beginning of the fishing season to determine which site each fisherman will use on the first day of the season.
- Each fisherman can fish at only his assigned site the first day. He can fish at only the next numbered site the next day, and he must move from one numbered site to another every day after that.

These rules are simple and therefore easily understood by everyone. They are also fair despite the complexities of good sites, poor sites and fish movements during the year. Every fisherman has an opportunity to fish good sites as well as poor ones.

human social institutions

The rules are also easy to enforce. If they are broken, it is usually when fishermen fish good sites on days that are not their turn. This is easy to detect because fishermen almost always go to good sites on the days when they are allowed to fish them. As a consequence, legitimate users of good sites are there to make sure that other fishermen do not use the site.

An example of successful common property resource use: traditional village forest management in Japan

For more than 1000 years, forests in Japan were the main source of essential materials such as water, wood for construction, thatch for roofs, food for domesticated animals, organic fertilizer (decomposing leaves) for farm fields and firewood and charcoal

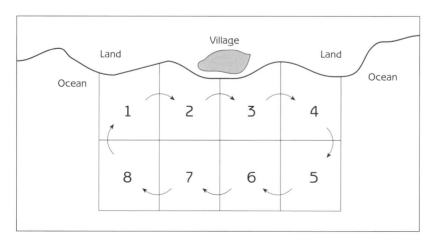

Figure 11.1
A system used to prevent tragedy of the commons in a coastal fishery in Turkey

for cooking and heating. The Japanese used their forests intensively, but they were able to prevent tragedy of the commons by managing their forests as a closed-access common property resource. The forest around each village belonged to that village. The village controlled who used the forest and how. Although agricultural land such as rice fields was in private ownership, the forest belonged to the village as a whole. Everyone agreed that common lands such as the forest should be managed to serve the long-term needs of the entire village.

While every family in a village had a right to use the forest, rules for forest use were decided by a village council with representation from families having decision-making authority by virtue of land ownership, land use rights or taxpaying obligations. Rules were designed to:

human social institutions

- limit the quantity of forest products that a family in the village could remove from the forest;
- provide equal access for every family in the village, while preventing overexploitation of the forest by the village as a whole;
- require as little effort as possible to implement and enforce;
- accommodate the roles that each forest product had in the village economy;
- fit with details of the local environment;

The extended family household was the basic unit of access to the village forest, and each household was assigned specific dates during which it could remove wood or other materials. For most materials, there was no limit on the amount that each household could remove during its scheduled time. In many villages, a number of households were organized into groups called *kumi*. Each *kumi* was assigned a different section of the forest for its use. In order to ensure fairness, the assignment was rotated each year so that each *kumi* could use a different part of the forest.

The way the rules worked can be illustrated by a typical procedure for removing animal fodder from the forest. Each household could send only one adult to cut the grass in its part of the forest on the scheduled day. Everyone in the same *kumi* formed a line to cut the grass in their part of the forest, and they could only start cutting after the temple bell sounded. They left the grass to dry after cutting. About a week later, two people from each household could go to the forest to tie the dried grass into bundles and place the bundles in piles of equal size (one pile for each household in the *kumi*). The piles were then distributed to all the households in each *kumi* by lottery.

Each village developed its own way of enforcing the rules. Because people were allowed to remove materials from the forest only on specified dates, anyone seen in the forest during other times was obviously breaking the rules. Most villages hired guards (a prestigious job for young men), who patrolled the forest on horseback in groups of two. In some areas all the young men in the village served as guards on a rotational basis. In villages that did not use guards, any member of the village could report seeing someone in the forest at the wrong time.

Each village had its own penalties for breaking the rules. The forest guards usually handled occasional violations in a quiet and simple manner. It was accepted practice for guards to demand a small payment of money or *sake* from the rule-breaker. If a violation was more serious, the guards confiscated the illegal harvest and any equipment or horses that the rule-breaker was using. Rule-breakers had to pay a fine to the village to recover their equipment or horses. The amount of a fine depended upon the seriousness of the offence, the willingness of the rule-breaker to make rapid amends and whether the rule-breaker had a history of violations.

human social institutions

People sometimes broke the rules because they desperately needed material from the forest at a time during which they were not allowed to remove it. One effective strategy for breaking the rules was to send the family's most beautiful daughter into the forest, because guards (being young men) were more lenient with young women. The punishment was not severe if people had a good reason for breaking the rules. For example, there is a story about a large number of villagers who entered the forest before the scheduled day to cut poles because they urgently needed the poles for vegetables on their farms. Otherwise the crop would be lost. These rule-breakers were given a light punishment because the village council realized that the date the council had scheduled for removing poles from the forest was too late. The rule-breakers were only required to make a small donation to the village school.

The social institutions for managing village forests in Japan were developed and refined over centuries, reaching their peak during the Tokugawa period (1600–1867). The management was successful because it was local. Even though Japan had a feudal and in many ways authoritarian social system, detailed rules for forest use were not imposed from outside the villages. It is also significant that forest access was based on households, not individuals. The share of wood and other materials that a household could remove from the forest did not increase if the household increased in number, and large households could not divide into two households unless they received special permission from the village. As a consequence, every household had a strong incentive not to have too many children, and there was almost no increase in the Japanese population during the Tokugawa period.

Japan's traditional system of forest management began to decline during the years after the Meiji Restoration (1868), and it deteriorated substantially with land reform and other social, political and economic changes following World War II. Forests are still important as a source of water for household, agricultural and industrial use, but the role of forests changed as Japan became a highly urbanized society integrated with the global economy. The importance of forests as a source of essential materials declined as Japan met the same needs by importing fossil fuels for heating and cooking, timber from other countries for construction purposes and chemical fertilizers for farms. Large areas of forest are now cut each year to make way for urban expansion, and the remaining forests have become increasingly important as weekend recreation areas for large urban populations.

human social institutions

The scale of sustainable common-property resource use

Most of the known examples of the sustainable use of common property resources are local in scale. The local level of resource use has many advantages, including the following.

* The resource is more uniform, and therefore easier to understand, when the scale is small.
* Local people have a more thorough knowledge of the resource and therefore a stronger basis for knowing what rules will be effective.
* Local people know each other well enough to have a foundation for trust.
* Local people desire sustainable use because they have a stake in the future of local resources.

An important question for human–ecosystem interaction is whether sustainable use of common property resources is possible on a large scale. So far, the experience with large-scale use has not been encouraging. Tragedy of the commons is typical for resources exploited by multinational corporations. Because large-scale resource use is a fact of life in today's global economy, the development of viable international social institutions to prevent tragedy of the commons is a major challenge of our time.

There are legitimate differences between local, regional, national and international interests when deciding on the use of natural resources. Government ownership of resources such as forested lands has been associated with sustainable management in some places but unsustainable management in others. Government administration has a general history of granting use rights for timber, livestock grazing or other resources to people with political influence at a price below the real value of the resource – and often without adequate attention to sustainable use. If large-scale control of resource use is unavoidable, it should be organized hierarchically so that national or global economic forces and government authorities do not exclude local participation.

coexistence

COEXISTENCE OF URBAN ECOSYSTEMS WITH NATURE

Chapter 10 described the conflict between urbanization and sustainable human–ecosystem interaction. Cities depend upon agricultural ecosystems for food and other products. They rely on natural ecosystems for water, wood, recreation and other resources and services. However, despite this dependence, as cities grow they tend to displace or damage agricultural and natural ecosystems, thereby diminishing the environmental support systems upon which they depend. Cities expand over agricultural lands and natural areas; and even where they do not displace agricultural or natural ecosystems, excessive demands for the products of those ecosystems can lead to overexploitation and degradation. Cities also expand indirectly at the expense of natural ecosystems because displacement of agricultural ecosystems and increasing demands for agricultural products can stimulate agricultural expansion far from the city, displacing natural ecosystems there. Modern urban ecosystems can have a strong impact on distant natural ecosystems because their **supply zones** extend to so many parts of the world.

Why do urban social systems show so little restraint in destroying or damaging the natural and agricultural ecosystems on which they depend? Part of the explanation (as discussed in Chapter 10) is alienation of urban society from nature, particularly if people have no contact with natural or agricultural ecosystems during childhood. The implications for design of urban landscapes are far reaching and profound. Urban landscapes that provide childhood experience with nature may be essential for an ecologically sustainable society. Until recently, virtually all cities contained a landscape mosaic of urban, agricultural and natural ecosystems that provided opportunities for direct contact with nature within walking distance of most people's homes. Unfortunately, many large cities today have become 'concrete jungles' in which this opportunity is no longer available. The result may be a positive feedback loop between an increasingly urbanized society and cities with fewer opportunities for childhood nature experience, creating adults whose lack of emotional connection with nature does not constrain them from damaging their city's environmental support system. Ensuring that natural ecosystems are retained as part of urban landscapes – or finding ways to restore green areas where they have already been lost – should be high on the agenda of urban communities.

coexistence

Is it feasible for natural ecosystems to survive in close contact with modern urban ecosystems? It can happen if the people in the area are concerned and active enough to ensure that the natural ecosystems are not polluted, destroyed or excessively disrupted. The coexistence of cities and **chaparral** in southern California provides an example. Chaparral ecosystems are characterized by a dense growth of tall shrubs and small trees about 2–3 metres in height. They have a rich assortment of birds and other small animals as well as larger animals such as deer, mountain lions (puma), bobcats (lynx), coyotes and foxes. The residential areas of some cities in southern California have convoluted edges that place a large number of homes in close proximity to natural chaparral ecosystems (see Figure 11.2a). These are sometimes shaped by foothills that form part of the terrain around the cities.

Figure 11.2
Landscape mosaics of urban and natural ecosystems

The dense chaparral vegetation restricts human activity to paths and roads, protecting the natural ecosystem from excessive human impacts while providing opportunities for hiking, mountain biking and other relatively unobtrusive activities.

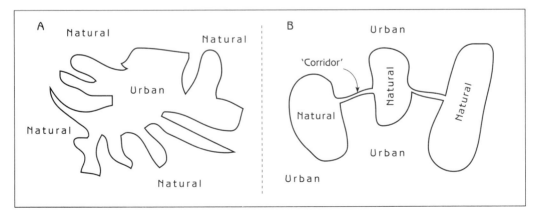

The size of a natural ecosystem is critical for maintaining its integrity in an urban area because in order to be fully functional a natural ecosystem must be large enough to provide habitat for all of its biological community. Large predators require territories of several square kilometres or more to provide them with food; they cannot survive if the ecosystem is too small. One way to ensure that natural ecosystems are large enough is to have natural ecosystem corridors that connect smaller patches together (Figure 11.2b).

Santa Monica mountains

coexistence

Even if urban and natural ecosystems can coexist next to each other, natural ecosystems will be lost if they are simply cleared away by urban expansion. The recent history of the Santa Monica mountains, a natural area of 900 square kilometres at the western edge of Los Angeles, illustrates how social institutions can control urban expansion over natural ecosystems. The Santa Monica mountains have a scattering of houses on a landscape mosaic that features chaparral on the hillsides with oak woodland ecosystems and temporary streams in the canyon bottoms. By the 1950s it was technically and economically feasible to level the granite hills in this area for residential development using earth-moving equipment originally developed during World War II for constructing airplane landing strips on mountainous Pacific islands. Mountains near cities often have a high priority for public ownership and protection because they are the city's source of water, but Los Angeles brings its water from rivers hundreds of miles away. In the mid-1960s more than 98 per cent of the land in the Santa Monica mountains was in private ownership, much of it in large parcels owned by land holding companies that intended to level it to construct thousands of houses. The rapid growth of Los Angeles during the 1950s and 1960s was extending high-density residential subdivisions into the mountains at a rate that threatened to cover much of the land with houses within a few decades.

The expansion of high-density housing into the Santa Monica mountains was controlled because of citizen initiatives that stimulated local, state and national governments to take decisive action to protect the natural landscape in the area. Starting in late 1960s, a highly organized, aggressive and persistent coalition of citizens groups in the western part of Los Angeles adjacent to the mountains, homeowners associations in the mountains themselves and environmental organizations such as the Sierra Club lobbied all levels of government for protection of the mountains. Energetic support from a few particularly sympathetic representatives in the

Los Angeles city council, the California state legislature, and the United States Congress led to action at all three levels of government by the end of the 1970s. Through negotiation and land condemnation, the state acquired 45 square kilometres of privately owned, undeveloped land adjacent to areas where residential developments at the edge of Los Angeles were expanding rapidly into the mountains. In 1974 this newly acquired land became Topanga State Park, in which residential and commercial development and highway construction were completely prohibited. In 1978 the United States government's National Park Service established the Santa Monica Mountains National Recreation Area to promote protection of nature throughout the mountains. In 1979 the state of California submitted a Comprehensive Plan for all of the Santa Monica mountains to the United States government. The state legislature created the Santa Monica Mountains Conservancy to implement the Comprehensive Plan, and all city and county governments in the area, while not legally bound to follow the plan, agreed to follow it in principle.

The Santa Monica Mountains Conservancy and the National Park Service were both charged with land acquisition, protection of nature on land they acquired, development and maintenance of recreational facilities such as hiking trails, and representation of the Comprehensive Plan at local government hearings regarding development of privately owned lands. The two levels of government have pursued their overlapping missions with somewhat different institutional strengths, priorities and management styles – the overlap and differences enabling them to accomplish together what neither could have accomplished alone. About 40 per cent of the land in the Santa Monica mountains is now under national or state ownership, and an additional 15 per cent is targeted for eventual acquisition. However, the total area with natural vegetation is diminishing gradually as the privately owned land is developed for residential housing or other remunerative purposes such as vineyards. Active involvement to promote compatible use of private lands has been a priority for the state and national agencies because private land use can have such far-reaching effects on the ecological health of nearby land under government protection. The process of influencing private land use has been overwhelmingly complex, with results at times successful and at others disappointing. Even if much of the privately owned land is eventually used for urban or agricultural development, the long-term commitment of state and national governments, local residents, recreational users and environmentalists to protecting the land ensures that the region's landscape will retain a substantial representation of natural ecosystems for generations to come.

coexistence

RESILIENCE AND SUSTAINABLE DEVELOPMENT

Resilience is the ability of an ecosystem or social system to continue functioning despite occasional and severe disturbance (see Figure 11.3). To understand resilience, imagine a rubber band and a piece of string tied in a loop. If the rubber band is stretched to twice its normal size, it returns to normal once the pressure is released. The rubber band is resilient because it can return quickly to its normal shape after being changed by a severe stress. The loop of string is very different from the rubber band because it breaks if stretched beyond its normal size and is therefore not resilient. Buildings are resilient if they are designed to withstand severe earthquakes. Social systems and ecosystems are resilient if they survive severe disturbances.

resilience

Resilient ecosystems are the backbone of a sustainable environmental support system. A key to resilience is anticipating how things can go wrong and preparing for the worst. There are many ways to achieve resilience:

- **Redundancy:** duplication and diversification of function provide backups for when things go wrong. This principle is most conspicuous in the design of modern spacecraft, which have extensive backup systems to replace parts of the spacecraft that fail to function properly. Redundancy is prominent in natural ecosystems. The presence of species with overlapping ecological roles and niches contributes to the resilience of ecosystems.
- Low dependence on human inputs: sustainable human–ecosystem interaction is associated with ecosystems that have small human inputs. Nature does most of the work. Large human inputs reduce resilience because sooner or later something will happen that interferes with a society's ability

Figure 11.3
Stability domain diagrams comparing high and low resilience

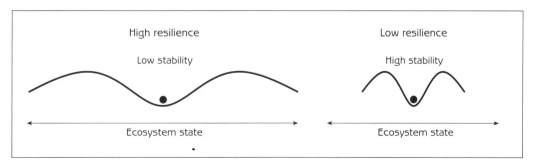

to provide the inputs. The collapse of Middle Eastern civilizations when irrigation ditches were clogged with sediment is an example (see Chapter 10).

Resilience is desirable, but it can conflict with other social objectives that are equally beneficial. Efficiency, for example, has become crucial for modern commercial enterprises because low operating costs are essential for survival. Economic efficiency and resilience are often in conflict because the redundancy that reinforces resilience requires extra cost and effort. Economic pressures to reduce resilience are increasing as competition tightens in the global economy.

resilience

Tradeoff between stability and resilience

Stability implies constancy – things staying more or less the same. Stability is desirable if it reduces unwanted fluctuations. For example, an income is stable if there is a paycheque every month. It is unstable if a person does not receive a paycheque on a regular basis. Figure 11.3 shows how greater stability can be associated with less resilience. Ecosystems and social systems that seldom change are more easily shifted to a different stability domain when external disturbances force them to accommodate change beyond their limited capacity.

Modern technology and large inputs of fossil fuel energy have given contemporary society the ability to build a high degree of stability into most people's lives by insulating them from fluctuations in their environment. Heating and air conditioning allow us to live and work in buildings with nearly the same temperature year round. The modern system of food production and distribution stocks supermarkets with an abundance of food at all times. The weakness of the system is dependence upon large energy inputs for heating and cooling buildings or producing and transporting food. Large inputs can increase stability but reduce resilience.

A common source of conflict between stability and resilience is the loss of resilience when a system is so stable that it does not exercise its ability to withstand stress. This is well illustrated by the disaster that accompanied a sudden fuel oil shortage in north-eastern United States some years ago. Americans normally enjoy an abundance of energy to comfortably heat their homes. Many people were not prepared when the supply of fuel oil broke down at a time of unusually severe winter weather. The result was an astonishing number of deaths from cold exposure when furnaces ran out of fuel. Some elderly people who seldom went outside during severe weather did not have appropriate clothing for low temperatures. Some people lacked a social support system to deal with this kind of emergency.

Floodplains provide another example of the loss of resilience when resilience is not exercised. A large percentage of the world's human population lives on floodplains because of the fertile soil, abundant supply of water and high capacity for food production. River water spreads over a floodplain for a short period each year, depositing a thin layer of mud that keeps the soil deep, fertile and highly productive for agriculture. However, floodplains also have an important drawback – floods can damage crops, houses and other property. During most years floods are mild and do not cause much damage, but sometimes flooding can be severe.

resilience

Floodplain societies typically structure their agriculture and urban ecosystems to minimize flood damage because their social systems have coevolved with the floodplain ecosystem. They grow their crops in areas that will not be badly flooded. If they cultivate rice, they use a special variety of rice with a stem long enough to hold the rice grains above the water so that the crop is not damaged. They build their houses above the ground so that floodwater flows under their houses; they store food in safe places so that they do not run out if a flood damages their crops; and they have social institutions to help flood victims deal with the damage that occurs when a flood is unusually severe. Floods can cause some damage despite these adaptations, but the damage is seldom very serious.

It is natural for people to desire no damage at all. In recent years, hydroelectric dams constructed to generate electricity have also helped to prevent floods. Other flood control measures such as levees, which increase the heights of riverbanks, keep water from spreading out of a river and over the surrounding floodplain. Flood control has reduced flood damage in the short term, but it has also made human–ecosystem interaction less resilient. Without floods, floodplain ecosystems gradually deteriorate because new soil is no longer deposited each year to maintain soil fertility. Farmers compensate for a reduction in soil fertility by applying larger quantities of chemical fertilizers, which reduces resilience because the agricultural ecosystems become dependent upon substantial fertilizer inputs. Agricultural production could decline drastically if fertilizer prices increase in the future, a real possibility because fertilizer comes from non-renewable resources.

Flood control can reduce the resilience of social system–ecosystem interaction in another way – the loss of social institutions and technologies that protect people and property from flood damage. A society with flood control 'forgets' how to structure its agricultural and urban ecosystems to withstand floods. Crops are grown in places where a flood could damage them, new houses are built at ground level on the floodplain, and other social institutions that reduce the impact of severe floods gradually go out of use. However, sooner or later – perhaps within 20–50 years – there is a year with so much rain that the river overflows the dams or levees. Despite the flood control, there is a flood with massive damage because the social system and the agricultural and urban ecosystems are no longer structured to reduce flood damage. The interaction of people with their floodplain ecosystem has lost its resilience – the ability to withstand severe floods – because the stability provided by flood control did not subject the social system to the smaller stress of annual floods.

resilience

The conflict between stability and resilience is important for ecosystems and social systems in many other ways. The example of forest fire protection in Chapter 6 was about the conflict between stability and resilience. Forest managers increased stability by putting out every fire, but they reduced resilience because continuous protection from small fires increased the vulnerability of forests to large-scale destructive fires.

The use of chemical pesticides to control agricultural pests has increased stability but reduced resilience. Traditional and organic farmers do not use pesticides to reduce pest insects that eat the crops; instead, they rely on natural control by predatory insects that eat the pest insects. Natural control is less than perfect because predatory insects do not eliminate pest insects completely; predatory insects and pest insects coexist together in the same ecosystem. Most of the time the crop damage in traditional or organic agriculture is moderate, typically 15 per cent to 20 per cent of the crop, because predatory insects prevent pest insect populations from increasing enough to inflict serious damage. However, sometimes there is more damage.

Modern farmers seek less insect damage and greater stability by using chemical insecticides to kill as many insects as possible. Unfortunately, the insecticides kill predatory insects as well as pest insects, so the natural control of pest insects by predators is lost. This makes farmers highly dependent upon insecticides. Without natural control, pest insect populations can increase to devastating numbers when insecticides are not in use. The situation becomes worse when pest insects evolve physiological resistance to insecticides. Farmers are forced to use larger quantities of insecticides, and a positive feedback loop – a 'pesticide trap' – is set in motion with more insecticides and more resistance. While insecticides can make agricultural production more stable as long as there is no insecticide resistance, resilience is reduced because insect damage can be devastating when resistance develops in agricultural ecosystems that lack predators to provide natural control. With some crops such as cotton the spiral of increasing insecticide use can continue until the cost of insecticides is so great that farmers can no longer afford to grow the crop.

Modern medicine has a similar problem with the use of drugs to control diseases such as malaria and tuberculosis. While drugs provide obvious benefits, their large-scale use can lead to drug-resistant strains of disease organisms in exactly the same way that large-scale use of insecticides leads to resistance in insects. The stability (low level of disease) achieved by modern medicine is accompanied by a loss of resilience due to dependence on drugs. The risk of epidemics with drug-resistant strains can be particularly serious when:

resilience

- the human population has lost its immunity to the disease;
- social institutions that provided other means of preventing the disease have been abandoned because they did not seem necessary.

The most serious conflict between stability and resilience concerns food security. Although wealthy countries have an abundant and stable food supply, food storage has declined drastically during the past decade. The abundant food supply lulls wealthy societies into an unrealistic sense of security. At the same time that modern science and economic development are increasing global food production, environmental deterioration and dwindling water supplies are reducing the potential. There are also possibilities of sudden and unexpected agricultural failure due to climate shifts induced by global warming. Nations such as Japan, which imports 60 per cent of its food, are particularly vulnerable.

The significance of stability and resilience for sustainable development can be expressed in terms of complex systems cycles. Harmony with nature by doing things 'nature's way' and preventing damage to the Earth's environmental support system is important for sustainable development; but sustainable development is not merely static equilibrium with the environment. Sustainable development is more than making the world function smoothly with no difficulties. Natural fluctuations and natural disasters are an unavoidable part of life. Design for resilience is an essential part of sustainable development. The key to resilience is the ability to reorganize when things go wrong, making dissolution as brief and harmless as possible.

What should we do about the conflict between stability and resilience? Both stability and resilience are desirable. It is best to have a balance. The social system should structure its interaction with ecosystems so neither stability nor resilience is overemphasized at the expense of the other. This means using resilient strategies to achieve an acceptable level of stability.

adaptive
development

ADAPTIVE DEVELOPMENT

Adaptive development is the institutional capacity to cope with change. It can make a major contribution to ecologically sustainable development by changing some parts of the social system so that social system and ecosystem function together in a healthier manner. Adaptive development is about survival and quality of life. Adaptive development builds resilience into human–ecosystem interaction. It does not simply react to problems; it anticipates problems or detects them in early stages, taking measures to deal with them before they become serious. Adaptive development provides a way to work towards sustainable development while simultaneously strengthening the capacity to cope with serious problems that will inevitably arise if sustainable development is not achieved.

The two basic elements of adaptive development are: 1) regular assessment of what is happening in the ecosystem; and 2) taking corrective action. The key to ecological assessment is the ability to perceive what is really occuring within ecosystems. The key to corrective action is a truly functional community. Adaptive development requires the organization, commitment, effort and courage at all levels of society to identify necessary changes and make them happen. A society examines its values, perceptions, social institutions and technologies and modifies them as necessary.

What values are important for ecologically adaptive development? An example is the significance we place on material consumption for the quality of our lives. We all need food, clothing and shelter; but how much more do we need? The scale of our material consumption has a critical impact on sustainable development because of the demands that consumption places on ecosystems. When people think deeply about what is most important to them, they usually identify social and emotional needs relating to family, friends and freedom from stress. Modern society has amplified material consumption in the belief that more possessions will help to meet these basic needs, a belief reinforced by advertising that emphasizes how various products can contribute to sexual gratification, friendship, relaxation, or other emotional needs. The result is a spiral of increasing consumption, intended to satisfy our basic needs but often failing to do so.

Modern values about material possessions are connected to our perception that economic growth is essential for a good life. Political leaders tell us that economic growth is their highest priority, while 'experts' addressing us through the mass media continually reinforce our belief as a society that a high level of consumption (consumer confidence) is essential for full employment and a healthy economy. The relation of economic growth to sustainable development is a major issue of our time because continual expansion of material consumption is ecologically impossible. What kind of economic growth is sustainable? How can we maintain a healthy economy and satisfy our human needs without placing excessive demands on ecosystems? Adaptive development maintains a public dialogue on key issues such as these and holds political leaders accountable for dealing with them.

adaptive development

Adaptive development for a sustainable society is caring about others – caring about community, caring about future generations and caring about the non-human inhabitants of the Earth. It requires real democracy and social justice because decisions and actions that value the future require full community participation. When a small number of rich or politically powerful people control the use of natural resources or other ecosystem services, they often do it for their own short-term economic gain. Societies are limited in their ability to respond adaptively if a few privileged people have the power to obstruct change whenever change threatens their privilege.

Strong dynamic local communities are at the core of adaptive development. Democracy has the fullest participation, and functions best, at the local level. All human interaction with the environment is ultimately local. Consider the exploitation of forests. Although deforestation is driven by large-scale social processes such as urban and agricultural expansion, international markets for forest products and the organization of commerce by multinational corporations, the trees are actually felled by the man with the axe or the bulldozer. When local people control their own resources, no tree can be destroyed unless local people allow it to happen. The same is true for cities that grow into impersonal concrete jungles. Local citizens can passively allow investors to change their urban landscape in ways that are profitable. Or they can control the growth of their cities by allowing only development that fits their vision of a humane and liveable city – a vision that usually includes a diverse and nurturing landscape with natural areas, parks and other spaces for community activity.

Crises involving concrete and compelling local issues can stimulate communities into action that eventually enables them to control their destiny on a broader front. While details can vary enormously, the following themes are illustrative of long-range action:

adaptive development

• Reversing undesirable trends: local communities take stock of their current social or ecological condition, as well as changes during recent decades. They strengthen support systems for the elderly, neighbourhood safety, constructive recreational activities for children, or whatever is most significant in their particular situation. They examine the balance of natural, agriculture and urban ecosystems within their city and in the surrounding regional landscape. If the landscape mosaic is out of balance or changing in that direction, they undertake initiatives to restore the balance.

• Anticipating disaster: communities prepare for earthquakes, floods, drought, food security or whatever else is appropriate at their location. Part of the preparation is for emergency response, but part consists of measures taken well in advance to reduce the severity of a disaster or the likelihood that it will even occur. For example, farmers can develop drought-resistant methods of cultivation in regions where droughts may increase in frequency due to global warming. Communities can reinforce local self-sufficiency in food production by forming consumer cooperatives in order to purchase local agricultural produce, establishing markets for local farmers in the process.

It is not necessary for community organization to focus on the environment in order to contribute to ecologically sustainable development. Community organization for any purpose will create the capacity to identify environmental concerns and act upon them. The first and crucial step is forming a vision of the kind of life that the community desires now and in the future – a vision that embraces the social and ecological environment. This kind of community vision is sensitive to the landscape. It is sensitive to possible problems in the future. Are food security or future water supply a concern? The vision addresses issues of dependence versus autonomy vis-à-vis the surrounding world. In what ways would greater or less self-sufficiency benefit the community? What are the significant needs that only the local community can deal with?

Acting on a community vision requires experimentation. The ability to clearly perceive and articulate alternative choices, and the creativity and imagination to form new possibilities, are essential. Adaptive development means experimenting with possibilities in ways that allow them to be expanded if successful or discarded if not. In today's world of global communications, adaptive development is networking to help others while learning from their experiences. It is stimulating neighbouring communities, as well as communities in distant lands, to become more sustainable and helping them to do so.

adaptive development

How can this happen? Much of the answer lies with environmental and community education. Modern education compels us to spend thousands of hours acquiring skills for professional success, but our ecological and community skills are limited. Ecological and community education is learning to form community visions and to think clearly about policy alternatives. It is the ability to think strategically about local ecosystems in terms of the whole system and connections among its parts – including connections between social systems and ecosystems.

Is adaptive development a Utopian dream? In fact, adaptive development is not new. Most adaptive development comprises common sense that has guided functional and sustainable communities for thousands of years. Adaptive development is not exclusively about the environment. It touches every way in which a society makes itself truly viable.

Of course, local community action has its costs in time, attention and the effort to deal with interpersonal relations. Many people feel that they lack the time or prefer to avoid the hassle, but once they enjoy the social rewards of doing useful things with neighbours, they usually find it more worthwhile. Community gardening is one way to promote community solidarity while incorporating an ecological perspective. Most people enjoy gardening with family and neighbours. They value the fresh food that a garden provides, and gardening puts them in touch with ecosytems in numerous ways. Organic gardening has particular potential to increase ecological awareness.

Can adaptive development for an ecologically sustainable society really happen? There are reasons for qualified optimism. Corporations are adapting to the environmental awareness of their customers by developing environmentally friendly products. The private sector is responding to environmental problems with new environmental technologies. Perhaps even more significant, an increasing number of corporations have added sustainable development as an institutional goal. They realize that future business success will depend upon the ecological health of the planet.

An example of the private sector's capacity for adaptation in the realm of technology is its collaboration with government to deal with depletion of the ozone layer. The 'ozone story' began with the discovery that chlorofluorocarbons (CFCs), used primarily for refrigeration, were breaking down the ozone layer, which protects the planet from ultraviolet radiation. Within a few years there were international agreements to replace CFCs with environmentally friendly chemicals, and industry followed through to implement the agreements. Similar stories appear to be unfolding in the energy industry as it responds to the Earth's limited supply of petroleum and natural gas. The use of hydrogen for energy storage and transport is in rapid development, and alternative energy technologies such as solar cells and windmills are growing rapidly. Such developments are positive but the ozone layer is not yet restored to health, and dependence on petroleum and gas is far from resolution. Alarmingly, some major industries continue to obstruct new environmental products and technologies that conflict with their existing markets.

adaptive development

There is less basis for optimism about adaptation that conflicts with the basic foundations of modern society. Global warming is an example. Reductions in greenhouse gas emissions, particularly carbon dioxide, strike at the heart of modern society's dependence on massive quantities of fossil fuel energy. In 1997 the Kyoto Protocol set an international goal to reduce the carbon dioxide emissions of industrialized nations by 5 per cent during the subsequent ten years. Some nations promoted this goal with enthusiasm while others accepted it with reluctance. Developing countries, including several large industrializing nations responsible for massive carbon dioxide emissions, refused to pledge any restriction on their emissions. Although the Kyoto Protocol is significant as a first step toward international cooperation on global warming, the actions specified by the Kyoto Protocol are far too modest to be of practical significance. Computer simulation studies have indicated that if every nation follows the Kyoto Protocol completely, greenhouse gases will continue to accumulate in the atmosphere, and the increase in average global temperature during the next fifty years will be reduced by less than 0.1°C compared to the increase expected with no Kyoto Protocol – almost no difference. The computer studies indicate that full compliance with the Kyoto Protocol would reduce the number of people facing an added risk of coastal flooding from rising seas during the next fifty years by only a few per cent. There would be virtually no impact on regional shifts in climate. Unfortunately, neither industrialized nations nor industrializing nations are willing to consider seriously the *major reduction* in carbon dioxide emissions that would be necessary for a genuine impact on global warming.

What can governments do for adaptive development? Of course they should face up to realities such as global warming and do their best to deal with environmental problems at regional, national and international levels. Equally important, governments should educate their citizens about environmental issues and provide educational and material assistance to strengthen the capacity of local communities to follow a path of adaptive development. Local communities should insist that governments assist them to develop this capacity. Governments can encourage and assist local communities to set up environmental districts similar in organization to the local school districts in many countries.

adaptive development

Non-governmental organizations (NGOs) have played a crucial role in developing a worldwide dialogue on environmental issues. The United Nations Conference on Environment and Development (known as the Earth Summit) in 1992 brought together governments, NGOs, industry and others. Though the process has not been smooth, such forums reinforce the interconnectedness of global and local issues and the need for collaboration at all levels.

NGOs can serve as catalysts for adaptive development. While recognizing that non-governmental organizations vary immensely in their organization and mission, one brief example will illustrate the possibilities. Nature conservation organizations have discovered that their efforts to protect natural ecosystems as reserves are frequently undermined by human activities in the surrounding area – including activities that are essential to people's livelihoods. In order to adapt to this, some conservation organizations are setting up businesses to learn and demonstrate how to pursue economic activities in ways that protect natural ecosystems. For example, they have embarked on joint ventures with timber companies to manage forests in ways that are not only sustainable for wood production but also maintain natural forest ecosystems as part of the landscape mosaic. They have developed cooperatives with coral reef fishermen to ensure a sustainable supply of fish while maintaining the unique biological diversity of the reefs. Some have formed cooperatives with local farmers to make farming compatible with natural ecosystems in the same watershed. Where silt from soil erosion threatens estuaries or other natural ecosystems, conservationist–farmer joint venture companies are providing the technical support

Box 11.1
Examples of
environments
and their
characteristics

adaptive
development

Social environment

Characteristics of social environments include:

*   education (for example, memorizing versus learning to think);
*   watching television and playing video games versus playing with friends outdoors;
*   safe neighbourhoods versus fear of street crime;
*   people working near home versus commuting long distances to work;
*   women having equal/unequal opportunities for professional careers.

Urban environment

Characteristics of urban environments include:

*   traffic;
*   air quality;
*   housing (for example, high-rise apartments versus single-family dwellings);
*   parks and natural areas in cities;
*   places for community activities.

Rural environment

Characteristics of rural environments include:

*   recreational opportunities;
*   forests as sources of clean water, timber, biological diversity, recreation, etc;
*   food supply and food security.

International environment

Characteristics of international environments include:

*   sources of food and natural resources;
*   travel and recreational opportunities;
*   impacts of the global pop culture;
*   impacts of the global economy.

and marketing to enable farmers to secure a satisfactory income with low-erosion crops and cultivation practices.

What can individuals do? They can bring a human ecology perspective and commitment to sustainable development to the workplace, and they can organize details of their daily lives to be in greater harmony with the environment. Equally essential, individuals can work for the viability of their local community – helping to form a community vision; assessing the ecological status of their region and changes in the local landscape; contributing to community support systems; and, in general, building long-term ecological health and resilience into the community and its landscape. Individuals can teach their neighbours about sustainable development and awaken their desire to participate in setting an ecologically sustainable course for their future. As the eminent anthropologist Margaret Mead once said, 'Never doubt that a small group of thoughtful, committed citizens can change the world; indeed, it's the only thing that ever does.'

THINGS TO THINK ABOUT

1. In what way do you build resilience in your personal life? What are the ways in which your society achieves resilience? What are the ways in which the resilience of your local community, your nation or the world is weak? What can be done to improve resilience in those instances?
2. Think of examples of the conflict between stability and resilience in your personal life and in the society in which you live. Are stability and resilience in balance? It not, what can be done to achieve a better balance?
3. Agreement about good rules for using a common property resource is essential for sustainable use of the resource. Think of concrete examples of social institutions that prevent tragedy of the commons from occurring, using information from newspaper or magazine articles or your own personal knowledge. Then think about your society's social institutions for using resources such as petroleum, minerals, water and the land. Are they effective for sustainable use? Are there ways in which you think they could be improved upon from this perspective?
4. For what kinds of public concerns is your local community (or city) organized? Are some of these concerns environmental? Are there environmental concerns that are not addressed, even though you think they should be? How do you think the community can be educated so that individuals establish appropriate priorities for their interactions with ecosystems?
5. What are the roles of city, state (prefectural, provincial) and national government in shaping human–ecosystem interaction in your country? What are the roles of corporations? What can citizens do to stimulate governments and corporations to follow more ecologically sustainable policies?
6. Strategic planning is a way to initiate constructive action in support of ecologically sustainable development in communities. Brainstorm with some friends to discover your opinions regarding the following essential steps for strategic planning:
   * *An ideal vision of your community 20 years from today:* what kind of life do you want for your children and grandchildren? What kind of environment do you want for your children and grandchildren so that they will have a good quality of life? A vision can include things that you want to keep the same and things that you want to

things to
think about

improve upon. Environment can have a broad meaning, including the social and urban environment as well as natural and agricultural ecosystems (see Box 11.1).

- *Obstacles to realizing the vision:* what environmental problems could prevent the kind of life that you have outlined in your vision? You can include problems that exist today and need improvement (such as air quality in cities). What environmental issues are not problematic today, but could be in the future? For example, today's destruction of forests or farmland by urban expansion may not yet have serious consequences in some areas but could if exploitation continues. What about current agricultural practices, environmental degradation and food security?
- *Actions to overcome the obstacles:* decide what your community can do about the environmental problems that you identified in 'obstacles to realizing the vision'. What can individuals do? What are the institutional obstacles to successful action and how can they be overcome? Can you act yourselves or do you need the cooperation of local or national governments, the private sector, or non-governmental organizations?

EXAMPLES OF ECOLOGICALLY SUSTAINABLE DEVELOPMENT

This chapter presents two case studies that illustrate many of the concepts in this book. The first is about eco-technology, and the second is about a regional environmental programme. I personally participated in both.

Today, so many contemporary trends seem to be away from ecologically sustainable development. How can we foster sustainable development in the face of these trends? These case studies start by showing how changes in the human social system changed human–ecosystem interaction in ways that in turn have changed the ecosystem with detrimental consequences for people. Each case study then demonstrates how people can translate ecological ideas into concrete actions to move human–ecosystem interaction in a healthier and more sustainable direction.

These examples show the rewards of paying attention to both ecological and social considerations in a balanced manner when dealing with environmental problems. Effective and enduring solutions to environmental problems cannot be expected when solutions focus only on political and economic considerations to the exclusion of ecological realities, or when they focus solely on ecological considerations to the exclusion of social realities. The case studies show how real people are responsible for innovative ideas and the entire process of transforming ideas to reality. Sustainable development is not something that others will do for us. It is something that together we must all do for ourselves.

DENGUE HEMORRHAGIC FEVER, MOSQUITOES AND COPEPODS: AN EXAMPLE OF ECO-TECHNOLOGY FOR SUSTAINABLE DEVELOPMENT

Dengue hemorrhagic fever is an 'emergent' disease known only since 1950. This case study shows how modernization can create new public health problems and how local community action with an ecological approach can contribute to sustainable solutions.

eco-technology

The disease and the mosquito

Dengue is a flavivirus related to yellow fever. It may have originated in non-human primates, which still provide a natural reservoir in Africa and Asia. Non-human primates do not show symptoms, but humans can become seriously ill. First-time dengue infections in children are usually mild and often unnoticed, but first-time infections in adults may be severe. Fatalities are rare, but high fever, chills, headache, vomiting, severe prostration, muscle and bone aches and severe weakness for more than a month after the fever subsides make dengue fever an illness that many adults remember as the worst sickness they ever experienced.

Dengue hemorrhagic fever is a life-threatening form of dengue. It is not caused by a separate viral strain; instead, it comes from the fact that the dengue virus has four distinct strains. Infection with one strain confers lifelong immunity to that strain but also creates antibodies that enhance infection with the other three strains. Dengue hemorrhagic fever typically occurs when infection with one strain is followed a year or more later by infection with another strain. About 3 per cent of second infections produce dengue hemorrhagic fever, and about 40 per cent of dengue hemorrhagic fever cases develop a shock syndrome that can be fatal. The most damaging symptom is fluid leakage from capillaries into tissues and body cavities, sometimes accompanied by severe gastrointestinal bleeding (hence the name hemorrhagic). There is no medicine to counter the virus, but the loss of fluids can be treated by getting water and electrolytes into the vascular system, administered orally in mild cases and intravenously in severe cases. Most dengue hemorrhagic fever victims are under 15 years old. If untreated, about 5 per cent of cases are fatal, but proper treatment can reduce fatalities to less than 1 per cent.

The mosquito *Aedes aegypti* is the principal **vector** of both dengue and yellow fever. Originally a tree-hole-breeding mosquito in Africa, it long ago acquired an urban life style by breeding in similar situations around human habitations. *Aedes aegypti* now breeds in man-made containers such as water storage tanks, wells, clogged rain gutters and discarded objects such as tyres, tin cans and jars that collect rainwater. The mosquito lays her eggs on the side of a container a few millimetres above the water level. The eggs can sit for months without hatching if they remain dry, but they hatch within minutes if covered with water. The fact that this normally happens only when more water is added to a container increases the probability that a container will have enough water for the larvae to complete their development before the container dries out.

eco-technology

While male mosquitoes feed only on plant juices, females suck blood from animals to get the nutrients they need to develop their eggs. When a female takes blood from a person infected with dengue, the virus multiplies in her body, and 7 to 15 days later (depending upon temperature) she has enough of the virus to infect people. Transmission of the virus is much higher in tropical climates, where rapid viral multiplication at higher temperatures makes it more likely for an infected mosquito to survive long enough to become infectious.

History of dengue

Starting in the 16th century with the expansion of European colonialism and trade, *Aedes aegypti* spread around the world by hitching rides in water storage containers on boats. Dengue and *Aedes aegypti* existed in Asia for centuries without serious consequences because the distribution of *Aedes aegypti* was limited by *Aedes albopictus*, an indigenous Asian mosquito that is physiologically capable of transmitting dengue but not associated with significant dengue transmission in practice. Asian towns and cities were well endowed with trees and shrubs, and *Aedes albopictus* competitively excluded *Aedes aegypti* wherever there was vegetation.

The situation in the Americas was quite different. *Aedes aegypti* thrived in cities and towns because no mosquito like *Aedes albopictus* restricted its distribution. We know *Aedes aegypti* was common in the Americas because of numerous yellow fever epidemics following the introduction of yellow fever from Africa by the slave trade in the 16th century. The historical record for dengue is not clear because its symptoms do not distinguish it from other diseases, but dengue was probably common throughout much of the Americas for centuries. Philadelphia had a dengue fever epidemic in 1780. Dengue fever was common in towns and cities on the Gulf and Atlantic coasts of the United States until the 1930s.

Dengue probably spread everywhere with *Aedes aegypti*, but it did not attract much attention, even where the infection rate was high, because most people were infected as children with mild symptoms. Devastating epidemics made yellow fever a very different matter. *Aedes aegypti* became an object of international attention when Walter Reed demonstrated in 1900 that this mosquito was responsible for yellow fever transmission. Campaigns were initiated in the Americas to get rid of *Aedes aegypti* by eliminating the places where it bred around people's houses. During the 1930s the Rockefeller Foundation mobilized a virtual army of house-to-house government inspectors in Brazil to find and eliminate every place *Aedes aegypti* might breed. Inspectors had legal authority to enter premises, destroy containers, apply oil or paris green (an arsenic mosquito larvicide) and impose fines. It was possible to consolidate the eradication of *Aedes aegypti* neighbourhood by neighbourhood, without reinvasion, because adult *Aedes aegypti* usually travels less than 100 metres in a lifetime. The campaign was so effective that *Aedes aegypti* was eradicated from large areas of Brazil by the early 1940s.

Although there were outbreaks resembling dengue hemorrhagic fever in Queensland, Australia, in 1897 and in Greece in 1928, dengue hemorrhagic fever was not a recognized disease until 1956 because it was unusual to have more than one strain in the same region. Everything changed with World War II, when large numbers of people and the four dengue strains were moved around the Asian tropics. There were numerous dengue fever epidemics during the war as the virus was introduced to new areas where people lacked immunity. Cases with dengue fever symptoms appeared in Thailand in 1950. The first recognized dengue hemorrhagic fever epidemic was in the Philippines in 1956, followed by epidemics in Thailand and other parts of South-East Asia within a few years. Uncontrolled growth of developing world cities during the following decades greatly expanded *Aedes aegypti*'s breeding habitat. Urban landscapes provided a bounty of water storage tanks and discarded containers collecting rainwater in neighbourhoods lacking basic services such as piped water and trash collection. The decline of vegetation in urban landscapes allowed *Aedes aegypti* to expand through Asian cities without competition from mosquitoes such as *Aedes albopictus*.

eco-technology

The spread of dengue hemorrhagic fever was probably delayed by the appearance of DDT in 1943. DDT was like a miracle. It was harmless to vertebrates at concentrations used to kill insects, and it was effective for months after application. In 1955 the World Health Organization began a global campaign to spray every house in malarial areas with DDT. Malaria virtually disappeared from many areas by the mid 1960s, and at the same time *Aedes aegypti* disappeared from most of Latin America and some parts of Asia such as Taiwan.

Failure of the DDT strategy

The incredible success of DDT was short-lived because mosquitoes evolved resistance that spread quickly around the world. Developing world governments could not afford to continue intensive spraying, particularly when alternatives to DDT such as malathion cost more than ten times as much. Malaria started to return in force by the late 1960s, and by the mid 1970s *Aedes aegypti* returned to most areas from which it had previously been eradicated. Dengue did not return to the United States because window screening and air conditioning led to an indoor life style that reduced contact between people and mosquitoes. However, the four dengue strains and dengue hemorrhagic fever spread rapidly through tropical Asia, settling into a permanent pattern of recurring local dengue fever outbreaks as the four strains continued to circulate. Dengue hemorrhagic fever entered the Americas in 1981 with an epidemic in Cuba that hospitalized 116,000 people in three months. Dengue quickly spread through much of Latin America, sometimes punctuated by dengue fever epidemics of hundreds of thousands of people, but dengue hemorrhagic fever was generally sporadic because most areas had only one strain. Although dengue was common in many parts of sub-Saharan Africa, it was not a major health problem because Africans are generally resistant to severe dengue infection.

The social and political situation for dealing with *Aedes aegypti* had changed immensely since the campaigns against yellow fever earlier in the century. A few wealthier countries such as Taiwan continued to spray houses with newer insecticides, and a few countries such as Cuba and Singapore initiated comprehensive house inspections and fines to get rid of *Aedes aegypti* breeding around people's homes. However, most countries lacked the political will and the financial and organizational resources to implement such programmes. Chemical **larvicides** that kill all the mosquito larvae, and later a microbial larvicide (*Bacillus thuringiensis*), were available to treat water storage containers. However, people were reluctant to put pesticides in their water.

eco-technology

Even if people are willing, larvicides must be applied on a weekly basis to be effective. The cost of purchasing larvicides and managing large-scale use proved beyond the capacity of every government that tried to implement it. Some governments tried to organize voluntary community participation to eliminate *Aedes aegypti* breeding habitats – advising housewives, for example, to clean their water storage containers weekly to interrupt development of the larvae – but without much success.

There is no vaccine or medicine for dengue; the only way to prevent the disease is to get rid of the mosquitoes. Today the main action against the mosquitoes is by individual families who purchase insecticide spray cans and mosquito coils to keep mosquitoes from bothering them at night. The effect on *Aedes aegypti* is limited, because this mosquito bites during the day and spends most of its time resting in places such as clothes closets beyond the reach of casual spraying. Vaccine development has been underway for years; but progress has been slow, and a vaccine could be risky because it might enhance susceptibility to dengue hemorrhagic fever, as happens after natural dengue infections. It is now typical in most places for governments to do little about *Aedes aegypti* until there is a dengue epidemic or dengue hemorrhagic fever appears. Then trucks drive up and down streets spraying malathion, with little impact in many instances because the epidemic is already well underway and female *Aedes aegypti* are inside houses where not much insecticide can reach them. Even if spraying manages to reduce the mosquito population, it must be repeated frequently to sustain the impact. *Aedes aegypti* can rebound to large numbers within a few days.

There has been no noticeable decrease in dengue fever or dengue hemorrhagic fever cases during the past 20 years. Worldwide, about 50 to 100 million people are infected with dengue each year. There are several million severe dengue fever cases and about 500,000 dengue hemorrhagic fever cases annually. Fatalities have remained high in some countries, but other countries have reduced fatalities dramatically by providing extensive medical treatment. Several hundred thousand people are hospitalized with dengue hemorrhagic fever in Vietnam and Thailand every year, but the fatality rate is less than 0.3 per cent. Nonetheless, the economic costs are high. Patients require one to three weeks of hospitalization, and parents lose work time while caring for sick children in hospitals. Global warming could eventually extend the geographic range of dengue as higher temperatures, and consequently shorter viral incubation times in mosquitoes, stimulate transmission.

eco-
technology

Copepods enter the scene

Although **biological control** with predators of *Aedes aegypti*
larvae offers the possibility of functioning without the frequently
repeated applications necessary for pesticides, it did not receive
serious consideration when the DDT strategy collapsed. Fish were
widely used against malarial mosquito larvae prior to the DDT era,
but the use of fish for *Aedes aegypti* control was limited because
fish were expensive and did not survive for long in most
containers. Besides, many people did not want fish in their water
storage containers, particularly if they used the water for drinking.
Many aquatic animals such as planaria, dragonfly nymphs and
aquatic bugs were known to prey on mosquito larvae, but none
had ever proved effective enough or practical enough to go into
operational use. Mosquito-control professionals and public health
officials, who relied heavily on chemical pesticides throughout
their careers, considered biological control a pipe dream.
Opportunities for profit were too remote to stimulate research and
development by the private sector.

eco-
technology

   This was the situation about 20 years ago, when scientists in
Tahiti, Colombia and Hawaii independently discovered that
virtually no *Aedes* larvae survived in water-filled containers if the
copepod *Mesocyclops aspericornis* was present. Copepods are tiny
crustaceans that are ecologically very different from other aquatic
invertebrates that prey on mosquito larvae. If mosquito larvae are
numerous, the copepods eat only a small part of each larva, giving
each copepod the capacity to kill 30 to 40 larvae per day, far more
than they actually eat. Even more important is their large
numbers. Copepods eat small animals up to twice their own size,
but they also eat phytoplankton, protozoa and rotifers – a diet that
provides enough food to make copepods the most abundant
predator in most freshwater habitats. The total capacity of a
copepod population to kill mosquito larvae is enormous. Most
species of copepods are too small (0.3–1.2 millimetres in body
length) to prey on even the smallest mosquito larvae, but
Mesocyclops aspericornis and other large species of copepods (1.2
millimetres or more in body length) attack and consume newly
hatched mosquito larvae without hesitation. About 10 per cent of
areas with water where mosquitoes might breed have natural
populations of *Mesocyclops* or other large copepods, which
drastically reduce the survival of mosquito larvae.

   The same thing that happens in nature can be achieved by
introducing appropriate copepod species to sites that do not
already have them. This principle applies not only to containers
where *Aedes aegypti* is breeding but also to aquatic habitats where

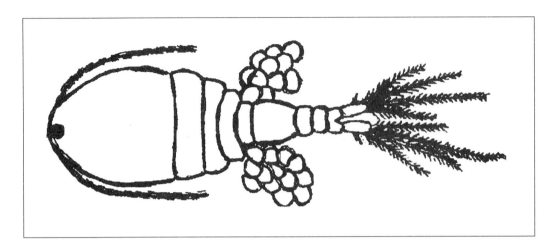

Figure 12.1
Mesocyclops
(actual length
approximately
1.5 millimetres)
Note: Copepods do
not have eyes; the
eyespot in the middle
of the forehead
detects light but does
not form an image.
Copepods move by
means of rapid oar-
like movements of
their large antennules
(the long structures
extending to each side
of the body from the
front). The antennules
contain mechanical
sensory organs that
detect vibrations in
the water so that
copepods know when
small animals such as
mosquito larvae are
close enough to be
captured as food.
Female copepods
carry egg sacs on
both sides of their
body for about three
days until young
copepods emerge
from the eggs.

Anopheles malarial mosquitoes breed. Malarial mosquito larvae are generally scarce in habitats that contain natural populations of large *Mesocyclops* species; *Anopheles* larvae disappeared when *Mesocyclops* were introduced to rice fields and small marsh areas in Louisiana. Unfortunately, the potential of *Mesocyclops* for malaria control has not been developed further because malaria control agencies have abandoned their efforts to control mosquitoes. Contemporary malaria control is based almost entirely on anti-malarial drugs, whose long-term effectiveness is doubtful due to drug resistance already widespread among malarial parasites.

The development of copepods for dengue control has been much more successful because copepods are effective and easy to use in the simple container habitats where *Aedes aegypti* breeds. It is unusual for copepods to get into man-made containers on their own; but they thrive in many kinds of containers when introduced, and they do so independently of the supply of mosquito larvae. Copepod populations range from hundreds in a rainwater-filled tyre to thousands in a water storage tank. The largest species usually kill more than 99 per cent of the *Aedes aegypti* larvae, and they usually stay in a container for as long as there is water. Even without water, they can survive as long as there is moisture.

The simple life cycle of copepods and their ability to thrive on a diet of protozoa make mass production easy and inexpensive. The production system uses bacteria on decomposing wheat seed as food for a small protozoan (*Chilomonas*) that provides food for young copepods and a larger protozoan (*Paramecium caudatum*) that provides food for the larger stages. The system is simple, inexpensive and highly resilient, functioning in open containers of any size or shape. One hundred adult female *Mesocyclops* produce about 25,000 new adult females within a month. Females are inseminated during adolescence and require no further contact with males to produce 50 to 100 eggs weekly during their several-month life span.

Once it was realized how effective copepods are, research was initiated in Australia, South-East Asia and the Americas to identify the best copepod species for mosquito control and how to utilize them. Suitable species were always available locally because copepods large enough to kill mosquito larvae occur naturally virtually everywhere that *Aedes aegypti* is a problem. *Mesocyclops aspericornis* is the most effective species in Polynesia, Australia and parts of Asia. *Mesocyclops longisetus*, the world's largest species of *Mesocyclops*, proved most effective in the Americas.

eco-
'technology

In order for a copepod to be effective at controlling *Aedes aegypti*, it must do more than kill mosquito larvae. It must also be good at surviving in containers. *Mesocyclops aspericornis* and *Mesocyclops longisetus* are good at surviving in sun-exposed containers in the tropics because they tolerate water temperatures up to 43° Celsius. Moreover, because they cling to the bottom and sides of a container, they survive in water storage containers from which people frequently scoop water. Copepods that swim in the water column quickly disappear from a water storage container. *Mesocyclops aspericornis* and *Mesocyclops longisetus* are effective in wells, cisterns, cement tanks, 200-litre drums, clay jars, flower vases and even bromeliads if they have water on a continuous basis. People do not object to copepods in their water storage containers because these tiny animals are barely noticeable. Besides, it is not unusual for other small aquatic animals to live in the water.

Copepods do not survive in small rainwater-filled containers or discarded tyres that dry out frequently, though they do well in tyres that are continuously filled with water during the rainy season. They do not survive in small cement tanks with rapid water turnover, particularly if the water is frequently run down the drain, and they are killed when bleach is left in a tank after cleaning or slopped into a tank while washing clothes next to the tank. A significant difficulty is the loss of copepods from water storage containers when they are cleaned. This is easily overcome by saving a small quantity of water from the container to restock it with copepods after cleaning. In small-scale pilot projects in Honduras and Brazil, housewives quickly learned to monitor their containers, maintaining *Mesocyclops* at their homes with pride. The key to success was personal attention from community organizers. Unfortunately, Latin American public health bureaucracies seem to lack the capacity for neighbourhood organization to expand the use of *Mesocyclops* on a larger scale.

Success in Vietnam

Dengue hemorrhagic fever is a serious concern in Vietnam because it has hospitalized nearly two million Vietnamese and killed more than 13,000 children since appearing there 40 years ago. The first demonstration of how effective *Mesocyclops* can be on a community scale began in 1993, when scientists at Vietnam's National Institute of Hygiene and Epidemiology introduced local species of *Mesocyclops* into all of the water storage containers in Phanboi, a village of 400 houses in northern Vietnam. Like most of rural Vietnam, the two main sources of *Aedes aegypti* in Phanboi were large cement tanks (several-thousand litre capacity), which nearly every house uses for long-term storage of rainwater from the roof, and clay jars (20- to 200-litre capacity) used to store water for immediate use. *Mesocyclops* thrived in the large cement tanks, which are seldom drained or cleaned. They did nearly as well in large clay jars but could not survive for long in small clay jars because the water was frequently poured out. Introduction of *Mesocyclops* to wells provided a reservoir that continually restocked clay jars used to store well water.

eco-technology

The *Aedes aegypti* population in Phanboi declined by about 95 per cent during the year after *Mesocyclops* introduction. However, *Aedes aegypti* was still breeding in small discarded containers such as jars, bottles and cans that collected rainwater but could not be treated with *Mesocyclops*. Villagers were encouraged to participate more actively, and motivation was high due to a prior history of dengue hemorrhagic fever outbreaks in the village. The socialist political system provided a basis for rapid, comprehensive and continuous community mobilization. The village women's union educated villagers about the use of *Mesocyclops* and organized villagers to stock any containers without *Mesocyclops* by pouring in a small quantity of water from containers that already had them. An existing recycling programme for discarded containers was reorganized to ensure they did not collect rainwater while waiting for pickup. *Aedes aegypti* disappeared within a few months, and no *Aedes aegypti* mosquitoes or their larvae have been sighted in the village during the subsequent seven years. The disappearance of *Aedes aegypti* was significant because it was the first time in more than 20 years that even a local eradication of any kind of mosquito had been documented anywhere in the world, and it was accomplished without pesticides.

Mesocyclops was then introduced to other villages in northern Vietnam, and *Aedes aegypti* disappeared from them as well. It is noteworthy that *Aedes aegypti* disappeared without having *Mesocyclops* in every container. Success was probably due to the 'egg-trap effect'. Egg-laying mosquitoes do not discriminate against containers with *Mesocyclops*, so they waste their eggs on containers with *Mesocyclops* instead of putting them in containers with better prospects for larval survival. Computer simulation studies indicate that a mosquito population will collapse if Mesocyclops is in more than 90 per cent of the containers. In contrast, getting rid of 90 per cent of the containers only reduces mosquito populations in the model by 90 per cent.

The successful demonstration at Phanboi was essential for mobilizing official government support and foreign financial assistance to distribute *Mesocyclops* to more communities in Vietnam. Television publicity and school education programmes are making *Mesocyclops* a household word. A government inquiry telephone line refers interested communities to health workers who can provide Mesocyclops and explain their use. A simple mass-production system at Vietnam's National Institute of Hygiene and Epidemiology uses 150-litre plastic waste pails to produce several hundred thousand *Mesocyclops* per month at very low cost.

eco-technology

The programme follows the Phanboi model. Central staff members train local health workers, who in turn use videotape documentaries to introduce *Mesocyclops* to the community. The health workers train local teachers to organize students for regular collection of discarded containers. From the village women's union, health workers recruit volunteer 'collaborators' with demonstrated reliability in ongoing house-to-house family planning and immunization programmes. Each collaborator is responsible for 50 to 100 houses and starts by introducing about 50 *Mesocyclops* into a tank at one of the houses. As soon as the copepods multiply to large numbers, the collaborator carries a bucket of tank water containing *Mesocyclops* around to all the other houses, pouring a glass of the water into every container. Collaborators explain the use of *Mesocyclops* to every family and return at least once a month to inspect the containers. The programme has trained about 900 health workers and collaborators, and *Mesocyclops* has been distributed to more than 30,000 households in northern and central Vietnam.

Most communities in the programme have repeated the scenario at Phanboi. *Aedes aegypti* disappears about a year after *Mesocyclops* introduction. The few exceptions have been urban communities, where *Aedes aegypti* has declined but not disappeared; the reason is incomplete coverage of the houses by local collaborators. It is sometimes necessary to recruit collaborators of unknown reliability in urban areas that lack ongoing house-to-house health programmes. While most new collaborators do a good job, some do not, and their task can be complicated by lower social cohesion in cities. With 12 million Vietnamese households in dengue areas, the potential number to be served is enormous. The bottleneck for national distribution of *Mesocyclops* is training health workers and local collaborators. Some provinces are setting up their own *Mesocyclops* production and training centres. The programme will face its greatest challenge as it extends to southern Vietnam, whose tropical climate is ideal for *Aedes aegypti* and dengue transmission throughout the year.

eco-technology

Transporting large numbers of *Mesocyclops* from production facilities to villages can be a problem because copepods quickly exhaust their food supply when crowded in a small quantity of water. Then they eat each other. An easy solution comes from the fact that *Mesocyclops* can survive for months suspended on damp foam rubber, where they cannot move to eat each other. Foam rubber cubes are stacked in small plastic containers for mailing to public health offices throughout Vietnam. The copepods are introduced to a water storage container by dropping a foam rubber cube with 50 copepods into the container.

Vietnam reported 234,000 dengue hemorrhagic fever cases in 1998, responsible for more deaths than any other infectious disease. In 1999 the government initiated a high-priority national dengue programme with *Mesocyclops* in a leading role, not only for dengue prevention but also for dealing with dengue outbreaks in areas where *Mesocyclops* is not yet in use. The government provides kits to local health workers for rapid blood analysis of suspected dengue cases so that an immediate emergency response can go into action wherever dengue is confirmed. As the supply increases, *Mesocyclops* will be routinely distributed to houses in outbreak areas.

Prospects for Mesocyclops *in other countries*

Can other countries use *Mesocyclops* as successfully as Vietnam? The prospects are particularly promising in South-East Asia, where dengue hemorrhagic fever is a major health problem, public concern is high and most *Aedes aegypti* breeding habitats are similar to the water storage containers that have proved ideal for *Mesocyclops* in Vietnam. Public motivation is not as strong outside of South-East Asia, and some of the breeding habitats are not as ideal for *Mesocyclops*. While dengue control in other areas will often require substantially more than *Mesocyclops* and container recycling, *Mesocyclops* can eliminate *Aedes aegypti* production from at least some kinds of containers almost everywhere that dengue is a problem.

The mechanics of production and distribution are not an obstacle to extending *Mesocyclops* to other countries. Production is inexpensive, and shipment to local distributors is easy. While production and distribution in Vietnam is by national, provincial and local government, distribution in other countries could use any combination of governmental department, non-governmental organization and the private sector that works under local conditions. The key to success is community organization. It is straightforward enough to put copepods in containers and restock the containers whenever copepods are lost, but it is essential to make sure that everyone does it. Success can proceed neighbourhood by neighbourhood. 100 houses that work together can free themselves of *Aedes aegypti* even if houses in the surrounding area do nothing.

eco-technology

The most promising strategy is to distribute *Mesocyclops* where local networks provide the greatest prospects for success. Vietnam has the advantage that most of its dengue is in rural areas where community organization is strongest and house-to-house health programmes are already functioning well. Fortunately, thousands of communities in other countries also have house-to-house networks of one sort or another for primary health care, family planning, paramedical malaria treatment, agricultural extension, religious charity and small business support. These same networks could serve as vehicles for distributing *Mesocyclops* and ensuring their proper use on a community scale. Even private marketing networks, which so effectively distribute insecticide spray cans and mosquito coils, could play a role if rewards based on community use are built into the incentive system. With each success, the demonstration effect should stimulate more communities to organize so that they can use *Mesocyclops* successfully.

Conclusions

What does the dengue hemorrhagic fever case study tell us? Firstly, it shows how human activities create environmental conditions that determine whether a disease will flourish or disappear. International transportation created dengue hemorrhagic fever by moving the four dengue strains around the world. Dengue disappears when people eliminate the opportunities for *Aedes aegypti* to breed in water-filled containers around their homes.

Secondly, it demonstrates how local mosquito eradication is possible with ecological management. An ecological disease-control strategy that integrates a variety of control methods is more effective than a strategy based exclusively on pesticides. We can expect ecological methods to be sustainable. It is unlikely that mosquito larvae will evolve resistance to *Mesocyclops*.

Thirdly, it demonstrates the level of effort necessary for success. The effort that prevails nearly everywhere in the world today does not meet that standard. Nor does it meet the standard of the yellow fever campaign that eradicated *Aedes aegypti* from much of Brazil 60 years ago, a campaign that owed its success to its intensity and its meticulous organization and management.

Finally, and most importantly, it highlights the central role of local community. Dengue hemorrhagic fever will be eliminated only through an intense and well-organized effort at the local level. The general lack of progress with dengue during the past 30 years is not unique. Social support systems in local communities have declined throughout the world as personal and public priorities have shifted in other directions. Numerous dimensions of human welfare that depend upon strong local communities have declined correspondingly. While responsibility for a strong and effective local community must reside primarily with local citizens, encouragement and assistance from national governments can be decisive. Ecologically sustainable development, including sustainable control of mosquito-transmitted diseases, will become a reality only when and where local communities are truly functional.

environmental management

THE BARATARIA-TERREBONNE NATIONAL ESTUARY PROGRAM: AN EXAMPLE OF REGIONAL ENVIRONMENTAL MANAGEMENT

Estuaries are ecosystems where rivers spread out over a large area as they run into the sea. Much of the water in estuaries is a combination of fresh and salt water mixed by the ocean tides. Estuaries are exceptional in their biological diversity, their biological productivity and the economic value of their biological resources. Estuaries are also among the world's most endangered ecosystems. Their wealth of natural resources encourages intensive use and overexploitation as well as conversion of the natural ecosystems to agricultural ecosystems. Many coastal mangrove ecosystems in South-East Asia have been converted to aquaculture ponds to satisfy the global market for shrimp, prawns and fish. Many of the world's largest cities are located in coastal areas, where fertile floodplain soils of nearby estuaries are used to produce food for the city. It is not unusual for growing coastal cities to expand over nearby estuaries.

The Barataria-Terrebonne estuary is the largest estuary in the United States. The entire estuary system covers an area of 16,835 square kilometres where the Mississippi River flows into the Gulf of Mexico (Figure 12.2). It is home to approximately 735 species of shellfish, fish, amphibians, reptiles, birds and mammals. Approximately 630,000 people live in the area, and its rich natural resources provide a livelihood to many additional people living outside the area. The Barataria-Terrebonne estuary provides an example of ecological problems that can arise when natural resources are exploited intensively and when natural ecosystems are deliberately modified or transformed to other kinds of ecosystems for human purposes. The Barataria-Terrebonne estuary case study is particularly instructive because the local people have developed a carefully designed programme of action to mobilize their community for dealing with the problems. It is a success story that illustrates adaptive development as described in Chapter 11, showing what it takes to make adaptive development a reality and what adaptive development can accomplish.

environmental management

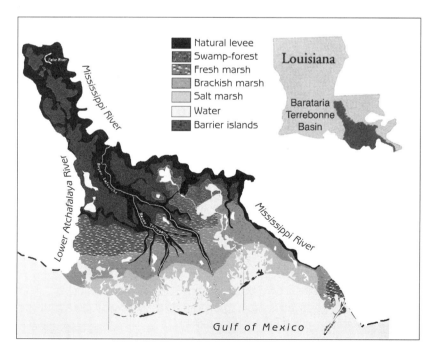

Figure 12.2
Barataria-
Terrebonne
estuary
Source: BTNEP
(1995) *Saving Our
Good Earth: A Call to
Action. Barataria-
Terrebonne estuarine
system
characterization
report*, Barataria-
Terrebonne National
Estuary Program,
Thibodaux, Louisiana

Forests		Marsh					
Deciduous forest	Swamp	Fresh	Brackish	Salt	Lagoon	Barrier Island	Ocean

Figure 12.3
Landscape profile showing the three major types of natural ecosystems in the estuary: swamp, marsh and open water
Source: BTNEP (1995) *Saving Our Good Earth: A Call to Action. Barataria-Terrebonne estuarine system characterization report*, Barataria-Terrebonne National Estuary Program, Thibodaux, Louisiana

Description and history of the estuary

Like other estuaries, the Barataria-Terrebonne estuary is a landscape mosaic that developed in response to moisture, salinity and other physical gradients extending from dry land through **wetlands** to open water, and from pure river water through **brackish water** to sea water. The estuary has three major types of natural ecosystems which occur along a gradient from higher to lower ground: **swamp**; **marsh**; and open water (Figure 12.3). The highest ground is dry enough for houses and farms and mixed deciduous forests characteristic of the region. Much of the higher ground is periodically flooded so that for most of the year the soil is wet or even under several centimetres of water. The natural ecosystem in this situation is swamp, a wetland forest dominated by cypress trees that can grow to a vast size during a lifetime of a thousand years. Swamp and deciduous forest ecosystems occupy 19 per cent of the estuary system. At slightly lower ground with more water, marsh ecosystems prevail, making up 22 per cent of the estuary system. Where the water is brackish or saline, marshes are typically characterized by a dense cover of coarse grasses 0.5–1 metre in height. Large animals in the swamps and marshes include bears, deer and alligators (which can grow to more than 4 metres in length). The open water covering the lowest ground is too deep for trees or marsh grasses to grow. Open water occupies 37 per cent of the estuary system and contains aquatic ecosystems.

The estuary contains an impressive array of natural resources including timber, wildlife and seafood. It is also the nursery for numerous species of commercially important fish in the Gulf of

Mexico. The integrity of natural ecosystems in the estuary is maintained by a dynamic equilibrium between sedimentation and sinking of the land. It is natural for wetland soils to sink a few centimetres each year. Because the soil has such a high organic matter content, some of the organic matter is decomposed and some is compressed by the weight of the soil above it. Sediment deposited during flooding compensates for the sinking by adding soil to the top. If there is enough sediment in the floodwater to entirely compensate for the sinking, the landscape topography and the resulting water regime of the estuary remain more or less the same from year to year.

As in the rest of North America, Native Americans inhabited the Barataria-Terrebonne estuary for thousands of years. Their population was small and their demands on the estuary's natural resources were modest. More intensive use began around 200 years ago with the arrival of European settlers who logged the cypress forests and cleared the higher (and drier) land for farming and construction of their homes. Since then, the different natural resources have been subject to intensive use at different times, as changing markets and the boom and bust of resource overexploitation and depletion have led the people in the area to switch their attention from one resource to another. Spanish moss, which hung from cypress trees in abundance, was harvested to provide stuffing for mattresses during the early years. Land was drained for commercial crops such as cotton. A prodigious supply of fish, shrimp, oysters and crawfish provided jobs for immigrant fishermen from numerous countries. Alligators were killed in large numbers for their valuable hides, and fur-bearing animals such as muskrats, mink and otter were trapped for their pelts. Nutria (coypu) were introduced from South America at the beginning of the 20th century to add a resource for the fur trade. The market for nutria pelts has declined with the anti-fur movement in recent years and, despite predation by alligators, nutria populations have exploded and seriously overgrazed marsh vegetation.

Exploitation of the estuary's natural resources changed the face of the landscape, but even greater changes resulted from developments that gained momentum during the 20th century. Most conspicuous was the network of canals constructed for navigational purposes. Intensive petroleum exploration and exploitation dating from the 1930s increased the number of canals, polluting and damaging natural ecosystems. Construction of levees and other public works for flood control completely altered the pattern of water circulation, flooding and sediment deposition that maintained natural ecosystems throughout the estuary. These changes set in motion numerous chains of effects

environmental
management

reverberating through the estuary ecosystem. Natural ecosystems were deteriorating at an alarming rate by the 1980s. The biological resources on which so many of the estuary's inhabitants depended for a living were seriously threatened. Some families were losing the land on which they built their homes.

Ecological problems

Change in water flow. Canals for navigation, as well as oil and gas exploration and extraction, create open channels for tidal movement of salt water further into the estuary. This **salt-water intrusion** increases the salinity in some parts of the estuary, changing the biological community to salt-tolerant plants and animals that previously lived only in saline areas closer to the ocean. Salinity can kill large numbers of cypress trees, particularly when salt water is carried into the estuary by powerful storm surges associated with hurricanes. Canals also increase soil loss from the estuary, as the erosion of canal banks by waves from passing boats expands the areas of open water. Material dredged to make canals is piled at the sides, obstructing water movement and causing accumulations of water in some places while preventing water and sediment from reaching other places. Flood control levees prevent river water and sediment from dispersing over the surrounding wetlands. Most of the sediment in the Mississippi River (200 million metric tons per year) is channelled through the estuary into the Gulf of Mexico.

Reduction in sedimentation. The Mississippi River carries 80 per cent less sediment today than it did a century ago. Soil conservation measures throughout the Mississippi River watershed have reduced the quantity of sediment flowing into the river, and numerous water control structures along the course of the river (eg, locks and dams) reduce water flow so that most sediment settles out of the river water before it reaches the estuary. Nonetheless, the Mississippi River contains enough sediment to build land that is not isolated from the river by levees. While floodwaters deposited sediment throughout the estuary in the past, many parts of the estuary now receive no sediment input from the Mississippi River because levees prevent floodwaters from reaching reach them.

Land loss and habitat changes. When natural sinking of the wetlands is not compensated by sediment deposition, the result is **land subsidence**. Water levels increase because lower land is

environmental
management

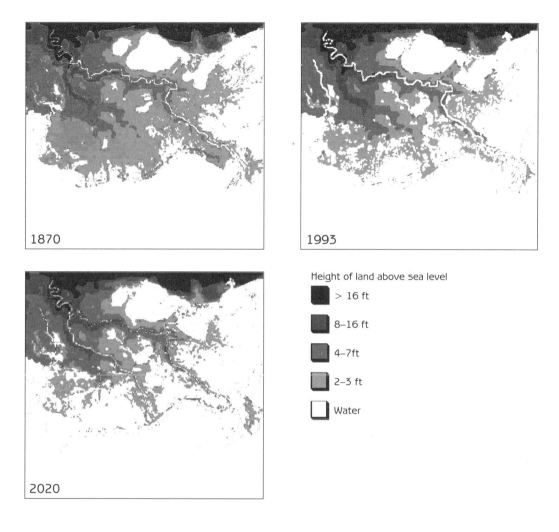

1870

1993

2020

Height of land above sea level

> 16 ft

8–16 ft

4–7ft

2–3 ft

Water

covered with deeper water, and changes in water level change the entire biological community. Swamps change to marshes and marshes change to open water (see Figures 12.4 and 12.5). This land loss has been exacerbated by erosion due to wave action, human activities such as dredging and canal construction, and the global rise in sea level attributed to global warming. Most of the land loss has been from salt marsh areas (Figure 12.2), which is the wetland closest to the ocean. Land loss is particularly severe where nutria eat up all the marsh grasses, leaving almost no vegetation to hold the soil. During the 1980s, 54 square kilometres of wetland (0.8 per cent of the total wetland area in the estuary) were lost each year. The rate of land loss declined during the 1990s, in part because much of the more easily eroded land was already gone.

Figure 12.4
Change in topography of Barataria-Terrebonne estuary during the past 130 years and projected 20 years into the future by a computer model
Source: data from Barataria-Terrebonne National Estuary Program, Thibodaux, Louisiana

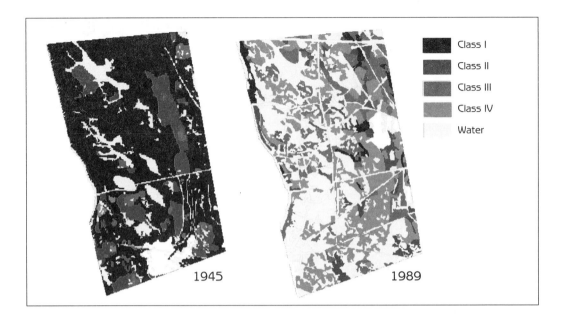

Figure 12.5
A 110-square kilometre section of the estuary that experienced dramatic transformation of marsh to open water during the past 50 years (Leeville, Louisiana)
Note: 'Water' in the map is canals and open water. 'Class 1' marsh has the least water and 'Class IV' marsh has the most water
Source: BTNEP (1995) *Saving Our Good Earth: A Call to Action. Barataria-Terrebonne estuarine system characterization report*, Barataria-Terrebonne National Estuary Program, Thibodaux, Louisiana

Eutrophication. Sewage and agricultural runoff contain plant nutrients such as nitrogen, phosphorous and silicates that stimulate blooms of algae and other plants which consume large quantities of oxygen at night and eventually remove even larger quantities of oxygen from the water when they die and decompose. The effects of low oxygen concentrations in the water are particularly conspicuous when low oxygen causes a massive fish kill.

Pathogen contamination. Sewage pollution contaminates the estuary with bacteria and viruses that concentrate in shellfish and other seafood, creating a health hazard for people and reducing income from these resources.

Toxic substances. Although the Mississippi River arrives at the estuary after industrial and household wastes have been dumped into it along its course of more than a thousand miles, the quantity of pollution has been reduced substantially during recent decades. While the river water contains higher than acceptable levels of nitrogen and atrazine (a herbicide used in cornfields upriver), the Mississippi River is not a significant source of pollution for the estuary. Virtually all of the pollution in the estuary comes from substances spilled into the estuary itself. These include: herbicides for controlling water hyacinth and other aquatic weeds that obstruct navigation in canals; emissions from petrochemical and chemical industries along nearby portions of the Mississippi River; pollution from boats, oil spills and other pollution associated with oil and gas production; agricultural and urban runoff including agricultural pesticides, chemicals for lawns and gardens and old automobile engine oil dumped on the ground; and seepage from disposal of hazardous wastes, including heavy metals and a variety of carcinogenic organic substances. Many of these substances accumulate in the food chain, where they can present hazards to human health.

Change in living resources. As the area of wetland declines, the number of plant and animal species associated with those wetland ecosystems declines correspondingly. Overexploitation and pollution can also have adverse impacts on the plants and animals. Bald eagles and brown pelicans nearly disappeared from the estuary during the 1960s because of DDT pollution from agricultural use. Populations of these two birds have recovered in recent years because DDT use stopped in the early 1970s. Introduced species of plants and animals compete with native species. Nutria consume nearly all the vegetation on about 4 square kilometres of marshland each year. In 2000, a *Spartina* grass die-back of unknown cause (called 'brown marsh') transformed about 80 square kilometres of salt marsh to mud flats and affected another 900 square kilometres of salt marsh to a lesser extent. The effects of ecological changes in the estuary on fisheries are not well understood, but some scientists think that further deterioration of the estuary could lead to a serious decline in fisheries. Despite these problems, no species of plant or animal appears to be in imminent danger of disappearing from the estuary.

environmental management

The solution: a regional environmental programme

In 1990, the United States government Environmental Protection Agency decided to develop environmental management plans for all major estuaries in the United States. A core team of seven full-time staff, assisted by numerous part-time volunteers, were responsible for the development of a management plan for the Barataria-Terrebonne estuary. The following mission statement provided terms of reference:

> *The Barataria-Terrebonne National Estuary Program (BTNEP) will work to develop a coalition of government, private, and commercial interests to identify problems, assess trends, design pollution control and resource management strategies, recommend corrective actions, and seek commitments for implementation. This coalition will provide the*

necessary leadership, will facilitate effective input from affected parties, and will guide the development of coordinated management procedures. The BTNEP will provide a forum for open discussion and cooperation by all parties that includes compromise in the best interest of natural resource protection.

The management plan was developed through a series of strategic planning workshops that utilized a 'technology of participation' developed by the Institute for Cultural Affairs. The planning process was designed around the following sequence of workshops over a period of nearly two years:

environmental management

- Vision for the future.
- Obstacles to realizing the vision.
- Actions to realize the vision.
- Coalitions to implement the actions.

The following description of what happened during each of these stages demonstrates how the design of a regional environment programme can evolve from broad goals, as in the mission statement above, to a specific set of actions to realize the goals.

The planning process was open to anyone who wanted to participate, such as representatives from national, state and local governments, corporations and commercial organizations and interested citizens. A group of about 250 participants was continuously involved during the three years it took to formulate and refine the plan.

The planning process started with a workshop to identify a *vision* for the future of the estuary. The key question for the workshop was 'What do we want the Barataria-Terrebonne estuary to be like in 25 years?' The brainstorming procedure was designed to include the diverse and often conflicting opinions of all participants while identifying broad themes on which everyone could agree. Participants put forward their ideas by writing each idea with a few key words on a piece of paper which was then stuck on a wall for everyone to see. Participants were allowed to request clarification of the meaning of a particular idea but there was no discussion of the merits of an idea. Every idea on the wall went into the final record of the workshop.

Several hundred ideas were submitted. After putting all of them on the wall and making sure that everyone understood them, the workshop participants worked together to sort the ideas into groups that had something in common. All the participants then decided together on theme titles for each group of ideas. The theme titles, as well as every idea associated with each theme,

Box 12.1
First Barataria-
Terrebonne
estuary planning
workshop: vision
statement

We the people of Louisiana and the Barataria-Terrebonne estuarine basins believe that the Barataria-Terrebonne ecosystem is a national treasure which represents a unique multi-cultural heritage. Furthermore, we recognize that our ongoing stewardship is critical to its preservation, restoration, and enhancement. This stewardship can only be maintained by active support of those who live in the basin, and those who use its abundant resources locally, statewide, and throughout the nation. Acknowledging the importance of this estuary to our environmental, cultural and economic well-being, the people living and working in these two basins believe that we should have a balanced ecosystem that includes:

- Public education and informed citizen participation.
- Local, state and national recognition and support.
- Maintained multi-cultural heritage.
- Sustained and restored wetlands that support viable fish and wildlife resources.
- Pollution abatement to protect the health of plants, animals and people.
- Environmentally responsible economic activity.
- Environmentally compatible infrastructure (roads, bridges, levees, railways, etc).
- Comprehensive, integrated watershed planning among all users.
- Harmonious use of the resources by many interests and resolution of user conflicts.

We pledge to work together to develop a plan to re-establish a chemical, physical and biological balance in the Barataria-Terrebonne estuary so that diverse plant and animal communities and human health and welfare can be improved and sustained for present and future generations.

environmental management

were put into a word processor and printed out as a record of the workshop. The results from the workshop were summarized as a vision statement (see Box 12.1) which listed the themes identified by the workshop.

The second workshop addressed obstacles and the challenges to overcome the obstacles. It followed the same procedure as the first workshop. Participants individually listed their ideas on cards that were placed on the wall. All participants then worked together to group the ideas and give theme names to the groups. The following obstacle themes and corresponding challenges are set out in Box 12.2.

The challenges identified by the second workshop served as points of reference for the next workshop, which brainstormed actions to deal with the challenges. More than 400 actions were suggested, and a list of all the suggestions was circulated to workshop participants and other interested persons. The workshop results are summarized in Box 12.3.

environmental
management

Box 12.2
Second
Barataria-
Terrebonne
estuary planning
workshop:
obstacles and
challenges

Obstacle theme	Challenge
• Conflicting agendas	Discover common ground within the management and user groups
• Parochial attitudes	Create a pathway toward regional pride and long-term stewardship of the estuary
• Distorted image	Assemble a promotion package which emphasizes unique elements of the estuary and provides in-depth factual background
• Inadequately informed public	Develop and implement a comprehensive programme to involve and inform all users
• Natural resource limits	Identify the limits of our resources and seek balanced use
• Adjustment to natural processes	Understand how to be compatible with natural change and use existing infrastructures to enhance the ecosystem and minimize impact of natural disasters
• Ineffective government	Involve all levels and political jurisdictions in long-range planning and implementation
• Mistrust and resistance to environmental regulations	Develop clear, fair, practical and enforceable regulations with strict penalties
• Data gaps and interpretations	Organize and interpret data into information readily accessible to decision-makers and public

After a period of four months to allow everyone time to think about the suggested actions, there was a workshop to identify *catalytic actions* – actions that would not only have desirable consequences in themselves but also generate other desirable actions. Identification of catalytic actions and grouping of the actions into four major programmes followed the same procedure as previous workshops. The major programmes were:

1 Coordinated planning and implementation.
2 Ecological management.
3 Sustained recognition and citizen involvement.
4 Economic growth.

The catalytic actions provided the basis for 51 *action plans* in the final environmental management plan. Participants who wanted to participate in implementing a particular major programme signed up as members of the alliance committed to its implementation. During the following year each alliance worked out the details of its programme. Details were planned only by the alliance committed to implementing that particular programme. At no time did anyone plan work to be done by someone else. The detailed programmes

Natural factor	Human factor	Management factor	Linking factor
Systems related to physics, biology or chemistry and the movement of water or land within the estuarine ecosystem. Address the science and technical problems and are tightly linked to one another	Socioeconomic systems which currently have the greatest impact on the estuary. Involves informed public participation and the cultural patterns and attitudes related to economic development and natural resource value	Systems of decision-making and management which involve integrating comprehensive, holistic environmental considerations into the planning, coordinating and regulating of the human and natural resources	Systems which serve as criteria to achieving environmental sustainability. Represents how the natural, human and management systems are dynamically linked and were referred to by the stakeholders as the 'heart or soul or conscience' of the ecosystem
Land mass Preserve and restore the wetlands and Barrier Islands by developing aggressive and effective programmes	**Economic development** Promote environmentally responsible economic activities and estuarine-based jobs that sustain estuarine resources	**Comprehensive databases** Create an accessible, comprehensive database with interpreted information for the public	**Balanced use** Formulate indicators of estuarine ecosystem and human health and measures of balanced use of natural resources
Diverse biological communities Realistically support diverse, natural biological communities	**National recognition and support** Gain national recognition through informed advocacy to attract federal funding and strengthen federal policies to support the estuary	**Effective Regulations** Create clear, fair, practical and enforceable regulations with balanced participatory input and interagency coordination by increasing quantity and quality of public participation	**Common-ground solutions** Discover common-ground solutions within management and user groups to ensure implementation and obtain voluntary protection of resources
Water quality Develop and meet water quality standards that adequately protect estuarine resources and human health	**Education and involvement** Implement comprehensive education and awareness programmes that enhance active public participation and maintain the cultural heritage	**Comprehensive watershed planning** Develop and maintain multi-level, long-term comprehensive watershed planning by establishing a tradition of upfront, inclusive stakeholder involvement in all planning efforts	**Compatibility with nature** Be compatible with natural, physical and biological change by using existing and future infrastructures, providing harmonious, socioeconomic activities, and minimizing the impact of natural disasters

were then combined to form the environmental management plan (see Box 12.4), which was published in 1996 as a four-volume *Comprehensive Conservation and Management Plan*.

Implementation of the plan began in 1996. A team of volunteer participants manages each action plan. Every team is open to

Box 12.3
Third Barataria-Terrebonne estuary planning workshop: challenges and actions

Box 12.4
The Barataria-
Terrebonne
National Estuary
Program
environmental
management
plan

**environmental
management**

BTNEP GOALS

* Forge common-ground solutions to estuarine problems.
* Maintain multi-level, long-term, comprehensive watershed planning.
* Create clear, fair, practical and enforceable regulations.
* Preserve and restore wetlands and barrier islands.
* Develop and meet water quality standards that adequately protect estuarine resources and human health.
* Realistically support diverse natural biological communities.
* Create an accessible, comprehensive database with interpreted information for the public.
* Formulate indicators of estuarine health and balanced usage.
* Implement comprehensive education and awareness programmes that enhance public involvement and maintain cultural heritage.
* Create national recognition and support for the Barataria-Terrebonne estuary.
* Be compatible with natural processes.
* Promote environmentally responsible economic activities that sustain estuarine resources.

ACTION PLANS

Programme 1: Coordinated planning and implementation

Programme implementation structure
* Continue the management conference.
* Establish points-of-contact throughout the state for Comprehensive Conservation and Management Plan implementation.
* Maintain the programme office and critical staff.

Coordinated planning
* Use participatory decision-making processes at Management Conference meetings; conflict resolution.
* Establish two Wetlands Permitting Information Centers in the estuary.
* Provide education and planning assistance to local officials and planners to ensure sustainable economic development within the estuary.
* Develop and implement a set of recommended procedures for agencies to involve the public in the development of state rules, regulations and guidelines.
* Establish a periodic evaluation process to assess implementation of the wetlands permitting process and regulations.

Programme 2: Ecological management

Habitat management
* Restore the natural hydrology of areas receiving freshwater inflows.
* Divert freshwater and sediment to decrease salinities and maintain or create marsh.
* Evaluate the effectiveness of reactivating Bayou Lafourche as a distributary channel of the Mississippi River.

- Use dredged material to create, maintain and restore marshes.
- Preserve and restore the estuary's barrier islands.
- Stabilize shorelines and induce sediment deposition to create, maintain and restore marshes.
- Evaluate marsh management and water control structures to stabilize water levels and salinity for marsh establishment and growth.

Water quality
- Quantitatively estimate sources and loads of nutrient, bacteria and toxic contaminants within the estuary.
- Reduce the number, volume and impact of petroleum-related fluid spills to the estuary.
- Reduce human sewage discharges to the estuary from treatment plants, rural homes, unsewered communities, commercial and residential vessels and waterfront camps.
- Employ existing Agricultural Management Plans to reduce loadings of nutrient and toxic contaminants.
- Reduce pollutant loadings associated with current stormwater discharge practices; enhance wetlands with stormwater.
- Create a Geographic Information System-based database of sediment contamination for management purposes.
- Determine risks and threats of toxic and noxious phytoplankton blooms to human health and fisheries industries.

Living resources
- Encourage landowners to manage their land as habitat for migratory and resident birds.
- Reduce adverse impacts of exotic plant species through regulation, education, management and control.
- Initiate a zebra mussel monitoring programme in the estuary and develop and disseminate new information about control techniques.

Accessible and compatible data set
- Create an accessible, centralized data management system.

Programme 3: Sustained recognition and citizen involvement

Citizen involvement and participation
- Develop a network of community leaders and teams to support and implement Comprehensive Conservation and Management Plan Action Plans.
- Regularly conduct meetings to involve the public in decisions on estuary issues.
- Provide citizen involvement opportunities for protecting and managing the estuary.
- Develop citizen monitoring programmes to produce data on water quality and living resources issues.
- Conduct and support activities that highlight the cultural heritage of the estuary to develop environmental awareness and stewardship.
- Assist and encourage communities to establish urban green spaces.
- Continue storm drain stencilling throughout the estuary.

environmental management

Public information and education
- Generate legislator support for estuary issues.
- Use the media for information dissemination.
- Organize a group of volunteer speakers and presentations on estuary issues.
- Provide educational materials on estuary issues for identified target audiences.
- Develop a targeted distribution campaign for information about the estuary and the Comprehensive Conservation and Management Plan.
- Create and promote the use of a toll-free number for the programme office.

environmental management

Curriculum
- Develop and disseminate curriculum materials to support estuarine education (Kindergarten through university).
- Provide continuing environmental education programmes.
- Develop an awareness of the need to finance environmental education; identify funding strategies and sources.
- Establish an estuarine educational resources network in the estuary.

Programme 4: Economic growth

Economic development
- Identify sources of funding for new environmentally-sustainable businesses.
- Encourage nature-based tourism and recreation.
- Develop a commercial market for nutria to reduce their impacts on wetlands.

Technology transfer
- Conduct an annual technology exposition to showcase environmentally-sustainable technologies.
- To develop new and expand existing markets, encourage and provide training in the exportation of environmentally-sustainable resources, products and technology.
- Identify existing, develop new and encourage the use of more environmentally-sensitive technologies and business practices.

Cooperative incentives
- Identify, promote and provide financial or tax incentives for environmentally-sustainable economic development.
- Develop and implement an education programme to explain the purpose of wetlands permitting to business and industry audiences.

anyone who wants to participate. A few of the most popular teams have more than a hundred people. Each action plan is strategic in character. The team decides on activities as the work progresses.

BTNEP's most important achievements to date have been:

- Focusing public attention on the estuary as an ecological system.
- Generating increased citizen involvement.
- Establishing credibility and trust in the programme.

An image of neutrality in a complex arena of competing public and private interests is essential for acceptance by the community. BTNEP does not favour any one particular group. It is only concerned with the ecological health of the estuary. A high level of professional integrity is essential for acceptance. People who live or work in the estuary can be confident that BTNEP's assessments and information packages are as complete and accurate as possible within the limitations of available information. BTNEP has a Data and Information Management System which draws on information from every available source, and a Sustainability Indicators Program which develops indicators to assess and communicate trends in the ecological health of the estuary.

environmental management

Many of the action programmes are concerned with preventing land loss in one way or another. The main thrust of on-the-ground actions to date has been the protection of land that is vulnerable to erosion by water. This includes extensive planting of mulberry, hackberry, live oak and other trees to hold the soil. In addition, brush fences have been constructed with thousands of used Christmas trees to protect the coastline from wave action. Dredged sediment has been used for small-scale marsh reconstruction. The programme's partners have also been doing the concrete planning and other groundwork for projects to divert river water in order to carry sediment to parts of the estuary where it is needed to build land or compensate for sinking soil or land erosion. The first large-scale river water diversion is due to begin in 2001. Results will be monitored carefully to guide ongoing adjustments to details of the diversion. Monitoring will also provide information for the design of other river water diversions – some using natural water flows and others using pipelines – that are online for sediment delivery to other parts of the estuary.

Many of the action programmes are also concerned with water quality. Small-scale sewage processing systems for houses and 'camps' (fishing cabins) scattered along the waterways in the estuary have been a high priority. In addition, some of the towns in the area have upgraded their sewage treatment facilities. High school students help to monitor levels of coliform bacteria (an indicator of human faecal contamination) in the water. An educational programme for farmers on alternative methods of controlling weeds, insects and other pests has helped them to reduce pesticide applications. The petroleum industry has upgraded equipment to reduce leaks and spills from oil platforms and pipelines.

An intensive programme of education for people of all ages has been crucial for success. Curricula and educational materials have been prepared for schools, and training workshops have been conducted for teachers. The Americorps and Delta Service Corps (government programmes that employ youths for community service projects) give presentations on estuary issues in local schools. A toll-free telephone number facilitates public inquiries. About 500,000 informational materials developed by the programme have been distributed to the public, including videos, booklets, CD-ROMs and maps such as those included in this chapter. The videos explain the history of the estuary, its ecological problems and what citizens can do to contribute to its ecological health. The Aquarium of the Americas in nearby New Orleans has displays about the estuary, and a Barataria-Terrebonne Wildlife Museum has recently been completed within the estuary area. Volunteer speakers explain estuary issues to civic groups, and educational workshops are conducted for the public. Information is continually supplied to the media, and copies of newspaper articles about estuary activities are provide to state legislators on a regular basis.

One of the greatest successes of the programme has been the high level of public participation. Businessmen's groups are contributing to marsh restoration. High school students and other groups of volunteers plant trees, build brush fences with old Christmas trees and make community parks. Special community activities such as a migratory bird celebration and annual ecology festival combine fun with ecological education and awareness. Public meetings are held to discuss special problems such as fish kills due to eutrophication, and major projects such as river water diversions are discussed in public meetings before being implemented.

environmental management

Conclusions

What can we learn from the BTNEP case study? Some of the ecological problems are unique to estuaries, but many are relevant elsewhere. Many elements of the vision outlined by the first planning workshop, such as pollution abatement, sustainable resource use and comprehensive planning, are similar to desires that would be expected from people anywhere in the world. Many of the obstacles identified by the second workshop, such as conflicting agendas of different actors in the region, information gaps, an inadequately informed public, ecological limits and ineffective government, are familiar to people everywhere, and the associated challenges are correspondingly similar.

One important lesson from this example is that, to be successful, regional environmental programmes need a full-time core staff, but they can be developed and implemented with modest resources. During the planning stage, BTNEP's staff comprised seven people; now there are only five. Their main functions are organizing, interpreting and communicating information and facilitating action. The human resources and funds for all the activities in the action plans come primarily from government agencies on a scale that is hundreds of times that of the human resources and budget of the BTNEP office. Volunteers have been essential. However, a larger programme staff would be desirable. The small size of BTNEP's staff compared to the large scale of the estuary, its ecological and social complexity and the large number of action plans that the staff are coordinating is a serious limiting factor for the programme.

environmental management

Openness and inclusion have been a key to BTNEP's success. This approach may not appeal to politicians and managers seeking to retain as much control as possible for themselves, but openness and inclusion make BTNEP far more effective and enduring by drawing fully on the wisdom of the entire community and generating a broad base of community 'ownership' of the programme that in turn leads to a corresponding commitment to its success. Another ingredient, which goes hand in hand with openness and inclusion, is a high technical standard for assembling and communicating ecological information about the estuary. Sound decisions, and public support for successful implementation, depend on an informed community with a realistic picture of what is happening and what can be expected from proposed actions.

Facilitation from outside the area played a critical role. The programme was developed in response to a request from the United States government which provided funds for both planning and implementation. Genuine community participation in the planning, which was central to a sound design and subsequent success in implementation, was facilitated by an outside non-governmental organization specializing in community organization and strategic planning. It is unusual for regional environmental programmes to develop spontaneously without outside assistance.

The exceptional ecological and economic value of the Barataria-Terrebonne estuary, as well as the magnitude and serious consequences of its ecological problems and the high rate of land loss, are undoubtedly responsible for the fact that an environmental programme of this quality was developed at this particular location. However, regional environmental programmes of similar quality are needed all around the globe. In the same way that a school council or regulatory body is necessary to ensure the standard of education for the children in its area, environmental programmes like BTNEP and the Santa Monica Mountains National Recreation Area (described in Chapter 11) are needed to ensure an ecologically healthy landscape for future generations and, where necessary, to restore the landscape to ecological health. It is a responsibility that cannot be ignored – a responsibility to ourselves, to future generations and to all the other biological inhabitants with which we share this planet.

things to
think about

THINGS TO THINK ABOUT

1. Explain how each of the following concepts is represented in the case study on dengue, mosquitoes and copepods: chain of effects through ecosystem and social system, carrying capacity, population regulation, community assembly, complex system cycle, human inputs to ecosystems, landscape mosaics, coadaptation, unexpected consequences from new technology, social complexity, sustainable management of common property resources, conflict between stability and resilience, adaptive development.

2. 'Environmental technology' typically brings to mind methods, processes or equipment for reducing pollution or recycling wastes. Although pollution abatement and recycling have an essential role in sustainable development, a much broader spectrum of technologies will be necessary for sustainable development to become a reality. The case study on dengue hemorrhagic fever and copepods illustrates biological control, an ecological technology that can help to deal not only with health pests but also agricultural pests. Can you think of other examples of ecological technologies (some of them very different from biological control) that can contribute to sustainable development? What role can local communities have in developing and implementing ecological technologies?

3. Local environmental management offers numerous benefits, but powerful obstacles must be overcome to make it a reality. Think of the landscape in your area along with other aspects of your local environment. What are the problems that deserve attention from the community? The case study on the Barataria-Terrebonne estuary shows how problems can be clarified to educate politicians and the general public in a way that mobilizes their support and participation for action to deal with the problems. What useful lessons did you extract from this example? How do they apply to mobilizing political and public support for ecological action in your own community?

GLOSSARY

adaptive development Social system evolution by a process of problem solving that includes broad community participation with monitoring to assess the effectiveness of human actions and corrective measures to bring the actions in line with community goals.

agricultural ecosystem See ECOSYSTEM.

Agricultural Revolution The beginning of agriculture about 10,000–12,000 years ago. Domestication and care of plants and animals as sources of food and other materials for human use.

agroforestry Agricultural ecosystems that include trees.

animism Belief that plants, animals and some non-living parts of nature have spirits or souls.

annual Plant that lives only one year or season

autonomous Free of outside control.

biological community All the living organisms (plants, animals, microorganisms) in an ecosystem.

biological control The control of pest organisms by altering their environment or introducing natural enemies such as predators or pathogens.

biological production (also called 'primary production') Total plant growth (due to photosynthesis) in an ecosystem. The quantity of plant growth determines the food supply for all other living organisms in an ecosystem.

biome A large-scale ecosystem associated with a particular climatic region.

biophilia An inborn emotional need of humans to have plants and animals as a part of their lives in one way or another.

brackish water A mixture of fresh water and salt water.

canopy The top layer of branches and leaves in a forest.

carrying capacity The maximum population number of a particular plant or animal species that an ecosystem can support on a long-term basis.

chaparral A biological community composed of shrubby plants adapted to dry summers and moist winters. Common in coastal Southern California.

clear-cutting Cutting all of the trees in a forest at the same time. The opposite of SELECTIVE LOGGING.

climax community The final stage of ecological succession.

coadaptation Adjustment of different parts of an ecosystem to one another.

coevolution Associated changes in two species of living organisms that have a close ecological relationship (eg, predator/prey), acting as agents of natural selection for one another.

commons A tract of land or other resource used jointly by the members of a community.

community assembly Self-organization of biological communities by selective addition of new species of plants or animals that arrive to an ecosystem.

complex adaptive systems Systems with feedback loops that enable them to adjust to fluctuations in their environment in ways that promote their survival.

consumer Animal or other living organism that feeds on plants, animals or microorganisms.

consumption The movement of organic matter (ie, carbon chains) through a food web as animals and microorganisms eat (or otherwise ingest) plants, animals or microorganisms to obtain the material and energy that they need to sustain their lives.

controlled burning Small fires set deliberately to reduce combustible material in a forest.

counterintuitive Opposite or contrary to expectations. The outcomes of human actions in complex adaptive systems such as ecosystems and social systems are often counterintuitive because complex chains of effects generate ultimate consequences that are different from immediate impacts.

decomposer A microorganism that feeds on dead plants, animals or microorganisms.

decomposition Consumption of dead plants, animals or microorganisms by microorganisms.

denial (cognitive dissonance) Refusal to believe information that conflicts with an existing belief system. Denial is a defence mechanism for reducing anxiety due to a conflict between reality and existing beliefs.

desertification Transformation of other kinds of ecosystems (eg, grassland) to desert. Typically associated with loss of topsoil and consequent reduction of plant life in semi-arid regions.

diminishing returns A benefit that beyond a certain point fails to increase in proportion to additional investments.

dispersal The spreading of plants, animals or microorganisms from one place to another by their own movement or when carried by wind, water, animals or machines.

division of labour Diversification of tasks or occupational roles in a society in order to improve working efficiency.

drift net Large-mesh monofilament nylon gillnet, typically miles long, used for ocean fishing. Fish are caught when they become entangled while trying to swim through the net.

ecological competition Use of the same resource by two different species of plant, animal or microorganism.

ecological niche The role of a particular species in the ecosystem. Ecological niche is defined in terms of the physical conditions and resources necessary for the species' survival and the species' position in the ecosystem's foodweb.

ecological succession A systematic progression of biological communities through time, each biological community replacing another due to natural ecological processes. See also HUMAN-INDUCED SUCCESSION.

ecology The science of relationships and interactions between living organisms and their environment.

economy of scale Reduction in unit costs as a consequence of increase in the scale of production.

ecosystem A system formed by the interaction of a biological community with its chemical and physical environment. An ecosystem includes everything at a particular location: plants, animals, microorganisms, air, water, soil and human-built structures. *Natural* ecosystems are formed entirely by natural processes. *Agricultural* ecosystems are created by people to provide food or other materials. *Urban* ecosystems are dominated by human-built structures.

ecosystem inputs Materials, energy or information that move into an ecosystem. *Human inputs* are human activities to organize or structure ecosystems.

ecosystem outputs Materials, energy or information that moves out of an ecosystem to another ecosystem or the human social system.

ecosystem services Materials, energy or information that people obtain from ecosystems for survival (eg, food, fibres, construction materials and water) or as amenities and experiences to enrich their lives.

ecosystem state Particular physical conditions, chemical concentrations, and numbers of each kind of plant, animal and microorganism that characterize an ecosystem at a particular place and time.

emergent property A characteristic of a system as a whole that comes into existence from the organization of the system's parts rather than from characteristics of any of the parts themselves.

endangered species A species of plant or animal in danger of extinction, typically as a consequence of human activities.

energy flow Movement of energy in the carbon chains of organic matter that passes through a food web as one organism consumes another.

environmental refugees People who move from a region because the ecosystem is no longer able to provide for their basic needs.

estuary The wide lower course of a river where its currents meet ocean tides. Much of the water in an estuary is a tidal mixture of fresh water and salt water.

eutrophication Pollution of water with minerals that stimulate plant growth.

exponential population growth Increase in population characterized by an increasingly larger population growth rate as the number of individuals in the population increases.

extended economic zone A marine area for which a nation claims sovereignty over all resources for a distance of 320 kilometres from its shores.

fallow Land that is left unused, without ploughing, planting or raising crops.

fisheries succession A change in the biological community of a fisheries ecosystem in which fish species that are intensely harvested disappear and other fish species (or other kinds of animals) take their place.

food chain A series of living organisms connected by one eating another. See also FOOD WEB.

food chain efficiency The percentage of carbon-chain energy at one step of a food chain that is available for consumption by the next step of the food chain.

food web A set of interconnected FOOD CHAINS which includes all the organisms in an ecosystem's biological community.

Green Revolution Increase in agricultural production through the introduction of high-yield crop varieties and application of modern agricultural techniques.

habitat The type of ecosystem in which a particular kind of plant, animal or microorganism normally lives.

hierarchical organization Organization of a system in such a way that each element of the system contains other elements within it. Biological systems have a hierarchy that extends from atoms and molecules to cells, tissues, organs, individuals, populations and biological communities. Landscape mosaics have a nested hierarchy of ecosystems extending from less than a square metre to the entire planet Earth.

high-yield varieties Genetically improved crops produced by modern breeding methods to have a high level of production under ideal environmental conditions.

homeostasis Negative feedback that maintains a living organism's body function within limits essential for the body to continue functioning properly despite external stimuli that have a tendency to disrupt the function.

human ecology The science of relationships and interactions between people and their environment.

human-induced succession A change in an ecosystem's biological community as a consequence of human activities. See also ECOLOGICAL SUCCESSION.

Industrial Revolution Changes in economic and social organization that began about 300 years ago in England with replacement of hand tools by power-driven machines.

land subsidence Sinking of the land due to processes such as organic matter decomposition and sediment compaction resulting from the weight of overlying sediments.

landscape mosaic A repetitive patchwork of different kinds of ecosystems across a land area. See also HIERARCHICAL ORGANIZATION.

larvicide A chemical or other agent for killing insect larvae.

leaf litter A layer of dead plant material on the soil surface.

legume Plants such as peas and beans with pods that split along both sides. Legumes commonly have root nodules with symbiotic bacteria that convert atmospheric nitrogen to a form that plants can use.

marsh A low-lying area, saturated with water, all or part of which is typically covered with moisture-tolerant grasses.

material cycling (also called 'nutrient cycling' or 'mineral cycling') Circulation of chemical elements through the food web, air, soil and water in an ecosystem.

metropolitan region A large city and its surrounding suburbs.

Minamata disease A severe form of mercury poisoning characterized by neurological degeneration. Called Minamata because of mercury poisoning from contaminated fish in Minamata Bay, Japan.

mineral cycling See MATERIAL CYCLING.

mineral nutrients Inorganic substances (eg, nitrogen, phosphorous, potassium, calcium, magnesium, sulphur, cobalt, copper, boron, manganese and zinc) that plants need for their growth.

monoculture An agricultural ecosystem with only one kind of crop.

mycorrhizae Fungi in symbiotic association with plant roots, facilitating phosphorous uptake by the roots.

natural capital All the natural resources on which a civilization depends to create economic prosperity. Natural capital includes water, minerals, air, soil, plants, animals and microorganisms in natural, agricultural and urban ecosystems.

natural ecosystem See ECOSYSTEM.

negative feedback A chain of effects through an ecosystem or social system that tends to keep particular parts of the system within certain limits.

nitrogen-fixing bacteria Bacteria responsible for nitrogen fixation – the conversion of atmospheric nitrogen to a form (eg, ammonia) that plants can use.

non-renewable natural resources Non-living resources such as petroleum, gas, coal and minerals.

nutrient cycling See MATERIAL CYCLING.

nutrient pump An ecological process in which trees take up mineral nutrients from soil too deep for crop roots to reach. The mineral nutrients pass into the leaves of trees, eventually falling onto the soil where they are accessible to crops.

organic farming Farming style that uses fertilizers of plant or animal origin and natural pest control methods instead of chemical fertilizers, pesticides, or growth stimulants.

overexploitation Use of an ecosystem service in excess of what the ecosystem can sustain on a long-term basis.

overfishing The OVEREXPLOITATION of a fishery by harvesting more fish than the fishery can yield on a sustainable basis.

overgrazing The OVEREXPLOITATION of pasture or rangeland resources by grazing more livestock than the grasses can sustain.

overshoot To pass beyond. In human ecology overshoot refers to (a) the increase of an animal or plant population beyond the carrying capacity of its environment or (b) the increase of industrial or other demands on an ecosystem beyond the ecosystem's capacity to provide services satisfying the demands.

parasite An animal that obtains its nutrition by living in close association with another kind of animal (the *host*) without killing it immediately. The host animal may be injured (and in some cases eventually killed) by the relationship.

pathogen A microorganism that causes disease in another kind of organism. This normally happens when a pathogen lives in close association with a host organism to procure the habitat and nutrition it requires for survival.

perception The way that people 'see' and interpret information. Perceptions are important for human ecology because they shape the way that information is used to agree on human actions.

perennial Crop or other plant that is present throughout the year because it lives for at least several years.

phytoplankton Microscopic plants that drift in the water of an aquatic ecosystem.

polyculture A mixture of crop species in an agricultural ecosystem.

population All the plants, animals or microorganisms of the same species in a particular ecosystem.

population pressure Stress due to scarcity of food or other resources when a population is close to, or greater than, carrying capacity.

population regulation Control of population number by negative feedback.

positive feedback A chain of effects through an ecosystem or social system that amplifies change.

precautionary principle A standard for human/environment interaction that emphasizes prudent action due to limited knowledge of the environment.

predator An animal that eats other animals.

primary production See BIOLOGICAL PRODUCTION.

redundancy Duplication or overlap of function that exceeds what is necessary.

renewable natural resources Resources that are continually replaced by material cycling and energy flow in an ecosystem. Most renewable resources (eg, forests, fisheries and agricultural products) are living resources, though some non-living resources (eg, water) are also renewable.

resilience The ability to return to an original form after severe stress or disturbance.

respiration Oxidation of carbon chains in the body of living organisms to extract energy for metabolic processes.

salinization Accumulation of toxic concentrations of salts in the soil as a consequence of irrigation. Irrigation water evaporates from the field, leaving dissolved salts to accumulate in the soil.

salt-water intrusion Tidal movement of ocean water inland because river flow to the ocean is interrupted.

satoyama A traditional system of village agriculture and forest management in Japan.

selective logging Cutting only some trees in a forest. Selective logging is a way to manage a forest on a sustainable basis. The opposite of CLEAR-CUTTING.

shifting cultivation See SWIDDEN.

slash-and-burn agriculture See SWIDDEN.

social institutions An established pattern of behaviour or relationships accepted as a fundamental part of a culture.

social organization The structure of social relations within a group, including relations among different subgroups and institutions.

social system Everything about human society, including its organization and structure, knowledge and technology, language, culture, perceptions and values.

soil erosion Loss of soil that is worn or carried away by wind or rain.

stability Constancy. Resistance to change.

stability domain A set of similar system states characterized by natural or social processes that tend to keep the system in those states.

subsistence farming Farming whose products provide basic family needs with little surplus for marketing.

supply zone See ZONE OF INFLUENCE.

sustainable development Doing things in a way that does not reduce the opportunities of future generations to meet their needs. *Ecologically sustainable development* depends upon human–ecosystem interaction that maintains the functional integrity of ecosystems in a way that allows them to continue providing ecosystem services.

swamp A forest ecosystem that is saturated with water.

swidden (also called 'slash-and-burn agriculture' or 'shifting cultivation') An agricultural system characterized by rotation between crops and natural vegetation. Fields are prepared for cultivation by cutting and burning natural vegetation (eg, forest). The field typically has crops for one to three years, after which it is left to fallow, generating natural vegetation that is eventually burned to prepare the field once again for crops.

symbiosis Mutually beneficial association between two different species of organisms.

tragedy of the commons The OVEREXPLOITATION of a natural resource because no one in particular owns the resource, resource use is open to anyone without restriction, and the resource is large enough for the actions of single individuals to have no significant effect on the supply of the resource.

trash fish Fish that have little commercial value.

unsustainable Not able to be continued for a long period. *Ecologically unsustainable* refers to human–ecosystem interaction that damages an ecosystem or depletes a resource in a way that diminishes the supply of the resource or the capacity of the ecosystem to provide a service.

urban ecosystem See ECOSYSTEM.

values Emotionally respected ideals, customs and institutions of a society.

vector An animal that transmits bacterial, viral, fungal or other disease.

watershed A region or area that drains to a stream, river, lake or ocean. Watersheds are the main source of water for cities and irrigated agriculture.

wetland A lowland area, such as a marsh or swamp, that is saturated with moisture.

worldview A person's comprehensive conception or image of the surrounding world and his relation to it. Worldviews shared generally by everyone in a society constitute the society's worldview.

zone of influence The area surrounding a city and affected by the city's authority or commerce.

zooplankton Small animals that live in the water of an aquatic ecosystem.

FURTHER READING

HUMAN ECOLOGY

Anderson, E (1996) *Ecologies of the Heart: Emotion, Belief, and the Environment*, Oxford University Press, Oxford

Borden, R, Jacobs, J and Young, G (eds) (1986) *Human Ecology: A Gathering of Perspectives*, Society for Human Ecology, College Park, Maryland

Borden, R, Jacobs, J and Young, G (eds) (1988) *Human Ecology: Research and Applications*, Society for Human Ecology, College Park, Maryland

Botkin, D and Keller, E (1999) *Environmental Science: Earth as a Living Planet*, Wiley, New York

Boyden, S (1987) *Western Civilization in Biological Perspective: Patterns in Biohistory*, Clarendon, Oxford

Brown, L R, Flavin, C and French, H (2001) *State of the World 2001: A Worldwatch Institute Report on Progress Toward a Sustainable Society*, Earthscan, London

Brown, L R, Flavin, C, French, H, Postel, S and Starke, L (2000) *State of the World 2000: A Worldwatch Institute Report on Progress Toward a Sustainable Society*, Earthscan, London

Brown, L R, Flavin, C, French, H, and Starke, L (1999) *State of the World 1999: A Worldwatch Institute Report on Progress Toward a Sustainable Society*, Earthscan, London

Bunyard, P (1996) *Gaia in Action: Science of the Living Earth*, Floris Books, Edinburgh

Campbell, G (1995) *Human Ecology: The Story of our Place in Nature from Prehistory to Present*, Aldine, Hawthorne

Clayton, A, and Radcliffe, N (1996) *Sustainability: A Systems Approach*, Earthscan, London

Cohen, J (1995) *How Many People can the Earth Support?*, WW Norton, New York

Daily, G (1997) *Nature's Services: Societal Dependence on Ecosystems*, Island Press, Washington, DC

Diamond, J (1997) *Guns, Germs, and Steel: The Fates of Human Societies*, WW Norton, New York

Drury, W and Anderson, J (1998) *Chance and Change: Ecology for Conservationists*, University of California Press, Berkeley

Ehrlich, P, Ehrlich, A and Holdren, J (1973) *Human Ecology: Problems and Solutions*, W H Freeman, San Francisco

Foreman, R (1995) *Land Mosaics: The Ecology of Landscapes and Regions*, Cambridge University Press, Cambridge

Gliessman, S (1997) *Agroecology: Ecological Processes in Sustainable Agriculture*, Lewis Publishers, Boca Raton

Gunderson, L, Holling, C and Light, S (1995) *Barriers and Bridges to Renewal of Ecosystems and Institutions*, Columbia University Press, New York

Hardin, G (1993) *Living within Limits: Ecology, Economics and Population Taboos*, Oxford University Press, Oxford

Hawken, P, Lovins, A B and Lovins L (1999) *Natural Capitalism: Creating the Next Industrial Revolution*, Earthscan, London

Hawley, A (1950) *Human Ecology: A Theory of Community Structure*, Ronald, New York

Hens, L, Borden, R and Suzuki, S (1999) *Research in Human Ecology: An Interdisciplinary Overview*, Vu University Press, Amsterdam

Holling, C (1978) *Adaptive Resource Management and Assessment*, Wiley-Interscience, New York

Homer-Dixon, T (1999) *Environment, Scarcity, and Violence*, Princeton University Press, Princeton

Hrdy, S (1999) *Mother Nature: A History of Mothers, Infants, and Natural Selection*, Pantheon, New York

Karliner, J (1997) *The Corporate Planet: Ecology and Politics in the Age of Globalization*, Sierra Club Books, San Francisco

Kormondy, E and Brown, D (1998) *Fundamentals of Human Ecology*, Prentice-Hall, New York

Lee, K (1993) *Compass and Gyroscope*, Island Press, Washington, DC

Levin, S (1999) *Fragile Dominion: Complexity and the Commons*, Perseus, Reading, Massachusetts

Lewin, R (1992) *Complexity: Life at the Edge of Chaos*, Macmillan, New York

Lovelock, J (1979) *Gaia: A New Look at Life on Earth*, Oxford University Press, Oxford

Marten, G (1986) *Traditional Agriculture in Southeast Asia: A Human Ecology Perspective*, Westview, Boulder, Colorado

McHarg, I (1995) *Design with Nature*, Wiley, New York

Meadows, D, Meadows, D and Randers, J (1993) *Beyond the Limits: Confronting Global Collapse, Envisioning a Sustainable Future*, Chelsea Green, Post Mills, Vermont

Miller, G (1998) *Environmental Science: Working with the Earth*, Wadsworth, Belmont, California

Moran, E (1982) *Human Adaptability: An Introduction to Ecological Anthropology*, Westview, Boulder, Colorado

Nebel, B and Wright R (1999) *Environmental Science: The Way the World Works*, Prentice-Hall, New York

Norgaard, R (1994) *Development Betrayed: The End of Progress and a Coevolutionary Revisioning of the Future*, Routledge, New York

Ostrom, E (1990) *Governing the Commons: The Evolution of Institutions for Collective Action*, Cambridge University Press, Cambridge

Rambo, A and Sajise, T (1985) *An Introduction to Human Ecology Research on Agricultural Systems in Southeast Asia*, University of the Philippines, Los Banos, Philippines

Rees, W, Testemale, P and Wackernagel, M (1995) *Our Ecological Footprint: Reducing Human Impact on the Earth*, New Society Publishers, Gabriola Island, British Columbia

Roseland, M (1997) *Eco-City Dimension: Healthy Communities, Healthy Planet*, New Society Publishers, Gabriola Island, British Columbia

Soule, F and Piper, J (1992) *Farming in Nature's Image: An Ecological Approach to Agriculture*, Island Press, Washington, DC

Spirn, A (1999) *Language of Landscape*, Yale University Press, New Haven

Steele, J (1997) *Sustainable Architecture: Principles, Paradigms, and Case Studies*, McGraw-Hill, New York

Suzuki, S, Borden, R and Hens, L (eds) (1991) *Human Ecology – Coming of Age: An International Overview*, VUB Press, Brussels

Tainter, J (1990) *Collapse of Complex Societies*, Cambridge University Press, Cambridge

Trefil, J (1994) *A Scientist in the City*, Doubleday, New York

Troxel, J (1994) *Participation Works: Business Examples from Around the World*, Miles Rivers Press, Alexandria, Virginia

United Nations Development Programme, United Nations Environment Programme, World Bank and World Resources Institute (2000) *People and Ecosystems: The Fraying Web of Life*, Elsevier, New York

Van der Ryan, S and Cowan, S (1996) *Ecological Design*, Island Press, Washington, DC

Watt, K (1973) *Principles of Environmental Science*, McGraw-Hill, New York

Watt, K (2000) *Encyclopedia of Human Ecology: New Approaches to Understanding Societal Problems*, Academic Press, New York

Wenn, D (1996) *Deep Design: Pathways to a Livable Future*, Island Press, Washington, DC

Wilson, E (2000) *Sociobiology: The New Synthesis*, Harvard University Press, Cambridge

Weeks, W (1997) *Beyond the Ark: Tools for an Ecosystem Approach to Conservation*, Island Press, Washington, DC

World Commission on Environment and Development (1987) *Our Common Future*, Oxford Paperbacks, Oxford

World Resources Institute (1997) *Frontiers of Sustainability*, Island Press, Washington, DC

Yes! A Journal for Positive Futures, PO Box 10818, Bainbridge Island, Washington 98110, USA

DENGUE HEMORRHAGIC FEVER, MOSQUITOES AND COPEPODS

Brown, M, Kay, B and Hendrix, J (1991) 'Evaluation of Australian *Mesocyclops* (Copepoda: Cyclopoida) for mosquito control', *Journal of Medical Entomology*, vol 28, pp618–623

Christophers, S (1960) *Aedes Aegypti (L.). The Yellow Fever Mosquito: Its Life History, Bionomics and Structure*, Cambridge University Press, Cambridge

Focks, D, Haile, D, Daniels, E and Mount, G (1993) 'Dynamic life table model for *Aedes aegypti* (Diptera: Culicideae): analysis of the literature and model development', *Journal of Medical Entomology*, vol 30, pp1003–1017

Halstead, S (1997) 'Epidemiology of dengue and dengue hemorrhagic fever' in Gubler, D and Kuno, G (eds) *Dengue and Dengue Hemorrhagic Fever*, CAB International, New York

Halstead, S (1998) 'Dengue and dengue hemorrhagic fever' in Feigin, R and Cherry, J (eds) *Textbook of Pediatric Infectious Diseases*, W B Sanders, Philadelphia

Halstead, S and Gomez-Dantes, H (eds) (1992) *Dengue – a worldwide problem, a common strategy, Proceedings of an International Conference on Dengue and Aedes aegypti Community-based Control*, Mexican Ministry of Health and Rockefeller Foundation, Mexico

Marten, G (1984) 'Impact of the copepod *Mesocyclops leuckarti pilosa* and the green alga *Kirchneriella irregularis* upon larval *Aedes albopictus* (Diptera: Culicidae)', *Bulletin of the Society for Vector Ecology*, vol 9, pp1–5

Marten, G, Astaeza, R, Suárez, M, Monje, C and Reid, J (1989) 'Natural control of larval *Anopheles albimanus* (Diptera: Culicidae) by the predator *Mesocyclops* (Copepoda: Cyclopoida)', *Journal of Medical Entomology*, vol 26, pp624–627

Marten, G (1990) 'Evaluation of cyclopoid copepods for *Aedes albopictus* control in tires', *Journal of American Mosquito Control Association*, vol 6, pp681–688

Marten, G (1990) 'Elimination of *Aedes albopictus* from tire piles by introducing *Macrocyclops albidus* (Copepoda, Cyclopoida)', *Journal of American Mosquito Control Association*, vol 6, pp689–693

Marten, G, Bordes, E and Nguyen, M (1994) 'Use of cyclopoid copepods for mosquito control', *Hydrobiologia*, vol 292/293, pp491–496

Marten, G, Borjas, G, Cush, M, Fernández, E, and Reid, J (1994) 'Control of larval *Ae. aegypti* (Diptera: Culicidae) by cyclopoid copepods in peridomestic breeding containers', *Journal of Medical Entomology*, vol 31, pp36–44

Marten, G, Thompson, G, Nguyen, M and Bordes, E (1997) *Copepod Production and Application for Mosquito Control*, New Orleans Mosquito Control Board, New Orleans, Louisiana

Riviere, F and Thirel, R (1981) 'La predation du copepods *Mesocyclops leuckarti pilosa* sur les larves de *Aedes* (*Stegomyia*) *aegypti* et *Ae*. (*St*.) *polynesiensis* essais preliminaires d'utilization comme de lutte biologique', *Entomophaga*, vol 26, pp427–439

Nam, V, Yen, N, Kay, B, Marten, G and Reid, J (1998) 'Eradication of *Aedes aegypti* from a village in Vietnam, using copepods and community participation', *American Journal of Tropical Medicine and Hygiene*, vol 59, pp657–660

Soper, F, Wilson, D, Lima, S and Antunes W (1943) *The Organization of Permanent Nation-wide anti-Aedes aegypti Measures in Brazil*, The Rockefeller Foundation, New York

Suarez, M, Ayala, D, Nelson, M and Reid, J (1984) 'Hallazgo de *Mesocyclops aspericornis* (Daday) (Copepoda: Cyclopoida) depredador de larvas de *Aedes* aegypti en Anapoima-Colombia', *Biomedica*, vol 4, pp74–76

BARATARIA-TERREBONNE NATIONAL ESTUARY PROGRAM

BTNEP (1995) *Land Use and Socioeconomic Status and Trends in the Barataria-Terrebonne Estuarine System*, Barataria-Terrebonne National Estuary Program, Thibodaux, Louisiana

BTNEP (1995) *Saving Our Good Earth: A Call to Action. Barataria-Terrebonne estuarine system characterization report*, Barataria-Terrebonne National Estuary Program, Thibodaux, Louisiana

BTNEP (1995) *Status and Trends of Eutrophication, Pathogen Contamination, and Toxic Substances in the Barataria-Terrebonne Estuarine System*, Barataria-Terrebonne National Estuary Program, Thibodaux, Louisiana

BTNEP (1995) *Status and Trends of Hydrologic Modification, Reduction in Sediment Availability, and Habitat Loss/Modification in the Barataria-Terrebonne Estuarine System*, Barataria-Terrebonne National Estuary Program, Thibodaux, Louisiana

BTNEP (1995) *Status, Trends, and Probable Causes of Change in Living Resources in the Barataria-Terrebonne Estuarine System*, Barataria-Terrebonne National Estuary Program, Thibodaux, Louisiana

BTNEP (1996) *The Estuary Compact: A Public–Private Promise to Work Together to Save the Barataria and Terrebonne Basins*, Barataria-Terrebonne National Estuary Program, Thibodaux, Louisiana

Spencer, L (1989) *Winning through Participation*, Kendall/Hunt, Dubuque, Iowa

Watts, J and Cheramie, K (1995) 'Rallying to save Louisiana wetlands' in Troxel, J (ed) *Government Works: Profiles of People Making a Difference*, Miles Rivers Press, Alexandria, Virginia

INDEX

Page numbers in *italics* refer to figures or boxes; terms in **bold** will be found in the glossary